Standing Room Only

A Contemporary Exposé of the
Roman Catholic and Evangelical Agreement

❦

PHILIP DE COURCY

AMBASSADOR-EMERALD INTERNATIONAL
GREENVILLE, SOUTH CAROLINA • BELFAST, NORTHERN IRELAND

Published by
Ambassador-Emerald International
1 Chick Springs Road, Suite 203
Greenville, SC 29609 USA

and

Ambassador Productions
16 Hillview Avenue
Belfast, Northern Ireland
BT5 6JR

Cover design © 1999 Grand Design
Cover and internal design by Matt Donovan
Some Cover photography © 1999 Photodisc

Printed in Canada

www.emeraldhouse.com

*To my parents, William and Elizabeth De Courcy
who nurtured me in the fear of the Lord and taught
me by precept and example a love for God's Gospel.*

CONTENTS

ACKNOWLEDGMENTS

No book is an island. Therefore I would like to acknowledge the more than a little help that I received from friends.

Since the basic content of this material was first delivered in sermon form to the congregation of Placerita Baptist Church, thanks must go to them for their encouragement and support in both the preaching of the sermons and the writing of the book. Special recognition goes to one of our deacons, Mr. James Cederholm who helped greatly in the preparation of the manuscript. My gratitude also extends to my fellow elders who were willing to make room and allow time for this project to be completed. Thanks also to James McCarthy for his time and effort spent reviewing my manuscript.

Friends also came in the shape of good books written on this subject and I would like to salute their role in providing a well of thought and material from which to draw help. A list of the most helpful ones can be found at the back of this book for your further study.

I am much in debt of Emerald House and Tomm Knutson for the opportunity to publish this material and for their perseverance even when I overshot the landing zone.

Last but not least, to my wife June and our little women, Angela, Laura and Beth the biggest thanks of all. Their willing sacrifice released me to write and their loving support revived me throughout this project.

CHAPTER 1

DIVIDED WE STAND, UNITED WE FALL

Jude 3-4

Martin Luther, fiery reformer of the sixteenth century, was a true man of courage. He defied the church of his day, the pope, and other religious and secular leaders. In 1521, he appeared before the German Diet in the city of Worms; though promised safe escort, he knew he risked his life by going. The same promise had been given to John Hus a century earlier, and they had burned him at the stake. Church leaders had promised Luther forgiveness if he would repent of his "errors" and return to the "true faith." Luther knew this promise had little value since the Church considered promises to heretics non-binding. He also knew the history of the two previous centuries, when thousands of Christians underwent torture and sometimes death during the infamous Spanish Inquisition.

Luther arrived safely, but the court allowed him no opportunity to defend his beliefs. Instead, he was presented with a list of his "errors." Knowing that the court could decide whether he lived or died, Luther nevertheless said the following when asked if he would recant:[1]

> Unless I am convicted of error by the testimony of Scripture (since I put no trust in the unsupported authority of pope or of councils, since it is plain that

they have often erred and often contradicted themselves), by manifest reasoning I stand convicted by the
Scriptures to which I have appealed, I cannot and will
not recant anything, for to act against our conscience
is neither safe for us, nor open to us. On this I take
my stand. I can do no other. God help me. Amen .[2]

The words of Martin Luther, "Here I stand" have given
voice to the protest by generations of believers who have stood
outside the Roman Catholic communion. Spanning more than
four hundred years, God's people have stood implacably against
and apart from the recognized errors of the Roman Church,
particularly against Rome's theology and practice which was
viewed as unsound and therefore a danger to the health of the
body of Christ. Their common conviction was that the Roman
Catholic gospel was another gospel and thus must be rejected
wholesale. By implication, Roman Catholicism was therefore
an enemy of the gospel, and every true soldier of the Cross of
Jesus Christ was put on a theological war footing with respect
to her. In fact, for a number of Protestants, Rome was viewed as
distinctly anti-Christian in both spirit and form.

Charles Haddon Spurgeon, the gifted and gallant 19th
century Baptist preacher, epitomized this spirit of protest and
theological stance when he stated:

It is the bounden duty of every Christian to pray
against Anti-Christ, and as to what Anti-Christ is
no sane man ought to raise a question. If it be not
the Popery in the church of Rome there is nothing
in the world that can be called by that name . . .
because it wounds Christ, because it robs Christ of
His glory, because it puts sacramental efficacy in the
place of His atonement, and lifts a piece of bread in

the place of the Saviour, and a few drops of water in place of the Holy Ghost, and puts a fallible man like ourselves up as the Vicar of Christ on earth; if we pray against it, because it is against Him, we shall love the persons though we hate their errors; we shall love their souls though we loathe and detest their dogmas, and so the breath of our prayers will be sweetened, because we turn our faces towards Christ when we pray.[3]

"Here I stand" was the polemic and position for previous generations when it came to the matter of communion and cooperation with the Roman system. Rome was judged to be an ecclesiastical Trojan horse that was not to be accepted within the walls of true biblical Christianity. Our Evangelical fathers and Protestant mentors considered Rome a spiritual adulteress and fervently argued that no faithful lover of Jesus Christ would be found courting her or wed to her.

As we shall see more fully in this chapter, Protestant dissent and disagreement was driven by doctrinal and Evangelical concerns over the person and work of Christ. In the mind of our Evangelical forebears, Rome's doctrine and practice undermined the four unshakable pillars of gospel truth: *that men are saved by grace alone through faith alone in Christ alone based upon the revelation of the same in Scripture alone.* It was their conviction that to *Sola Scriptura* (Scripture alone) Roman Catholicism had added human and Church tradition. To *Solus Christus* (Christ alone) Rome had added the pope, Mary, the priesthood and the saints. To *Sola Gratia* (Grace alone) Rome had added human merit and the sacraments. To *Sola Fide* (Faith alone) Rome had added works and good deeds as a means of attaining eternal life. Therefore, the subsequent prevailing opinion in the light of these facts was that Rome, like the Judiazers in Paul's day, had corrupted and perverted the gospel, and was worthy of the anathema and reproach of all true Christians (Gal.1:5-9; Phil. 3:1-11). Rome, much like the Pharisees and Scribes of Jesus' day, had denuded the Word of God through layers of human tradition and had earned the scorn of Christ Himself (Matt. 15:3,6,14).

That was yesterday, but what about today? Are Evangelicals still standing in opposition and non-conformity to Rome? Is Rome still viewed as the old enemy? Sadly, the answer to that question is no. Today, as never before, we are witnessing joint enterprises between Roman Catholics and Evangelicals in areas of worship, evangelism, and social crusades the likes of which would have been thought impossible a generation ago. It would seem that the gulf created by the Protestant Evangelical Reformation almost five hundred years ago is closing quickly. Present-day Evangelicals would rather be seen sitting in communion with Rome rather than standing in opposition to Rome. They prefer the dialogue of consensus rather than the monologue of protest. Prominent Evangelical leaders and Christian periodicals are advocating peace with Rome rather than war against Rome. Advocacy is given for the need for Evangelical Protestants to come in from the cold and place their feet to the ecumenical fire. After all, Christianity isn't a contest so why the protest?

To lend credence to what I have just said, consider the following quotes from two renowned Evangelical leaders from both sides of the Atlantic that epitomize this spirit of accommodation and change of heart. Speaking of the New Catholic Catechism (1994), the well-known Evangelical writer Alister E. McGrath, in an article for *Christianity Today* entitled "Do We Still Need the Reformation?" wrote:

The catechism's robust and committed defense of orthodoxy will be a major consideration for Evangelicals as they reconsider their attitude to Roman Catholicism. It indicates that an important ally could be at hand in the struggle for the restoration of doctrinal orthodoxy to the mainline denominations.[4]

David Watson, a British Evangelical charismatic, who exercised considerable influence over British Evangelicalism in the 70's and 80's, when addressing the 1977 National Evangelical Anglican Congress (NEAC) in Nottingham, England, spoke of the Reformation as "one of the greatest tragedies that ever happened to the church."[5]

Let us pause for a moment and taste the flavor of these statements; because they represent a strategic shift within Evangelicalism towards Rome. In the McGrath quote, Rome is judged an ally and not an enemy of Evangelicalism. In the Watson quote, the Protestant Reformation is viewed as a tragedy and not a triumph. Changed days and changed opinions, would you not agree?

Implied in these statements and the statements of others (noted throughout this book) is the belief that it is time to fill in the trenches and call a truce between Evangelicalism and Catholicism. It is suggested by many leading figures on both sides of the divide that Evangelicals and Catholics must come of age and be willing to show a maturity which was lacking in previous generations, and grow out of the doctrinal tantrums which divided and plagued their forefathers. In the face of a collapsing western culture and increased intellectual attack upon orthodox Christian belief, many believe it is time to circle the Christian wagons and end the bickering within Christ's camp before it is too late. Through Evangelical presses and personalities we are being told that the enemy to be fought is not Christians of another tradition, namely Roman Catholics, but the common enemy of godless secular humanism, materialism, and immorality.

In the light of past testimonies and present trends already noted in this chapter, every one of us must therefore ask ourselves a rather serious question, *do we prefer to stand or sit?* Shall we line up with our forebears and stand against Rome and its theological departure from the gospel, or shall we join our contemporaries in sitting down with Rome and mutually reach an agreed future together? Is the centuries old controversy justified or a childish squabble that ought to end? That question is a serious one which this book sets out to answer. Put differently, as Watson quoted, was the reformation unnecessary and tragic, or was it a tragic necessity because Rome had so erred from the truth?

Your two options are either obstruction or construction. Obstruction in that you believe Roman Catholicism to be a purveyor of a false gospel, and therefore stand opposed to reunion and participation with Rome. Construction in that you believe Rome to be an orthodox Christian Church worthy of respect and assistance. In the first option you work to build a wall of separation, in the second option you work to build a bridge of cooperation.

As for this author, it will be my contention throughout this book, which has drawn from the study of God's Word and considers the historical issues, that *"Here I Stand"* is the correct stance. This is not the time to declare a cease-fire in the name of a false peace. The table we are invited to sit at is a table of surrender in which the gospel will become a casualty. The concerns that drove and occupied our fathers with regards to Rome's erroneous teaching have not evaporated with the mists of time. Following Vatican II and the New Catechism, Roman Catholicism may be wearing a new face, but the old Tridentine heart remains. In fact, I hope to prove in subsequent chapters that nothing in substance has changed since Trent, and if the truth were told, Rome has added to her sins through additional theological aberrations. It is my conviction that Roman Catholicism has been and remains a deceptive, aggressive and massive system that stands by its theology and history opposed to the gospel and church of Jesus Christ. This is not the time, if ever, to whitewash the scarlet woman. When weighed in the balance of Scripture, the doctrines of Rome are to be found wanting. Since I believe this to be true, I find the present goal of union and communion with the Vatican nothing less than a desertion of the gospel and a betrayal of the martyrs.

Scripture declares that there is one sacrifice and that it is Calvary (Heb. 1:3). There is one confessional and that is the throne of grace (Heb. 4:14-16). There is one mediator and he is our Lord Jesus Christ (Heb. 7:24-25). The Roman Catholic mass, confessional, and the veneration of Mary are but insults in the face of our Lord Jesus Christ, who appeared to put away our sin by the sacrifice of Himself and now appears in heaven for us (Heb. 9:23-28). Consequently, to seek union with the holy father of Rome and his Church would be to lose the favor of our one true Father in heaven (2 Cor. 6:11-18).

In continuing to introduce the content and intent of this book, let me underscore the reality that the issue at hand is not an academic one. Big issues hinge on our response and attitude to the faith of the Vatican. This issue of reconciliation with Rome is unavoidable for at least three reasons:

1. *The Issue of Unification* Whether we like it or not the ecumenical train is gathering speed and collecting more passengers by the day. Each of us therefore needs to decide whether we want to climb on board or remain on the platform of

protest. For years there was what we might call "ivory tower ecumenism" where leaders and theologians locked behind closed doors and away from the public eye traded compliments regarding each other's respective traditions. Today, however, through the charismatic movement and cooperative evangelism, ecumenism has changed shape and become "grass roots" in its expression. Evangelicals and Catholics are drinking of the "same spirit," working together in reaching the lost, and joining hands in protest outside abortion clinics.

The question is, do we want to be party to this renewed push for ecumenical endeavor? Is this movement an answer to Christ's own prayer for unity in John seventeen and worthy of our involvement? Or is it a fulfillment of prophecy concerning apostasy spoken of by Paul in his second letter to Timothy and therefore worthy of our condemnation? Mixed in with this is the historical position of Rome in considering the Protestant a schismatic having separated himself from the one true church, founded by Christ in apostolic succession under the primacy of Peter. Is it not therefore time for the separated brethren to find their way home and into the arms of the mother Church?[6]

2. *The Matter of Salvation* To put it crudely, Rome considers itself our best bet for salvation. It is believed and stated that through the treasury of the Catholic Church, Christ dispenses salvation through the means of the sacraments. The New Catechism repeats the conviction of the Second Vatican Council that "through Christ's Catholic Church alone, which is the universal help toward salvation, that the fullness of the means of salvation can be obtained."[7] The New Catechism also repeats the tenet that "they could not be saved who, knowing that the Catholic Church was founded as necessary by God through Christ, would refuse either to enter it or remain in it."[8]

In his 1989 book, *Towards a Civilization of Love*, Cardinal Hume, leader of the Catholic Church throughout England said:

> "The Council document on ecumenism is at pains to state; 'The Catholic Church possesses the wealth of the whole of God's revealed truth and all the means of grace. It is unable to concede a similar status to others'".[9]

As a further attestation to Catholicism's pivotal and primary role in the matter of salvation and its attainment, Pope John Paul II writes:

> "Christ is the true active subject of humanity's salvation. The Church is as well, inasmuch as it acts on behalf of Christ and in Christ. Christ . . . asserted the need for the Church, when men enter through baptism as if through a door. For this reason men cannot be saved who do not want to enter or remain in the Church, knowing that the Catholic Church was founded by God through Christ as a necessity."[10]

Consequently, if these claims were true in any way then for the health of our souls we ought not to be apart from the Catholic Church, for it alone as the one True Church of Christ possess all the means of grace. The heart of this matter therefore is the gospel, what it is, and where it is to be found. The question of union and reunion with Rome has eternal happiness hanging in the balance.

In J. C. Ryle's *Five English Reformers*, the schism over Rome's monopolistic position as dispenser of grace, is vividly told in the account of John Hooper's death. As the Bishop of Gloucester under Bloody Mary, Hooper was burned as a heretic for his Protestant faith and rejection of the Mass. Bishop Ryle recounted the scene:

> When Hooper arrived at this spot, he was allowed to pray, though strictly forbidden to speak to the people. And there he knelt down, and prayed a prayer which has been preserved and recorded by Fox, and is of exquisitely touching character. Even then a box was put before him containing a full pardon, if he would only recant. His only answer was, "Away with it; if you love my soul, away with it!" He was then fastened to the stake by an iron round his waist, and fought his last fight with the king of terrors.[11]

Out of love for our souls should we not too come to a definitive view concerning Rome and its status as a Christian Church preaching the Christian gospel? Cardinal Hume has put Protestantism in its place; is it not time once again for Evangelicals to make their mind up as to where Rome belongs? The true proclamation and possession of eternal salvation rides on this question. Is salvation mediated through the sacraments of the Catholic Church or not?

3. *The Topic of Evangelization* Evangelism should be the heartbeat of the true church that is alive to the purposes of God in all generations (Matt. 28:18-20). Christ makes it clear in His high priestly prayer that we are in this world to call people out of this world until the end of this world (John 17).

Consider then the matter of evangelizing Roman Catholics. Should you consider Roman Catholicism to be a false religion devoid of the saving message of God's grace toward sinful men, you then are charged with the duty to reach with the gospel the almost 900 million Roman Catholics in the world. However, should you on the other hand, side with those

10

who wish to recognize Catholics as brothers and sisters in Christ, the field of operations is drastically reduced in that you potentially fence off twenty percent of the world's population for evangelism.

Should you discount the reality of what I am outlining, read the following report as it appeared in the June 1995 edition of the Dallas/Fort Worth Heritage paper:

> Mike Gendron, a Dallas Theological Seminary graduate who leads an Evangelical outreach to Roman Catholics, recounted a March 25 encounter with some Texas state Promise Keeper executives attending a Dallas workshop for various ministries. Gendron told The Heritage that while manning his ministry booth he was openly criticized by PK staff members who said that Catholics were "already saved, so what's the need for this [Gendron's] ministry?"

The topic of evangelism makes the focus of this book a real life issue. Are we to allow our Catholic friends or neighbors to go merrily on their way assuming they are Christians, or are we to graciously confront them about their need of trusting in the finished work of Christ alone for their hope of heaven (1 Cor. 9:16; 2 Cor. 4:3-6)?

For these three reasons you cannot perch yourself on the fence and choose not to decide whether the current Evangelical-Catholic dialogue and reconciliation is correct and virtuous. This book ought not to be put down or its questions avoided because weighty matters hang in the balance of your response.

Before proceeding further, I must add two things by way of explanation that will help clear the path to a better understanding of this book's content and this author's intent.

First, my controversy with Roman Catholicism is not to be understood as me being anti-Catholic. The subject material of this book is an issue of belief and truth, not individuals and personalities. I have many friends and acquaintances that are Roman Catholic, and I value their friendship and support dearly. We know that Roman Catholic neighbors are no better or worse than Protestant ones. If offence is given by this book I pray it will be the offense of the Cross and not the authors ignorance or arrogance (Gal. 5:11, 6:14).

Second, my understanding of what Roman Catholicism stands for will be taken from the official statements and dogmas of the church. Some people today might disagree, arguing that these statements are in general out of date and believed only by a minority. If that is so then now is the time that what is officially declared as true should be made to match what is generally believed to be true. But until that happens, we have to work from what officially exists and what has not been officially denied as declared in Rome's doctrinal statements. Should I fail to take this approach, all objectivity will be lost, and the argument will descend into individual squabbling rather than dealing with historical and theological controversy. It is my intention to engage Roman Catholicism on the basis of its Catechism and confessional teaching and not with a handful of facts and a bucketful of conspiracies.

Having laid the foundation for this book and the issues involved, I will build upon the introductory remarks in considering the stand of yesterday and the retreat of today.

The Stand of Yesterday

It is clear from the teaching of God's Word that once we have sided with Christ through faith in Him, the bounden duty of the Christian is to stand in opposition to moral evil and theological error (Eph. 6:12-13; Phil. 1:27-28; 2 Thess. 2:15). In these references the word "stand" means to "hold your ground, to resist successfully". In these exhortations there is a call to arms particularly directed to the defense of the gospel in its simplicity and sufficiency (Phil. 1:7, 27-30; Gal. 1:6-9; Jude 3, 4). The New Testament church was admonished to stand guard over the gospel and cross swords with anyone or thing that sought to vandalize the truth of Christ in the gospel (1 Tim. 6:12, 20-21).

Taking this admonition seriously, our Evangelical forebears crossed swords with Roman Catholicism. Until recently, Protestant Evangelical ministers and ministries stood opposed to the papacy, in the belief that Rome preached a corrupted gospel and was a hoax of the devil to deceive souls. Like an army phalanx, this former generation locked their shields of faith in a united front against what they saw as a capricious enemy of the gospel.

This was true of the 16th century Reformed movement, the 17th century separatist and Baptist movement, and the 18th and 19th century Evangelical movement. There was a common belief that Rome was an adversary. Their protest and opposition was manifest through the shedding of their own blood, the spilling of ink, and the preaching of sermons.

In a day of softening attitudes toward Rome, consider again the opinions and observations of men upon whose shoulders we Evangelicals stand. The ground may be shifting in our day but their stand was clear and uncompromising and should act as a bulwark against this movement toward Rome.

Speaking of conferences and dialogue that sought to heal the rift between Protestantism and Catholicism, Martin Luther quipped:

Let them go on, we shall not envy the success of their labors, they will be the first who could ever convert the devil and reconcile him to Christ ... The scepter of the Lord admits of no bending and joining; but must remain straight and unchanged, the rule of faith and practice.[12]

Now consider the comments of the great reformer John Calvin, who was well acquainted with Rome and its Popes, in his commentary on Galatians:

Paul charges the Galatians with defection, not only from his own teaching, but from Christ ... Thus they were removed from Christ, not in that they entirely rejected Christianity but because in such a corruption only a fictitious Christ was left to them. So today the Papists choose to have a half Christ and a mangled Christ and so none at all and are therefore removed from Christ. They are full of superstitions which are directly opposed to the nature of Christ. Let it be carefully observed that we are removed from Christ when we accept that which is inconsistent with His mediatorial office; for light cannot be mixed with darkness.

In August 1746, The great evangelist George Whitefield, was in Philadelphia when news arrived that "Bonnie Prince Charles," the Jacobite (and Catholic) pretender to the British throne, had been roundly defeated at the battle of Culloden. Whitefield immediately preached a sermon thanking God for rescuing the British from the multiplied woes of a Catholic monarchy. He said:

How soon would our pulpits every where have been filled with these old anti-Christian doctrines, free-will, meriting by works, transubstantiation, purgatory, works of supererogation, passive obedience, non-resistance, and all the other abominations of the whore of Babylon.[13]

It should be understood that Charles Spurgeon entertained throughout his life, a very negative attitude toward Romanism. For example, a fellow Baptist once told Spurgeon that he had attended a Catholic Mass in Paris and had "felt very near the presence of God." Spurgeon replied that this proved the text, "If I make my bed in hell, behold thou art there."[14]

In his classic work on Roman Catholicism, Lorraine Boettner gives voice to generations of believers when he writes concerning Rome:

That the Roman Catholic has within it much truth it is not to be denied. It teaches the inspiration of the Scriptures, the deity of Christ, the virgin birth, the miracles, the resurrection of the body, the future judgement, heaven and hell, and other Scripture truths. In every instance, however, it nullifies these truths to a considerable extent by adding to or subtracting from what the Bible teaches. . . . The Roman Church thus has such serious inherent defects that over the broad course of history it cannot possibly emerge successful. Clearly it had lost its power to evangelize the world, and instead has become so confirmed in its present course that it cannot be reformed either from the within or from without. In the main it is as antagonistic and as much an obstacle to Evangelical Christianity as are the pagan religions

... Its interpretation of the Scriptures is so erroneous and its principles are so persistently unchristian that over the long period of time its influence for good is outweighed by its influence for evil. It must, therefore, as a system be judged to be a false church.[15]

D. Martyn Lloyd Jones, the wonderful British expositor of Scripture in step with his Welsh Evangelical heritage, wrote to explain the cause of confusion among so many Protestants, and to warn against any rapprochement with Rome:

> In one sense ... You might well think that the Roman Catholic Church is the most orthodox Church in the world ... [It] believes that Jesus of Nazareth was the eternal Son of God; it believes the Virgin birth; it believes in the Incarnation; it believes in His miracles; it believes in His substitutionary work upon the cross and His resurrection [etc] ...
>
> But at this point the subtlety comes in and the difficulty arises. To all that [orthodox truth] she "adds," with a damnable plus, things which are utterly unscriptural and which, indeed, become a denial of the Scripture. So she lands us eventually in a position in which, if we accept her teaching, we are believing a lie!

Lloyd Jones further protested:

> There are movements afoot ... which are trying to bring a rapprochement between Roman Catholicism and Protestantism ... This [Roman Catholic] system is altogether more dangerous than is Communism itself ...

Roman Catholicism is the devil's greatest masterpiece! It is such a departure from the Christian faith and the New Testament teaching that ... her dogma is a counterfeit; she is, as the Scripture puts it, "the whore." ...

Let me warn you very solemnly that if you rejoice in these [ecumenical] approaches to Rome you are denying the blood of the martyrs! ... There are innocent people who are being deluded by this kind falsity, and it is your business and mine to open their eyes ... [16]

From the sample of quotes and comments taken (and many more could be added) we are not left to wonder where our Evangelical fathers stood in regard to the faith of the Vatican. Their stance was an unflinching disapproval of the Roman system. Within these statements, it is the manifest fact that our forebears' disapproval was biblically and theologically driven. Romanism was to be rejected because she rejected the clear and consistent teaching of the Word of God, especially the tenets of the gospel. This centuries old controversy was not centered upon ecclesiastical politics but doctrinal purity.

Again from the quotations, it is to be seen that Protestants and Evangelicals took issue with Rome on a number of serious fronts. Over the centuries the controversy has raged around the following disagreements:

- The duality of tradition and Scripture in which practically the Word plays second fiddle to tradition as opposed to the principle of *Sola Scriptura* in which Scripture conducts all matters of faith and practice.

- The blasphemy of the Mass that purports to be a propitiatory offering of Christ as opposed to the once-for-ever in time death of Christ for His people.

- The tyranny of Purgatory which teaches the purging of sin through after death suffering as opposed to complete propitiation of our sin in what Christ did upon the cross.

- The curse of Sacramental Salvation which teaches that grace is received and found in the token of the Lord's Supper or participation in baptism, as opposed to the testimonial and commemorative aspects attributed to these ordinances according to the Bible.

- The scandal and universal authority of the papacy as opposed to the biblical portrait of Peter and the revelation of local New Testament leadership.

- The anathema of incomplete and Progressive Justification made possible by faith and works throughout life, as opposed to the complete and forensic justification of a soul at the moment of conversion by faith alone.

- The elevation of Mary to a place of perfection and intercession alongside her Son as opposed to the biblical revelation of a woman of faith used by God for a special task , but was nevertheless a sinner, redeemed in a similar manner to all Christians.

- The restriction of the Priesthood to an elite group of men who have power to absolve sin, as opposed to the corporate priesthood of all believers under the one great High Priest, Christ Himself, who alone can forgive sin.

- The preposterous claims of the Catholic Church to be the one true Church established by Christ in apostolic succession through the primacy of Peter, the first pope, as opposed to locally assembled congregations under the headship of Christ and godly leadership who preach apostolic doctrine and follow apostolic patterns of Church life.

Upon reflection of the preceding comments, any honest evaluation on our part of the historical and theological disagreements would have to conclude that the issues that divide are issues of fundamental importance. The division is fundamentally a disagreement over what the gospel is. Is salvation found through grace alone, by faith alone, in Christ alone, based upon the revelation of the same in Scripture alone (Eph. 2:8-9)? Or is salvation found through Mary, the sacraments, purgatory, and the one true Catholic Church? Are we justified by faith alone in Christ as Paul teaches (Rom. 3:28)? Or are we being justified by faith in Christ plus works and the sacraments, and never to be sure of the fact, as Rome teaches?

It is indisputable that our Evangelical predecessors stood opposed and outside the Roman system because they believed fervently that Rome taught another gospel. The faith once delivered to the saints was absent in the precincts of the Vatican thus striking discord between our spiritual ancestors and Rome (Jude 3-4). This antipathy toward Catholicism reaches back to the middle decades of the sixteenth century and was maintained with virtual unanimity into the 1960s.

Were these contentious Evangelicals right about Rome being wrong? Or is now the time for a change of heart? I, for one, stand shoulder to shoulder with them in denouncing Roman Catholic theology as a false gospel. Rome's attempt to modernize its theology through Vatican II and the New Catechism (1994) creates the appearance of a new look, but it is nothing more than a cosmetic exercise to hide her true face. New style Catholicism may have removed the anathemas of Trent, but it retains Trent's doctrines, which remain the heart of the division.

As a matter of support for the historical stance of true Evangelicalism toward Rome, let us delve into the New Catechism, so much appreciated by Mr. McGrath, to see if Rome has changed.

The Catechism of the Catholic Church is of special significance in this matter. It demonstrates clearly that Rome has not modified the teaching of the Council of Trent. One might quote at length from the catechism to show how closely it agrees with the conclusions of Trent and historic Catholicism. However, since reference will be made to the catechism and the unchanging nature of Catholic doctrine throughout this book, a few examples will suffice just now—namely tradition and Scripture, transubstantiation, justification by faith and purgatory. On the issue of tradition and Scripture, like Trent, the catechism calls for both to be accepted and honored with equal sentiments of devotion and reverence.[17] On the issue of the real presence of Christ in the mass, the catechism quotes directly from Trent: "In the most blessed sacrament of the Eucharist 'the body and blood together with the soul and divinity of our Lord Jesus Christ and therefore the whole Christ is truly really and substantially contained.'"[18] With regard to justification, The New Catechism again defers to Trent in that 'Justification is not only the remission of sins, but also the sanctification and renewal of the interior man.'[19] On purgatory there is like agreement. In fact, the catechism affirms that "The Church formulated her doctrine of faith on Purgatory especially at the Councils of Florence and Trent."[20]

Are you encouraged? Is this indeed a new day? Is it time for Protestants to come out of the cold and warm their feet at the ecumenical fire? Is it time to take our seat at the conference table with Roman Catholics? Is this an opportune moment for Evangelicals to moderate their stance? I think not. In a day when many Evangelicals are warming up to Rome, theological obstacles remain and call us to make a continued stand against this deceptive system of belief. This is not the time to redraw the boundaries of our fellowship to include Rome (Rev. 18:4-5). The fight of faith is still being waged with the Vatican and now is not the time to abandon the fight (Num. 32:6). We must not give up our heritage and the ground taken by our spiritual fathers (1 Kings 21:3; 20:34).

Steve Farrar, in his book *Standing Tall*, tells the following story:

> The story is told of the old Persian ruler who wanted to impress a visiting dignitary. He showed the official a glass cage and inside the cage a lion was resting comfortably next to a little lamb. The guest couldn't believe his eyes. "How can a lion and lamb coexist?" he asked. "I believe that it is possible for natural enemies to find peace," replied the ruler. "But how can a lion and a lamb possibly get along in the same cage?" asked the guest. "It's simple," said the ruler. "Every morning I put in a new lamb."[21]

Despite the euphoria of our day, like the story, any show of unity with Rome will undoubtedly come with a sacrifice of truth. It is therefore incumbent upon Evangelicals to stand fast in the liberty of the gospel as have previous generations and not go back to the bondage of Rome (Gal. 5:1). Divided we must stand, for if united, gospel truth will fall.

The Retreat of Today

In spite of the former comments and conclusions many contemporary Evangelicals are retreating from the position held by those upon whose shoulders they stand and whose doctrinal mantle they claim. Rome is now regarded as a friend and not an enemy, as an ally and not an adversary. Only a generation ago, Evangelicals keeping spiritual company with Roman Catholics would have been rare, yet now we see Protestants and Roman Catholics together in prayer, studying Scripture and worship. Numerous Evangelicals are proclaiming spiritual identity with Roman Catholics (1 Kings 22:3-4; 2 Chr. 19:2). The Evangelical church is turning its back on the Reformation and pointing its face towards the Vatican. Certain Evangelicals are advocating that now is the time to reacquaint ourselves with our long lost Christian cousins in Rome. No longer are we angry neighbors, but good citizens of one spiritual kingdom. Things are not as they were.

What is truly disturbing are the significant Evangelicals who are advocating reconciliation with Rome. Their willingness to compromise with Rome is antithetical to God's Word, and for their preeminent position within Evangelicalism, nothing less than egregious.

This recent shift within Evangelicalism is best illustrated in the release and acceptance in many quarters of the 1994 document *Evangelicals and Catholics Together: The Christian Mission into the Third Millennium*. This document was offered with much fanfare and publicity, and was immediately trumpeted as a defining moment in Protestant-Catholic relations. Included in the thirty signatories were well-known Evangelicals Pat Robertson, J.I. Packer, Os Guiness, and Bill Bright. Leading Catholics such as John Cardinal O'Connor, Bishop Carlos Sevilla, and Catholic scholar Peter Kreeft joined them. The renowned Evangelical author and speaker Charles Colson, and Richard Neuhaus, formerly a Lutheran minister who defected to Catholicism in 1990 headed the whole project and process. At the heart of the search, as outlined by Charles Colson, was "the unity of true Christians as an essential prerequisite for Christian evangelism."[22]

Progress was certainly believed to have been made. In the section "We Affirm Together" the following statement is to be found:

> All who accept Christ as Lord and Savior are broth-
> ers and sisters in Christ. Evangelicals and Catholics
> are brothers and sisters in Christ. We have not cho-
> sen one another, just as we have not chosen Christ.
> He has chosen us, and he has chosen us to be his
> together (John 15). However imperfect our com-
> munion with one another, we recognize that there is
> but one church of Christ. There is one church
> because there is one Christ and the Church is his
> body. However difficult the way, we recognize that
> we are called by God to a fuller realization of our
> unity in the body of Christ (5).[23]

Similar declarations of unity are peppered throughout the
document along with urgent appeals for more visible manifes-
tations of unity between the two. The document also highlights
areas of common faith between Catholics and Evangelicals but
curiously and yet not surprisingly the central tenet of the reformation "justification by faith alone" is conspicuously absent in
the flow of the accord. The document's appeal with regards to
the Christian mission is that Protestant and Catholics turn the
guns they have been pointing at each other towards the enemies of common morality and Judeo-Christian culture. The
common mission is one that is socio-political rather than Evangelical. This joint agreement represents a watershed in that for
the first time in generations leading Evangelicals have been
willing to reclassify Roman Catholics as brothers and sisters in
Christ.[24] As one song, put it, "the times are a changing."

Perhaps they have been changing for quite some time if
one considers the ministry of Billy Graham. Dr Graham has for

decades been fostering cooperation with Catholicism through his methodology of cooperative evangelism in which all the churches in a particular locality, whether Protestant or Roman Catholic, are invited to help and take part in outreach. A classic example of Graham's cooperation with Rome can be viewed in the following transcript of a letter from Cardinal Hume's house in London regarding Graham's 1989 Mission England.

ARCHBISHOP'S HOUSE,

WESTMINSTER, LONDON, SWIP 1QJ

July, 1989

Please forgive the delay in writing back to you for your letter of 9th July concerning the Mission of Dr. Billy Graham to London just ended.

Roman Catholic involvement in Mission 89, from the point of view of Cardinal Hume and within the diocese of Westminster, Southwark and Brentwood, the three areas covering the Missions of Dr. Graham (West Ham FC, Crystal Palace and Earls Court—and indeed the added Wembley) has been very good indeed. It truly is difficult to speak for what I do not know in other areas of our country. From an 'official' point of view, the Bishops of England and Wales (RC) joined with other Churches in 'inviting' Dr. Graham to London to give a Mission. Bishop Charles Henderson of Southwark was the bishop appointed by our Bishop's Conference to represent them. Cardinal Hume issued an official statement to his priests which was mailed to all the other bishops in England and Wales and indeed I know that this was sent to some of the bishops in Scotland and indeed in Ireland—asking for "prayer and co-operation" for the Mission.

Because, very sadly, of certain "fundamentalist Protestants" the Billy Graham Mission Team asked us to keep our participation very 'cool'— we did not want to anger people with our participation any more than they were! It was a sad state of affairs.

Dr. Graham called on Cardinal Hume the day before his Mission on June 13th and the Cardinal attended with myself the Mission at Earls Court on Monday, June 26th—this also with the Bishop of London (Anglican).

Some 2100 Catholics "went-forward" at the Missions evenings in London which was excellent— from nearly all our Parishes in Westminster! I am not certain as to "Livelink"— but I am told of support in the Liverpool area. I certainly don't think Catholics have been anti-Livelink! Billy Graham has helped our Church greatly and many have "renewed" their faith under his great ministry. I do not know myself of Catholic Counselors—just one or two perhaps. This does not mean however lack of support for the Mission! It is not our way you could say. Well, I hope that helps you a little with information, do write again if I can help.

Rev. Michael Seed, S.A., S.T.D.
Ecumenical Advisor to The Cardinal[25]

Please bear in mind that this is the Cardinal Hume mentioned earlier who would not concede to Protestantism the same status possessed by the Catholic Church, as the one true body of Christ. Sadly, Dr. Graham has been a great help to him and his Church.

In addition to the aforementioned example, a couple of years ago I had the privilege of hosting author and speaker Dave Hunt in the Baptist church I was pastoring at the time in Belfast. While there, he related that he was returning home to the States to argue for the inclusion of a story about Billy Graham's compromise with Rome in his up and coming book "A Woman Rides the Beast." The publishers would have preferred the offending story left out as a courtesy to Graham, but Dave Hunt won the day and related the story in his published book. He wrote:

> The BGEA [Billy Graham Evangelistic Association] acquired the printing rights [for a special edition] of . . . the classic Henry H. Halley Bible Commentary entitled, Pocket Bible Handbook . . . [It] described [Rome's] martyrdom of millions . . . [In its 1962 Billy Graham Crusade Edition] the Graham Association . . . removed all these pages . . .[26]

The same deletions were made from the additional special Crusade editions in 1964 and 1969. As a result, readers were denied dozens of pages of vital historical fact. Those pages documented the evil of a number of popes as well as of Rome's persecution and slaughter of Christians for centuries prior to the Reformation. That Billy Graham has helped swell the ranks of the Catholic Church and glossed over facts about her hatred of God's people and gospel, is conspicuous and disheartening. For it is this same gospel that he confesses to dearly love.

Another evidence of change is the reticence of Evangelical apologists to name Roman Catholicism as a cult, which was once the practice. In his 1973 book *Cults and Isms*, J. Oswald Sanders placed Catholicism at the top of the list of "heresies," but the chapter was dropped in his 1981 edition. Campus Crusader Josh McDowell's *Understanding the Cults* lists 11 characteristics of cults, all of which are found in Roman Catholicism, yet it is not listed as a cult.

In broadening the scope of observation, few would deny the growth and impact of the Charismatic Movement upon the Evangelical Church. Whether you agree with it or not, the importance of this movement cannot be denied. If it is a shaker within the Evangelical world, its views regarding Rome are therefore pertinent to this issue of Evangelical lapse. Let me quote some words from prominent names within that movement.

In his book "Charismatic Chaos", John MacArthur quotes the words of John Wimber, founder of the Vineyard Movement, given at a "Church Planting Service" in 1981 which are rather revealing. Wimber stated:

> The pope . . . by the way is very responsive to the Charismatic movement, and is himself a born-again Evangelical. If you've read any of his texts concerning salvation, you'd know he is preaching the gospel as clear as anybody is preaching it in the world today.[27]

Pat Robertson, another high-profile charismatic and host of the TV show the 700 Club, has declared his desire for unity with Rome. His own newsletter reported:

> After CBN founder Pat Robertson met with His Holiness, Pope John Paul II . . . [he] described their meeting as warm. "I think this meeting was historic," said Robertson, who joined with other Christian religious leaders [including Don Argue of the National Association of Evangelical, Chuck Colson, and J.I. Packer] in greeting the pope at the New York residence of His Eminence, John Cardinal O'Connor.

The meeting . . . came just hours after Robertson
[led] an Ecumenical Procession at the Papal Liturgy
[and was given a seat of honor at the Papal Mass] in
New York's Central Park. Robertson called the pope,
"a humble and caring servant of the Lord." . . .
Robertson presented a . . . letter to the Pontiff
underscoring CBN's commitment to work for
Christian unity and world evangelization.

Robertson also wrote that he was "encouraged" by
the pope's recent encyclical on Christian unity, *That
All May Be One*, and praised the Pontiff for his recent
call to Catholics to "be more committed to prayer for
Christian unity . . .'[28]

Speaking of TV personalities, Paul Crouch, the head of
the vast charismatic TBN television ministry, has declared on
his program "Praise the Lord":

I have come to the conviction that Martin Luther
made a mistake. He should have never left the Roman
Catholic Church. I am eradicating the word Protestant
out of my vocabulary. I am not protesting anything. It
is time for Catholics and non-Catholics to come
together as one in the Spirit and one in the Lord.[29]

Opening our eyes wider we note the unprecedented mobi-
lization of men within Evangelical churches under the leadership
Bill McCartney and the "Promise Keepers Movement." As an
expression of the movement's might, rallies are held nationwide
during which men are called to headship in the home, leadership
in the church, discipleship in Christ; which for this emphasis
they are to be applauded. However, this movement like Evangelicalism at large seems intent on embracing Catholicism.

For example, in the book, *Seven Promises of a Promise Keeper*, Jack Hayford a leading charismatic pastor and Promise Keeper speaker, writes concerning a Promise Keeper's first duty to worship God through Christ. Hayford stated:

> Redeeming worship centers on the Lord's Table. Whether your tradition celebrates it as Communion, Eucharist, the Mass, or the Lord's Supper, we are called to this centerpiece of Christian worship.[30]

Note the astounding inclusion of the Mass as a centerpiece to Christian worship. Changed days indeed. Many English Reformers were put to death by Bloody Mary for their very denial of the Roman Mass as a centerpiece to Christian worship as outlined in J.C.Ryle's book, *Five English Reformers*.

Of additional interest is the sixth promise, which calls upon men to reach beyond racial and denominational barriers to demonstrate the power of biblical unity. Mark for yourself who is to be included in this drive to biblical unity. In the words of the founder, Coach Bill McCartney, his inclusion is noteworthy:

> Now, I don't mean to suggest that all cultural differences and denominational distinctiveness are going to disappear. But what I know is that Almighty God wants to bring Christian men together regardless of their ethnic origin, denominational background, or style of worship. There's only one criterion for this kind of unity: to love Jesus and be born of the Spirit of God. Can we look one another in the eye—black, white, red, brown, yellow, Baptist, Presbyterian, Assemblies of God, Catholic and so on—and get together on this common ground: 'We believe in salvation through Christ alone, and we have made Him

the Lord of our lives'? Is that not the central, unifying reality of our existence? And if it is, can we not focus on that and call each other brothers instead of always emphasizing our differences? Men, we have to get together on this![31]

Again we find an Evangelical leader redrawing the line to include Roman Catholics within the Christian community. In this statement, Bill McCartney's contradictory words should be noted concerning the necessity of believing in salvation through Christ alone—and then including Roman Catholics as "brothers" in spite of the fact that they do not believe in salvation through Christ alone, adding sacraments and good works as requirements for salvation. Unfortunately, this is yet another example of big-hearted, softheaded Evangelicalism that's lacking theological resolve and has lost its historical roots in the matter of Roman Catholicism.

Finally, on the political front we are also witnessing a convergence of Protestantism and Catholicism. Read carefully the words contained in this Associated Press release dated October 12, 1995:

> The Christian Coalition urged Roman Catholics yesterday to unite with Evangelical Christians in pushing a conservative agenda. It's time for the two groups to come together because the "darkness has become so pervasive and the social pathologies have become so cancerous," said Ralph Reed, executive director of the Christian Coalition.
>
> Reed said Catholics and Evangelical Christians could find common ground in opposing abortion, opposing pornography, supporting school choice

and "believing that the family is the most important unit in society." He added, "We can no longer afford to be divided. It is a luxury that is no longer ours."

Underscore Ralph Reed's inferred description of the theological battles of the Reformation as "a luxury that is no longer ours." Our response is that the division over the truth of the gospel is hardly a luxury. The New Testament Church, which existed in a hostile culture, is our paramount example when they refused political alliance with Judaism, knowing it would occur at the expense of the gospel of Jesus Christ.

Indeed, more could be said to both alert and alarm to the mutation taking place within the body of Evangelicalism regarding the status of Roman Catholicism. In the details given, the pope is described as a born again Evangelical, the Mass a centerpiece of Christian worship, and the Church of Rome an equal partner in the cause of Christ.

Why this ecumenical fervor? Have the theological walls crumbled and the doctrinal disagreements been resolved? The New Catechism, which declares and defends the past errors of Catholicism, answers with a resounding no! Rome continues to build its theology upon something other than the four pillars of gospel truth: *Sola Scriptura, Solus Christus, Sola Gratia* and *Sola Fide.* Surprisingly, ECT realistically declares that deep differences remain in the dialogue between Evangelicals and Catholics. Consider the following quotation from the ECT document:

We note some of the differences and disagreements that must be addressed more fully and candidly in order to strengthen between us a relationship of trust in obedience to truth. Among many of the points of difference in doctrine, worship, practice and piety that are frequently thought to divide us are these:

+ The church as a integral part of the Gospel, or the church as a communal consequence of the Gospel.

+ The church as a visible communion or an invisible fellowship of true believers.

+ The sole authority of Scripture (*Sola Scriptura*) or Scripture as authoritatively interpreted by the church.

+ The "soul freedom" of the individual Christian or the Magesterium (teaching authority) of the community.

+ The church is a local congregation or universal communion. Ministry ordered in apostolic succession or the priesthood of all believers.

+ The Lord's Supper as Eucharist sacrifice or memorial meal.

+ Remembrance of Mary and the saints or devotion to Mary and the saints.

+ Baptism as a sacrament of regeneration or testimony to regeneration (9-10).

The document even acknowledges the solemn importance of many Catholic-Evangelical differences. The signatories expressly confess that some of the differences are so profound that they impinge on the Gospel itself:

On these questions, and other questions implied by them, Evangelicals hold that the Catholic Church has gone beyond Scripture, adding teachings and practices that detract from or compromise the Gospel of God's saving grace in Christ. Catholics, in turn, hold that such teachings and practices are grounded in Scripture and belong to the fullness of God's revelation. Their rejection, Catholics say, results in a truncated and reduced understanding of the Christian reality (10-11).

We could add to these differences the kernel of this debate namely the principle of *Sola Fide* which, as noted earlier, is conspicuously absent in the dialogue of this document. Yet what is amazing in all of this is that Protestants are asked to consider Roman Catholics as part of the family of God, despite the fact that no clear agreement was reached on the gospel itself. Is it not unforgivable that the very ground of justification before God was by-passed by these supposed pioneers of new relationships between Protestantism and Catholicism? A right relationship with each other must be grounded in a right relationship with God (1 John 4:1-3).

All this reminds me of a humorous story concerning a Catholic and Jewish couple who lived side by side in a duplex. For the Catholics, every Friday was "fish only," but for the Jews it was barbecue-steak-in-the-backyard night. To eat fish to the aroma of barbecued steak Friday after Friday was more that the Catholic couple could bear. Finally, after much deliberation, the only solution seemed to be to convert the Jewish couple to Catholicism and thus have them join the fish-on-Friday ritual. After several weeks their objective was reached, and with joy they watched the holy water sprinkled and heard the word of the officiant, "You were born a Hebrew, raised a Jew, but I baptize you a Catholic." What a victory! What a relief! No more smell of barbecued steak on Friday.

The next Friday rolled around. To the Catholic couple's dismay, the same aroma of barbecued steak came drifting through the apartment from the backyard. Horrified, they ran out to see what could have brought about such sudden backsliding. To their surprise, the Jewish husband was standing over a simmering steak on the outdoor grill, sprinkling it with barbecue sauce and saying in solemn tones, "You were born a calf, raised a cow, and I baptize you a fish."

Is there not a moral in this story for the purposes of our discussion? Just because some people say there is unity and brotherhood among Evangelicals and Catholics doesn't make it so. On the basis of the information already gathered, with more to come, it must be said that the change we are witnessing is Evangelical compromise and surrender. What we are witnessing is not a new beginning, but rather a sad departure from the faith of the Gospel (Gal. 1:6; 2 Tim. 4:1-5).

By way of conclusion and challenge, observe these words of warning by Northern Ireland Presbyterian minister, Donald Gillies:

> The rank and file of Protestantism must be warned. The ecumenical climate is depressing and soporific. It is slowly drying up our Evangelical fervor. The soft winds of false doctrine are lulling us to sleep and carrying us slowly but surely in a Romeward direction. The cause of true Protestantism is at stake. The work and sacrifice of Reformers and martyrs are in danger of being brought to naught. Like Paul, let us refuse to be subjected to attempts to destroy the sufficiency of Christ for salvation; unlike Peter, in a weak moment, let us not be intimidated by the fashionable ecumenism into surrendering our Christian liberty. Better even that the Protestant Church should perish than be reunited with Catholic error, superstition and idolatry. 'Flee from idolatry', the Word of God warns us (1 Cor. 10:14). Ecumenism is the new idolatry of the day. As a cli-

mate and obsession, with its efforts to achieve union at the cost of essential truth, with its pursuit of union for the sake of union, ecumenism has come between the souls of men and the God of truth. That is idolatry.[32]

1. Michael Yousef, *The Leadership Style of Jesus*, (IL: Victor Books, 1986) 43-44.

2. T.M.Lindsay, *A History of the Reformation*, (Charles Scribner's Sons) 257.

3. Michael de Semlyen, *All Roads Lead to Rome?*, (England: Dorchester House Publications, 1991) 182.

4. *Christianity Today*, December 12, 1994.

5. John Capon, *Evangelicals Tomorrow*, (Glasgow: Collins).

6. *Catechism of the Catholic Church*, (Missouri: Ligouri Publications, 1994) para. 813-822.

7. Ibid., para. 816.

8. Ibid., para. 846.

9. Michael de Semlyen, *All Roads Lead to Rome?* (England: Dorchester House Publications, 1991) 16.

10. John H. Armstrong, *A View of Rome*, (Chicago: Moody Press, 1995) 113.

11. J.C.Ryle, *Five English Reformers*, (London: Banner of Truth Trust, 1960) 16.

12. James Buchanan, *The Doctrine of Justification*, (London, 1961) 150-152.

13. George Whitefield, *Sermons on Important Subjects*, (London: William Baynes, 1825) 56.

14. Lewis Drummond, *Spurgeon: Prince of Preachers*, (Grand Rapids: Kregel Publications, 1992) 46.

15. Loraine Boettner, *Roman Catholicism*, (New Jersey: P&R, 1962) 455-460.

16. D.Martyn Lloyd Jones, *Roman Catholicism*, (Grand Rapids: Evangelical Press) one in a series of "Pastoral Booklets," 1-4, 16.

17. *Catechism of the Catholic Church*, para. 80-82.

18. Ibid., para 1374.

19. Ibid., para. 1989.

20. Ibid., para 1031.

21. Steve Farrar, *Standing Tall*, (Oregon: Multonmah Books, 1994) 61.

22. *Evangelicals and Catholics Together: Comments from Charles Colson and Prison Fellowship Ministries*, news release from Prison Fellowship dated 15 June 1994.

23. *Evangelicals and Catholics Together: The Christian Mission into the Third Millennium*, (29 March 1994) All page numbers refer to the 25-page version of the document as originally distributed by Prison Fellowship. Hereafter all quotations from this document are cited in parentheses with a page number only.

24. For a critique of this document see Chapter 5 of John MacArthur's excellent book *A Reckless Faith*.

25. Dr Ian Paisley, *Nearer my Pope to Thee, Nearer to Thee!* Pamplet published by Martyrs Memorial Publications, 356-76 Ravenhill Road, Belfast 6, N.Ireland.

26. Dave Hunt, *A Woman Rides the Beast*, (Oregon: Harvest House, 1994) 391.

27. John MacArthur, *Charismatic Chaos*, (Grand Rapids: Zondervan, 1992) 148.

28. *The Berean Call*, April 1996.

29. "Praise the Lord" program, TBN, October 17, 1989, hosted by Paul and Jan Crouch—quests were two Catholic priests, Fr. John Hamsch and Jesuit Fr. Herbert De Souza, and leading Catholic laywoman, Michelle Corral.

30. *Seven Promises of a Promise Keeper*, (Focus on the Family, 1994) 19.

31. Ibid., 160-161.

32. Donald Gillies, *Unity in the Dark*, (London: Banner of Truth Trust, 1964) 104.

CHAPTER 2

SLEEPING WITH THE ENEMY

Galatians 1:5-9

When World War I broke out, the War Ministry in London sent a coded message to a remote British outpost in the heart of Africa: "War declared. Arrest all enemy aliens in your district." This prompt reply was received: "Have arrested ten Germans, six Belgians, four Frenchmen, two Italians, three Austrians, and one American. Please advise immediately who we are at war with."[1]

In anything but coded terms the Bible declares war on error. The God of truth calls upon His people to engage in the battle over the truth of His gospel and our common salvation (Jude 3; Phil 1:7). Again and again the New Testament apostles issue a call to arms over the threat that false doctrine and spurious teachers pose to the gospel (2 Cor. 11:13-15; 1 Tim. 4:1-2; Acts 20:28-30; 2 Pet. 2:1-2; 1 John 4:1; Jude 3-4). Christians are called to be soldiers of the cross and to guard the treasure of the gospel (1 Tim. 6:20-21).

This war effort is hampered; however, when just like the British outpost in the heart of Africa, Christians can't distinguish friend from foe. Truth is endangered when the Church doesn't know whom to count as an enemy. The security of the gospel is compromised when the body of Christ is found sleeping with the enemy and unaware of it.

This possible lapse in security was precisely the problem among the saints at Galatia as Paul addressed them in the first chapter of his epistle (Gal. 1:6-9). To his utter shock and bewilderment, the Galatians were to be charged with leaving their post and fraternizing with the enemy. The words 'turning away' come from a Greek word, which signifies 'to transfer one's allegiance'. It was used of soldiers in the army who revolt or desert and was punishable by death during a time of war.

Paul accused the Galatians of turning away. They were Evangelical turncoats, spiritual deserters. They had turned away from Him who had called them in the grace of Christ and had embraced another gospel. In Acts 20:24, Paul writes of the true gospel when he described it, "the gospel of the grace of God". It is the glad and good news of a God who is gracious to undeserving sinners. In grace, God spared not His own Son but delivered Him up to the cross to die for us. In grace, He calls us to Himself. In grace, He justifies freely and forever all that will place their trust where He has placed their sin, on and in the person of Jesus Christ. "All is from God", as Paul wrote in 2 Corinthians 5:18, meaning, "all is of grace". Nothing is due to our efforts, merits, or works; everything in salvation is due to the grace of God.

But the Galatian converts, having received this gospel of grace, were now deserting it for another gospel, a gospel of works. When this news from the front reached Paul, his heart died, and his mouth fell open. The Greek word in verse six translated *amazed*, used to describe Paul's reaction to the news received, is very strong. It is used in the Gospels to communicate the crowd's reaction whenever they witness a miracle by Jesus—"We can't believe it" or "It is astonishing." It is a word that conveys outright surprise. But found here in Galatians, it has a twist of shock to it. Paul is stunned that this battalion of foot soldiers for Christ, this outpost for the Christian Gospel in Asia Minor, is to be found guilty of sleeping with the enemy.

Paul charges them with betrayal in joining forces with those who preach a different gospel. He is shocked at this surrender of the gospel. Orthodoxy has been supplanted by heterodoxy. How could this be? Where was the gap in their defenses?

The apparent success of the enemy, the Judaizers, in winning over the foolish Galatians was in cloaking their error in the tunic of truth. They had a gospel with a difference, but that made it a different gospel (Gal. 1:6-7). The Galatian Church had been tricked into letting the enemy slip in under the guise of Christianity. The Judaizers had added the keeping of the Jewish law to the gospel of God's grace (Acts 15:1). They did not deny that you must believe in Jesus for salvation, but stressed that one must be circumcised and keep the law as well. In other words, you must let Moses complete what Christ has begun. Or rather, you yourself must finish, by your obedience to the law, what Christ has begun. You must add your works to the work of Christ, which remained unfinished.

In his Commentary on Galatians, John MacArthur elaborated on the breech in defense at Galatia:

> The Judaizers who plagued the early church claimed to be Christians, and much of their doctrine was orthodox. They must have recognized Jesus as the promised Messiah and even acknowledged the value of His sacrificial death on the cross—otherwise they would never have gotten a hearing in the church. They claimed to believe all the truths that other Christians believed. They did not purport to overtly deny the gospel but to improve it by adding the requirements, ceremonies, and standards of the Old Covenant to the New. But anything added to grace destroys it just as surely as does anything

taken from it. When law—even God's own law—is added to His grace, His grace ceases to be grace (cf. Rom. 11:6).[2]

Aware of the threat posed by this subtlety, Paul dispatched this war correspondence to the Galatians, calling on them to return to their post and to once again take up the cause of defending the Gospel of God's grace by putting the Judaizers to flight. Paul tells the Galatians to repel this hellish invasion and enemy beachhead from within the borders of true Christianity (Gal. 1:5-9; 2:18). Legalism and ritualism challenge the survival of grace and therefore must be opposed bitterly by the Church of Christ. The Galatians were told to kill any thought of accommodating law and grace, faith and works.

Given the Biblical account of Paul's strong rebuke of the wayward Galatians, should it not be with a similar sense of shock and bewilderment that we view the recent movement of Evangelicals toward Rome? As demonstrated in the previous chapter, present-day Evangelicals are deserting in droves from front-line opposition to Rome, which had been established by generations of faithful saints, in a renewed desire for peace with the papacy. What is all the more amazing is that they freely admit that Rome has a gospel that is different; and yet like the foolish Galatians, they want to make room for it within the walls of biblical Evangelicalism. It seems, therefore, that the Evangelical church is opening itself up to an attack similar to that first perpetrated upon the work of the gospel at Galatia, the acceptance of an amended gospel as an authentic gospel. That is the clear and present danger.

To this augmentation of the Gospel, John MacArthur cautioned in his commentary on Galatians:

The most destructive dangers to the church have never been atheism, pagan religions, or cults that openly deny Scripture, but rather supposedly Christian movements that accept so much biblical truth that their unscriptural doctrines seem relatively insignificant and harmless. But a single drop of poison in a large container can make all the water lethal. And a single false idea that in any way undercuts God's grace poisons the whole system of belief.[3]

A red alert must be sounded within Evangelicalism because Catholicism is this type of gospel. To the essential truths and core beliefs of the gospel, they add and append doctrines, which subtract from Christ and His sufficiency. To the Bible they add tradition. To the headship of Christ over the church they add the pope. To justification they add sanctification, making them both the same. To Christ as our high priest they add Mary and the saints. To grace they add merit. To faith they add works. To heaven and hell they add purgatory. To one atoning sacrifice of Christ they add the mass. To the throne of grace they add the confessional box. The Judaizers of Paul's day were mere amateurs compared to the Romanists of today in supplementing and supplanting the gospel of Jesus Christ with a mongrel gospel.

Paul's admonition to the Galatians, therefore, comes with renewed force to this present generation of Evangelicals who are courting the scarlet woman of Rome. Are they going to help build again a system that the Gospel itself destroyed in the sixteenth century (Gal. 2:11-21)? Are they going to give credence to another gospel, which is not a gospel and bears upon it the anathema of God's curse (Gal. 1:6-9)? Are they going to return to the yoke of ritualism and the entanglement of ceremony

(Gal. 5:1-6)? Are they about to shift ground on the great truth that a soul is saved through faith alone in Christ alone on the basis of grace alone (Gal. 3:1-9)?

Perhaps we would do well to heed the warning of Spurgeon in his application of the solemn message of Joshua 6:26 to those in his day who sought to restore or further the fortunes of Rome:

> Since he was cursed who rebuilt Jericho, much more the man who labors to restore popery among us. In our father's days the gigantic walls of popery fell by the power of their faith, the perseverance of their efforts, and the blast of their gospel trumpets; and now there are some who would rebuild that accursed system upon its old foundations.
>
> We must warn with judicious boldness those who are inclined towards the errors of Rome, we must instruct the young in gospel truth and tell them of the black doings of popery in the olden times. We must aid in spreading the light more thoroughly through the land, for priests, like owls, hate daylight.

In the light of such intention in our day toward Rome, we are left like Paul to ponder the why and wherefore of our fellow Evangelicals' actions (Gal. 5:7-8). Why in our generation this quantum leap from opposition to cooperation? Why this blurred line between friends and foes, a line so much clearer in a past generation? Upon reflection, I would like to suggest four factors that I believe have contributed to this diversion by present-day Evangelicals from the path of obedience to the gospel and unto the dead-end street of false ecumenism.

A Lack of Doctrine

To put it simply, it is hard to know what error is when one is not sure about truth itself. People can become blind to false doctrine when they take their eyes off the truth. It is not difficult to be seduced by error when one has lost his or her love and loyalty for what's truth. C.H. Spurgeon, speaking of his own day, made an unconscious commentary of our day when he said, "Everywhere there is apathy. Nobody cares whether that which is preached is true of false. A sermon is a sermon whatever the subject; only the shorter it is the better."

The common theme today among the vast majority of Evangelicals is that doctrine is boring, divisive, and only for seminarians. More than one pastor has been told by his congregation, 'Don't give us doctrine, just give us the Bible.' Sadly, fewer and fewer Christians know what they believe and why they believe it (Luke 1:1-4; 2 Tim. 1:12). The average Christian is a theological kindergartner lacking a basic knowledge of Christian doctrine. Most are staking their hope for heaven on a wing and a prayer. They will tell you that Christ died for them, but can't explain the atonement. They will tell you they are saved, but can't explain the doctrine of justification. When it comes to doctrine, this is a day of the lowest common denominator. Congregations want preachers to play on their hearts not to tamper with their minds. Ours is a time when people want to feel God and know God without having to think biblically about God.

Read the following from Erwin Lutzer, as he magnifies what I have just said:

> In days gone by, many believers were tortured, eaten by wild beasts, or burned at the stake because of their doctrinal convictions. Theology was appropriately

43

called "the Queen of the Sciences" because men believed that one's relationship with God dwarfed all other considerations. After all, what can compete with ultimate questions: Is Christ qualified to be a Savior? Does baptism wash away sins? Can we be sure of eternal life? How is God's grace received by sinners? How many books are in the Bible? Does God choose who will be saved? Once saved, can we be lost?

Today opinion polls suggest that the Queen of the Sciences needs a new dress; perhaps she has even lost her crown. Only a small percentage of those who claim to be born again know who preached the Sermon on the Mount or can recite at least three of the Ten Commandments. The wag who said that most Americans think that the Epistles are the wives of the apostles was not very wide of the mark![4]

Sadly, Lutzer's comments reflect a grave departure from New Testament Christianity and is something the Bible warns us about (2 Tim. 4:1-4). In the early church doctrine, conviction, belief, and teaching were considered to be something of utmost importance. Truth to those first believers was very precious. Truth marked the character of Christ (John 1:14; 14:6). Truth was a liberating power (John 8:32). The work of the Holy Spirit was to be characterized and identified by truth (John 16:13; 1 John 5:17). The pastor's greatest joy was seeing Christians obedient to the truth (3 John 4). Pastors needed to be expert in the handling of the Word of Truth and give themselves to the pursuit and practice of doctrine (2 Tim. 2:15; 1 Tim. 4:15-16). Bible study had the acquisition of doctrine as one of its goals (2 Tim. 3:16-17). The New Testament Christian had settled convictions about Christ, His person and His work, convictions that were set in concrete (Eph. 4:14-15). Their knowledge of God was based upon revealed truths about God (John 20:31; 1 John 5:13). Truth and doctrine became the basis of their unity and the measure of their fellowship (John 17:17,20-21; Jude 3; Rom. 16:17; 2 Tim. 3:5-9).

Doctrinal neutrality is not only a grave departure from biblical Christianity, but also a grave danger. When a love for doctrinal truth reigns in the church, error and apostasy are banished from the borders of God's kingdom. But when truth is no longer guarded with jealousy, error returns from exile and troubles the Lord's kingdom. It would, therefore, be true to say that error could only survive in a climate of doctrinal ambiguity. False unity can only be constructed when true theological foundations are destroyed. Compromise can only take place when truth is taken from the judge's chair and given a seat in the observation gallery.

Theological ambiguity and doctrinal equivocation marks and drives the movement of Evangelicals and Catholic's together, both officially and unofficially. Before it is too late, it must be grasped by all that this proposed marriage of Protestantism and Catholicism is predicated upon Evangelicals divorcing themselves from long held and cherished biblical beliefs. The cup of united communion with Catholicism will necessitate the dilution of doctrine and force compromising Evangelicals to surrender significant biblical doctrine. This is the flaw and sin of this anticipated union. To allow the ecumenical train to move forward, doctrine must be shunted onto a side track, which is precisely the case with *Evangelicals and Catholics Together* (ECT). The following paragraphs will lend support to this assertion.

First, to read ECT is to soon discover that any discussion it seeks to have on theological and doctrinal matters is rather imprecise. Many theological concepts are introduced, but few doctrinal definitions are given. Initially, there is no definition of the "Christian mission" around which the document is based (pp.2, 4). While a concept of "Christian mission" is suggested on page twelve, there is no clear biblical definition anywhere in this paper. In fact, the joint mission focuses upon "the right ordering of society" (p. 12). The mandate they seem to assume is cultural and temporal, not spiritual and eternal. Furthermore, there is no definition of the concept of New Testament missiology, which would give opportunity to evaluate the proposed efforts of Evangelicals and Roman Catholics. To beat this drum again, we note that there is no definition of the "mission" and "faith" which are agreed upon (p. 4). Neither is there a definition of what it means to "accept Christ'" (p. 5). Throughout the document, important words such as "church" (p.6), "unity" (p.7), and "being Christian" (p.22), remain undefined and undetermined.

What we have therefore in ECT is a call to Protestants and Catholics to hold hands in the midst of a theological fog and doctrinal mist, something simply not entertained in the New Testament. Is this not unity for the sake of unity, not unity for the sake of truth? ECT is for this reason, dangerous because it uses the right terminology without the correct theology, and is peppered with hollow words empty of doctrinal weight.

Second, we note that the Apostles' Creed is held up as a rallying point for Christian unity and doctrinal agreement (p.6). The Apostles' Creed is reproduced in its entirety as part of the document. Let me share it with you:

> I believe in God, the Father almighty, creator of heaven and earth.
>
> I believe in Jesus Christ, his only Son, our Lord. He was conceived by the power of the Holy Spirit and

born of the Virgin Mary. He suffered under Pontius Pilate, was crucified, died, and was buried. He descended into hell. On the third day he rose again. He ascended into heaven, and is seated at the right hand of the Father. He will come again to judge the living and the dead.

I believe in the Holy Spirit, the holy catholic Church, the communion of saints, the forgiveness of sins, the resurrection of the body, and the life everlasting. Amen.

The Apostle's Creed is presented within ECT as a theological cornerstone for Protestants and Catholics to build better relationships. The Apostles' Creed, by implication, facilitates a united doctrinal front from which ecumenical endeavors can proceed. As the old maxim states "unity in the essentials," therefore ECT hopes to employ the Apostles' Creed to develop ecumenical cohesion between Protestants and Catholics.

The conviction of this writer is that such a hope is ill founded. The Apostles' Creed is not safe ground upon which to build unity simply because it is minimal theology. The problem with the Apostles' Creed is not with what it says, but with what it fails to say. It is indistinct and therefore attractive to ecumenically minded Protestants and Catholics who are anxious to reduce essential doctrines to a minimum in the interests of agreement and union among the churches. Upon examination, however, it fails to explain the doctrines of grace, the nature and purpose of Christ's death, the place and efficacy of the sacraments (if any), or the means of attaining unto the resurrection of the just.

One of the most vigorous and decisive exposures regarding the Apostles' Creed as a possible platform for Evangelical and Catholic unity came from the pen of Dr. William Cunningham, one of the greatest divines that Scotland ever produced. In his "magnum opus", *Historical Theology*, he wrote the following words that deserve our careful consideration:

> An essay was once written by a Lutheran divine, in which he exhibited in parallel columns the Lutheran, the Calvinistic, and the popish interpretations of all the different articles in the Creed. And it certainly could not be proved that any one of them was inconsistent with the sense, which the words bear, or in which they might be reasonably understood . . . Nay, it is well known that Arians, who deny the divinity of the Son and the Holy Ghost, have no hesitation in expressing their concurrence in the Creed . . . These considerations are quite sufficient of themselves to prove that the Apostles' Creed, as it is called, is not entitled to much respect, and is not fitted to be of much use, as a summary of the leading doctrines of Christianity. A document which may be honestly assented to by Papists and Arians, by the adherents of the great apostasy and by the opposers of the divinity of our Savior, can be of no real utility as a directory, or as an element or bond of union among the churches of Christ. And while it is so brief and general as to be no adequate protest or protection against error, it does not contain any statement of some important truths essential to a right comprehension of the scheme of Christian doctrine and the way of salvation. It is quite true that, under the different articles of the Creed, or even under any of the earlier creeds which

contained merely a brief profession of faith in the Father, the Son and the Holy Ghost, we might bring in, as many authors have done, an explanation of all the leading doctrines taught us in Scripture; but it is not the less true that they are not stated in the document itself, and that there is nothing in its words which is fitted to bring them to our notice.[5]

Essentially, this creed is simply ill equipped to become the measuring rod for orthodoxy or unity around the fundamental doctrines of Christianity. It is much too light and flimsy to anchor any true drive towards biblical union among the churches of this nation or any other nation. Biblical unity demands and deserves nothing short of a precise, detailed, and involved statement of the Christian Gospel, which is totally lacking in this document.

Third, in his book *Reckless Faith*, Dr. John MacArthur released some of the correspondence he received from the very signatories of the ECT document in answer to his concerns about this betrayal of the Christian gospel. Upon reflection, Dr. MacArthur notes a common thread running throughout the responses, namely that "this document is not about doctrine."

Quoting from one of these personal letters, Dr MacArthur uncovers for us the thinking that lay behind this accord as one of the signatories to ECT writes:

This document is not about theology or doctrine. From the outset we admit that there are doctrinal differences that are irreconcilable and we specifically identify many of these. This document is about religious liberty (i.e., the right of all Christians to share their faith without interference from church or state), evangelism and missions (e.g., not only the right but the responsibility under the Great Commission of all Christians to share Christ with all nations and all people), and the need all Christians have to cooperate, without compromise, in addressing critical moral and social issues, such as abortion, pornography, violence, racism, and other such issues.

In our battle for that which is good and godly, we must stand with those who will stand at all.[6]

Concerning the lack of doctrine determining the ministry and direction of modern Evangelical churches, please underline the language of this Evangelical leader. Without shame, this unnamed signatory, admits that the proposed coming together is not based on doctrine, but will be made with anyone who will stand at all. In my opinion, this is nothing short of a betrayal of the New Testament's prescription for fellowship and cooperation among believers. Doctrine was, and remains so today, the basis for unity and the measure with which you associated. In this regard, the first century church was vigilant in their discernment concerning any agreements that might be signed.

Unless one is willing to draw a line theologically, men and women will not know when they are crossing over into compromise. Doctrinal fences must be erected and maintained for they help us to know whose back yard we are in, whether it be God's or Satan's.

In his 1966 book, *Winds of Doctrine*, Addison Leitch astutely warns us about the dangers of avoiding sharp theological distinctions, which is exactly the case with ECT.

Try the following exercise on any denomination and consider its relationship to its own creeds. What, for example, is a Presbyterian? . . . Either a Presbyterian is one who is loyal to the Westminster Confession or he is something else. If he is not loyal to that confession, in what way shall he be defined? The answer is usually as follows: "Don't put us in a theological straitjacket; let's not have theological witch-hunting." This kind of response I consider to be an "out" rather than an answer. But suppose we accept the freedom from definition as a principle. After all, the important thing is to be a Christian, not a Presbyterian. Very well, a Protestant or a Romanist Christian? Will not the attitude that refuses to draw lines between Presbyterians and Baptists or between Protestants and Romanists eventually blur the distinctions between Christians and Buddhists and Moslems? It will, and it does.[7]

Ecumenical compromise takes place when the theological distinctives are blurred and the doctrinal landmarks removed or buried (Prov. 22:28). The parties to ECT unfortunately give us an unforced confession that this is exactly what they have done. Doctrine was not the issue for them, but it ought to be for us and all who seek true unity.

A Lack of Discernment

Yet another reason that we are witnessing today the auctioning off of our glorious faith, much like what happened at Galatia, is due to the devaluation of discernment. Christians, to a large extent, are unwilling to judge, scrutinize, and evaluate all that comes to them in the name of Jesus. The love for peace and quiet (not Christ) is driving most churches and believers to avoid controversy over issues, especially doctrinal ones. The argument employed by such individuals is that it cuts against

51

the grain of Christian love to make a judgment on the rights and wrongs of another's belief. In the church today, it seems the virtue of love has been stretched to include a charitable consideration of error (see 1 Cor. 13:6). Sadly, the average Evangelical church possesses no more discernment when confronted by error than Little Red Riding Hood possessed when faced with the wolf dressed up as her Grandmother. We seem willing to accept anything so long as it's dressed up in Christian language and tradition.

Lack of discernment fosters an environment that is ready-made for error to grow and live. Error and falsehood plead tolerance and advocate freedom from censorship. Error preaches a relaxation of the laws of comparison and contrast; whereas falsehood dislikes any kind of rule of faith. The lack of discernment thus creates a darkness that exists apart from the light of biblical scrutiny.

Such freedoms and liberties cannot, however, be afforded. The Word of God calls the child of God to be discerning and discriminating between light and darkness, truth and error. In his letter to the Thessalonians, Paul calls upon those believers to prove all things, and distinguish between what's good and what's bad (1 Thess. 5:21). The verb "prove" or "test" is a favorite with Paul and speaks of testing, examining, and approving that object under consideration. It was a word used to describe the ability of those in commerce to detect a spurious coin from the true mint. The thought then would be that the readers must become experts in discerning the true value of that which presents itself as spiritual currency.

Under the direct guidance of The Holy Spirit, Paul taught the church of Jesus Christ that ignorance and untested acceptance of all that claims to be from God is not demanded in any area of the Christian life. Believers are specifically warned, "Believe not every spirit, but prove the spirits, whether they are of God" (1 John 4:1). God's people are called to spiritually judge things by the criterion of the Word (1 Cor. 2:14; Acts 17:11). The Holy Spirit functions in the life of a believer as an early warning detection against error (John 14:26; 16:13; 1 John 2:20-27). It is, therefore, neither unloving nor unchristian to challenge and police the teaching and advice of fellow Christians and others.

In his book, *A Call to Discernment*, Jay Adams brings us to consider what he calls the principle of antithesis as we find it woven into the fabric of God's revelation. He points out that it is fundamental to genuine discernment:

> In the Bible, where antithesis is so important, discernment—the ability to distinguish God's thoughts and God's ways from all others—is essential. Indeed, God says that "the wise in heart will be called discerning" (Proverbs 16:21).

> From the Garden of Eden with its two trees (one allowed, one forbidden) to the eternal destiny of the human being in heaven or in hell, the Bible sets forth two, and only two ways: God's way and all others. Accordingly, people are said to be saved or lost. They belong to God's people or the world. There was Gerizim, the mount of blessing, and Ebal, the mount of cursing. There is the narrow way and the wide way, leading either to eternal life or to destruction. There are those who are against and those who are with us, those within and those without. There is life and death, truth and falsehood, good and bad, light and darkness, the kingdom of God and the kingdom of Satan, love and hatred, spiritual wisdom

and the wisdom of the world. Christ is said to be the way, the truth, and the life, and no one may come to the Father but by Him. His is the only name under the sky by which one may be saved.[8]

Thus discernment, hardly unchristian, is in fact a mark of godliness. God wishes His people to be antithetical in their thinking and to view things in terms of right and wrong, light and darkness, life and death. Like Solomon, we must pray for this ability that we might order the affairs of God's kingdom correctly (1 Kings 3:7-10). Solomon's desire for discernment pleased God. Error craves toleration, but God desires scrutiny and investigation on the part of His people.

The ECT document, to its shame, lacks discernment and fears scrutiny. Its egregious content encourages tolerance and disowns the principle of antithesis. On page 23 of the ECT, the authors address the context of uncharitable comments toward those of other faiths or viewpoints:

> Similarly, bearing false witness against other persons and communities, or casting unjust and uncharitable suspicions upon them, is incompatible with the Gospel. Also to be rejected is the practice of comparing the strengths and ideals of one community with the weaknesses and failure of another.

That last sentence is wholly untrue, and undermines the commands of Scripture both in the New and Old Testaments for God's people to be discerning. Such a statement appears to be nothing more than a self-justification for their own lack of doctrine and discernment.

Please do not misunderstand me. I am not advocating a censorious spirit or a pharisaical attitude. A love of controversy is unworthy of any Christian. Christ calls us to be salt, not caustic soda. Charles Spurgeon warned his ministerial students about holstering a theological revolver everywhere they went, and using it upon everyone and anyone whom dared to disagree with them.

Yet while I would make such qualification, the words of J. C. Ryle are none the less true, and help bring this section to a close:

> It is hard enough to fight the Devil, the world and the flesh without private differences in our own camp. But there is one thing that is even worse than controversy, and that is false doctrine tolerated and permitted without protest and molestation. It was controversy that won the battle of the Protestant Reformation. If the views, which some men hold were correct, it is plain that we ought not to have had a Reformation at all. For the sake of peace we should have gone on worshiping the Virgin, and bowing down to images and relics to this day. The Apostle Paul was the most divisive and controversial character in the entire book of Acts, and because of it he was beaten with rods, stoned and left as dead, chained and left in a dungeon, dragged before magistrates, barely escaped assassination, and so pronounced in him were his convictions that it came to a point when the unbelieving Jews in Thessalonica declared: "These that have turned the world upside down are come hither also." God pity those pastors whose main objective is the growth of their organizations, and whose main concern lest their "boats be rocked." They may escape involvement in controversy, but they will not escape the judgment seat of Christ.[9]

A Lack of Dependence

Pressing the issue further, what alarms me the more I read ECT and the justifications of the signatories, is what I perceive as a lack of dependence. The ecumenical thrust and trust in our day not only lacks doctrine and discernment but also manifests a lack of dependence upon God.

Advocates of ECT, and similar endeavors, are loudly voicing their concern over the moral and social slippage that is self-evident in western culture, especially in the United States. Leaders from both sides advocate through the medium of ECT the need for a united Christian crusade to take America back for God. The old enemies of Protestantism and Catholicism now see a common enemy in the pornographer, abortionist, atheistic professor, and liberal congressman. The message of this common mission calls upon us to forget the theological battles of four centuries ago in an effort to win the present cultural war. Therefore, the engine that drives this movement for Evangelical and Catholic cooperation is fueled not by doctrinal passion but social concern. It can be said that the mission into the third millennium as defined by ECT is socio-political, not Evangelical. By their own admission (as demonstrated in chapter one) the parties to ECT are divided on issues that impinge upon the very Gospel itself, therefore negating the possibility of a true Evangelical mission together.

Evangelicals, seized by a spirit of panic caused by this nation's moral decline, are throwing doctrinal caution to the wind. Today they are to be found promoting a broad Christian coalition inclusive of Catholics in an attempt to head off the destruction of our Judeo-Christian culture.

As witness to this trend we need only consider the words of J.I. Packer as he advocates the validity of the ECT document and the need for it in light of the times in which we live. Contributing to the book edited by Charles Colson and Richard Neuhaus and entitled *Evangelicals and Catholics Together*, Packer states:

The present needs of both Church and community in the Western world (not to look further for the moment) cry out for an alliance of all who love the Bible and its Christ to stand together against the slide into secularism and paganism that is so much a mark of current culture. Vital for the Church's welfare and the well-being of society itself at this time is the building of the strongest possible transdenominational coalition of Bible-believing, Christ-honoring, Spirit-empowered Christians who will together resist the many forms of disintegrative theology— relativist, monist, pluralist, liberationist, feminist, and the rest—that plague organized Christianity, and the many forms of postmodern subjectivity that are disintegrating the educational, familial, and political heritage of the West. Such a coalition already exists among Evangelicals, sustained by parachurch bodies, media, mission programs and agencies, and a wide range of literature. The stand for truth and wisdom would be stronger if this coalition were in closer step with the parallel Roman Catholic activities that have begun to emerge, aiming at similar goals.[10]

He further writes in the same article:

It is similarly vital for the health of society, specifically in North America, that adherents to the key truths of classical Christianity—a self-defining Triune God who is both Creator and Redeemer, this

God's regenerating and sanctifying grace, the sanctity
of life here, the certainty of personal judgment hereafter, and the future return of Jesus Christ to end history—should link up for the vast and pressing task
of reeducating our secularized communities on these
matters. North American culture generally has lost
its former knowledge of what it means to revere God
and hence it is in process of losing its values and standards, its shared purposes, its focused hopes, and
even its knowledge of what makes human life
human. Materialism, hedonism, and nihilism,
lumped together and miscalled humanism, is all it
now has left. Again, it is the theological conserva-
tionists, and they alone, who have resources for the
rebuilding of these ruins, and domestic differences
about salvation and the Church should not hinder us
from joint action in seeking to re-Christianize the
North American milieu. But the apologia for Christian values in society is only going to carry credibility
if the view of reality in which it is rooted takes hold
once more of people's minds. So propagating the
basic faith remains the crucial task; and it is natural
to think it will best be done as a combined operation,
with a combined call to Christian commitment as its
focal center. Maximizing togetherness in witness at
all levels will therefore be a timely move.[11]

Are not these astounding words from a renowned Evangelical thinker? Astounding because in them we discover the
mission of the church redirected and the trust of the church
misdirected. What do I mean? His words clearly articulate that
the mission of the church is to be redirected toward the saving

of the culture rather than the discipling of the nations (Matt. 1,
28:18-20). Note also the idea, that this rescue mission is to be
undertaken by a transdenominational ecclesiastical body, that
sets aside doctrinal differences about salvation, in seeking to re-
Christianize North America.

As a missions statement, Jim Packer's words are void of
New Testament instruction concerning our witness to the
world. The New Testament knows nothing of a Christian society but speaks of a Christian church—an assembly of
redeemed and converted people meeting and ministering
together within the society (Phil. 1:1; 1 Thess. 1:1-2). According to the words of Jesus Christ, the role played by the church
within society is to win men and women for Himself and to
encourage them to go back into that society to win others for
the same divine cause (John 17:14-21; Phil. 2:14-16). It is
plainly evident in Scripture that the focus of the New Testament church was the resurrection of spiritually dead men, not
the reformation of socially sick nations (Eph. 2:1-10, 3:8-13; 1
Thess. 1:5-10). The mission of the church is to go into the
entire world and preach the gospel, which means for Christians, the evangelizing of North America, not re-Christianizing
it. The gospel is neither a social program nor a political mani-
festo, it is the powerful message of the cross through which
God is pleased to save (1 Cor. 1:18-25; Rom. 1:16-17). The
Cross must not become an addendum to what is thought to be
more pressing agenda, namely the cultural war.

Although there is room to become involved in the political
process, we must be careful to keep our distance, fighting evil
and encouraging good wherever it is to be found. Ultimately the
ballot box cannot save us, only God can. Although we are
admonished to pray for those in authority, it is the Cross that
remains the centerpiece of His agenda (1 Tim. 2:1-5). Only

when the Cross stands alone, unencumbered by other religions, philosophies, or political ideologies, does it retain its power.

In his book, *Hitler's Cross*, Erwin Lutzer documents the demise of the Christian church in Germany during the Second World War due to its capitulation to a social agenda rather than a spiritual one. The cross was supplanted by the swastika, and the gospel was lost amidst the din of political rhetoric and upheaval. Near the end of the book, Lutzer makes a telling application to our day, which is so pertinent to the point I have been making, as he writes:

> Have we—I speak to those of us who are committed Christians- have we forgotten that God's power is more clearly seen in the message of the Cross than in any political or social plan we might devise? Might not our search for some antidote to our grievous ills be symptomatic of out lost confidence in the power of the gospel to change people from the inside out? Do we cling to the Cross with the deep conviction that it is not simply a part of our message to the world, but rightly understood it is the whole of it?

> We have witnessed increasing hostility against Christianity from society in general and from state institutions in particular. The restraints of our Christian past are being cast aside with cynical arrogance. In an effort to be "relevant," we now face the temptation of being diverted from our mission to become involved doing what is good while bypassing what is best.

> What, after all, is the meaning of the Cross about which we speak? Why should Christians "cling to the

old rugged cross" as the old hymn reminds us to do? Surely, we might think we have outgrown such sentimentality. But it is exactly here that Christianity stands or falls; it is the meaning of the Cross that gives Christianity power.[12]

But not only does Jim Packer redirect the mission of the church, he along with many other Evangelical statesmen, misdirects the trust of the church. Alarmed by pervading cultural darkness, Jim Packer and the defenders of ECT place Evangelicals in a state of emergency and encourage us to seek the solace and support of the Catholic Church. Packer tells us that the "stand for truth and wisdom would be stronger" if we join forces with the parallel activities of the Catholic Church.

Surely Packer's belief in the sovereignty of God must be shrinking as he anchors our hope to this trans-denominational coalition, which is devoid of doctrinal unity concerning the Gospel. My question in the light of Packer's proposition, is to ask why there is such small faith on the part of present Evangelicals in the Lord of the Church? Does our hope for survival depend upon alliance with the forces of the "holy father" in Rome, or rather in our Father who reigns in heaven and is able to accomplish His will on earth (Matt. 6:9-10)? Did the early church find it necessary to seek an alliance with Judaism in an attempt to roll back the forces of paganism?

Roman Catholicism, despite the gloss put on it by the words of J. I. Packer, remains an enemy of the Gospel, and is neither a friend of God nor His people. It is shameful that the Church of Christ be called upon in this manner to rely upon Rome for ammunition and manpower in the war against evil and error.

Although spoken in another context, when communism was the perceived threat of the culture, the words of Donald Gillies in *Unity in the Dark* are timely and pertinent. He wrote:

> We have no warrant from God to support one evil in order to destroy another. Judah was severely rebuked by the Lord for doing exactly this—seeking help against Assyria from the old enemy Egypt. "Woe to the rebellious children that walk to go down into Egypt, and have not asked at my mouth; to strengthen themselves in the strength of Pharaoh and to trust in the shadow of Egypt! Therefore shall the strength of Pharaoh be your shame, and the trust in the shadow of Egypt your confusion" (Isa. 30:1-3). The leaders of Judah, in forming this alliance, were guilty of trusting in an arm of flesh instead of in the Lord (Jer. 17:5), and also of disobeying the distinct command of the One who had delivered them out of Egypt, and who said, "Ye shall henceforth return no more that way" (Deut. 17:16). If, therefore, we still believe that the Reformation was of God, then to seek the help of the Church of Rome, which quite openly remains the enemy of the Evangelical Protestant faith (she can do no other), to meet the threat of Communism is sheer rebellion against the Lord.

In chapter 31 of his prophecy, Isaiah continues his rebuke against those of his countrymen who were bent on going down to Egypt for help. He tells them plainly that when the Lord shall stretch out His hand, both helper and helped shall fall, but His faithful people will be defended and preserved by

the power of the Lord. He then calls for a return to
the Lord and for true repentance manifested in the
casting away of all idols. "Then shall the Assyrian
fall with the sword, not of a mighty man" (v. 8). So
may it be in our day.[13]

The church must in these days keep to her mission of personal evangelism and seek to fulfill the great commission in
dependence upon God. Whatever the social or spiritual threat,
the Lord is our refuge and strength, an ever present help in
troublesome times (Psalm 46:1, 90:1).

A Lack of Dissent

In the courtroom of human opinion, a gag order has been
issued to stop the proclamation of the absolute and exclusive
truth of the Gospel of Jesus Christ. The mood of the times, evident both in the church and outside of the church, is that one
belief is as good as another. Therefore, when it comes to personal belief and theological conviction, live and let live, and to
say that someone or something is wrong is increasingly viewed
as wrong itself. The new morality defines right as agreeing that
the other opinion is not wrong. It is believed that everybody has
a right not to be accused of being wrong (Isa. 5:20). To dissent
from this universal law and cultural code is to be immediately
branded a bigot, extremist, and a troublemaker (1 Kings 18:17-
18). Respect and tolerance for everything and anything is the
order of the day.

This unquestioned liberty in belief and behavior is yet
another trend within the framework of this new ecumenism
that concerns me greatly. For example, in the paragraphs preceding the conclusion, the ECT document admonishes Evangelicals
to assiduously respect those who hold to a view of baptism that

includes the reception of the new birth (pp. 22-23). The belief that grace is imparted and sin is removed in the sacrament of baptism is, according to ECT's authors, a doctrine deserving of respect and credence within the Christian community. Thus, people who believe that they are "born again" because they were baptized Catholic "must be given full freedom and respect" to remain Catholic, and they should not be confronted by Evangelicals and told that no amount of sacraments or good works can make them acceptable to God. Dissent and opposition to the falsehood of baptismal regeneration is considered wrong, despite New Testament teaching that baptism does not save, but rather follows one's personal faith in Jesus Christ (Matt. 28:19-20; Acts 2:40-41, 8:36-37, 16:33-34; 1 Cor. 1:17; Titus 3:4-7).

Setting aside the issue of baptismal regeneration, a principle emerges from this statement of tolerance that seems to rule out the possibility of strong protest and dissent towards those with whom you disagree theologically and doctrinally. With the prevailing attitude that accepts separate, yet divergent doctrines, the new breed of Evangelical ecumenists advocate the silencing of dissent in the spirit of Christian fellowship. This suspicion is evidenced by ECT's omission concerning justification by faith alone. Such avoidance of the real issues between Roman Catholicism and historic Evangelicalism creates the impression that cooperation and communion is based upon a vow of silence regarding the big issues.

But is such silence and muted fellowship biblical? Is it wrong to confront someone with his error rather than to close your eyes and mouth to his mistake? Is it right to pursue Christian fellowship while at the same time leaving the outstanding issues of theological divergence behind? I think not!

Isaiah was told to cry aloud and spare not in his denunciation of the people's sin and error (Isa. 58:1). He did not seek peace at any price, but rather sought righteousness at any cost. Likewise, Paul did not assiduously respect Peter's right to fraternize with the Judaizers and their false gospel (Gal. 2:11). Paul was more concerned about the integrity of the gospel and the purity of the church than a patchwork coalition with the Judaizers for the benefit of the nation. It was hardly an exercise in ecumenism when Jesus pronounced his woes upon religious leaders of His day (Matt. 23:13). And according to the New Testament, an apostolic ministry must actively refute those who contradict the Bible (Titus 1:9), and be willing to contend for the gospel (Jude 3 and 4). Pastors ought to be theological and spiritual watchmen who cry a warning to the church of approaching danger, and fearless in their duty of spotting the enemy and defending the church (Ezek. 33:1-6; Mark 8:15; Luke 20:46; Acts 20:26-31; Phil. 3:2; 1 Peter 5:8; 2 John 8).

The active defense of God's Word and biblical doctrine is unpopular today. It is frequently said that pastors must always be positive in their teaching, never negative. But those who say this have either not read the New Testament or, having read it disagree with it. As previously noted, the Lord Jesus and His apostles have set forth the obligation to be negative in refuting error. Is it not possible that the neglect of this very ministry is one of the major causes of theological confusion and false ecumenical fusion in the church today?

A mute church is a weak church. God's men doing God's ministry weren't called to be diplomats, but rather as prophets to clearly and loudly trumpet the truth (1 Cor. 14:8). ECT is the work of diplomats who will have peace at any price even if it means gagging the truth. One might even suppose that should such a trend continue, ECT's authors would have us respect the devil and his doctrines if needed to maintain unity around the shrine of ecumenism. With respect to the issues at stake, we have a solemn duty to protest and publish our dissent against the Gospel's betrayal and the attempt to make vain those martyred for its safeguard. Protestantism was born in protest, and we must continue to live unashamed for the defense of the gospel.

A. W. Pink's comments on the description given by Ahab to Elijah as the "troubler of Israel" makes a statement that is applicable to the argument for Evangelical dissent with heretical doctrines. He wrote:

> It is no unusual thing for God's upright ministers to be spoken of as troublers of people and nations. Faithful Amos was charged with conspiring against Jeroboam the second, and told that the land was not able to bear all his words, Amos 7:10. The Savior Himself was accused of "stirring up the people," Luke 23:5. It was said of Paul and Silas at Philippi that they did "exceedingly trouble the city," Acts 16:20, and when at Thessalonica they were spoken of as having "turned the world upside down," Acts17:6. There is therefore no higher testimony to their fidelity than for the servants of God to evoke the rancor and hostility of the reprobate. One of the most scathing condemnations that could be pronounced on men is contained in those terrible words of our Lord Jesus to His unbelieving brethren: "The world cannot hate you; but Me it hateth, because I testify of it, the works thereof are evil," John 7:7. But who would not rather receive all the charges which the Ahab's can heap upon us than incur that sentence from the lips of Christ!

> It is the duty of God's servants to warn men of their danger, to point out that the way of rebellion against

66

God leads to certain destruction and to call upon them to throw down the weapons of their revolt and flee from the wrath to come. It is their duty to teach men that they must turn from their idols and serve the living God, otherwise they will eternally perish. It is their duty to rebuke wickedness wherever it be found and to declare that the wages of sin is death. This will not make for their popularity, for it will condemn and irritate the wicked, and such plain speaking will seriously annoy them.[14]

The Scottish Highland evangelist, John Kennedy, adds to this point when he wrote:

"No Christian can be true and faithful on whose brow the world shall not brand the name bigot. But let him bear it. It is a mark of honor, though intended to be a brand of shame. In every age from the beginning, when the cause of truth emerged triumphant from the din and dust of controversy, the victory was won by a band of bigots who were sworn to its defense."[15]

Biblical Christianity ought not, therefore, to run shy pursuing the defense of truth for fear of being branded as sectarian. If a man is earnest about truth, he will be sectarian. Scriptural truth by nature is intolerant of error, thus we have no right to make room for views that are incompatible with the Bible. As Pink and Kennedy rightly point out, the church and her leadership must unashamedly stand with the truth and oppose its detractors. Silence towards those who attack the gospel is high treason and a dereliction of Evangelical and pastoral duty. Yet today, the mantle of protest and dissent, which has marked the Evangelical church over the centuries, has fallen to the ground. Truth has lost its teeth. Protestantism is silent towards the Church of Rome and its heretical excesses.

In summary, I ask the following. Why are we witnessing this retreat today from the stance of yesterday? What are the factors contributing to this present course of action which gives credence to another gospel thereby repeating the mistake the Galatians made concerning the Judaizers?

a) Evangelicalism has lost its backbone—no doctrine.

b) Evangelicalism has lost its sight—no discernment.

c) Evangelicalism has lost its nerve—no dependence.

d) Evangelicalism has lost its voice—no dissent.

1. Roy B. Zuck, *Devotions for Kindred Spirits*, (Illinois: Scripture Press Publications, 1990) 275.

2. John MacArthur, *Commentary on Galatians*, (Chicago: Moody Press, 1987) 13-14.

3. Ibid., 14.

4. Erwin W.Lutzer, *All One Body—Why Don't We Agree?*, (Illinois: Tyndale House, 1989) 13-14.

5. Donald Gillies, *Unity in the Dark*, (London: Banner of Truth Trust, 1964) 59-60.

6. John MacArthur, *A Reckless Faith*, (Illinois: Crossway Books, 1994) 131.

7. Addison H. Leitch, *Winds of Doctrine: The Theology of Barth, Brunner, Bonhoeffer, Bultman, Niebuhr, Tillich.* (New Jersey: Revell, 1966) 30.

8. Jay E. Adams, *A Call to Discernment*, (Oregon: Harvest House, 1987) 31.

9. Michael de Semlyen, *All Roads Lead to Rome?* (England: Dorchester House Publications, 1991) 217.

10. Charles Colson and Richard Neuhaus, *Evangelicals and Catholics Together,* (Dallas: Word Publishing, 1995) 171.

11. Ibid., 172.

12. Erwin W. Lutzer, *Hitler's Cross*, (Chicago: Moody Press, 1995) 192.

13. Gillies, 70.

14. A.W. Pink, *Elijah*, (Edinburgh: The Banner of Truth Trust, 1956) 113.

15. de Semlyen, 216.

CHAPTER 3

BY WHAT AUTHORITY?
PART I

2 Timothy 3:14-17

So far in our text we have drawn the doctrinal and historical battle lines that have existed between Protestantism and Catholicism. We have given notice to the recent betrayal and conspiracy afoot in the camp of Evangelicalism. Rather than diligently guard their posts, many Evangelicals would rather give up the fight and settle for a compromise through accommodation with Rome—an accommodation, however, that in reality means a surrendering of the gospel and its principles.

In this chapter, it is my aim to take you beyond the battle lines and into the thick of the fight with Roman Catholicism. Although the Protestant Reformation originally set out to address several abuses within the Catholic Church, such as *indulgences*, the conflict and skirmish escalated over a period of three years into a fiery and furious theological war. By the 1520s, the Reformers had opened two fronts of engagement with Rome around two major doctrinal points.

In his book, *A View of Rome*, John Armstrong details the burgeoning rift between Catholics and the Reformers.

> By the 1520s the central issues of the debate revolved around two major doctrinal points. These two points were known as the formal and material

69

principles of the Reformation. The formal principle, or that which formed the Reformation, was the doctrine of Scripture. What is authority? Where is it found? In the church or in the Bible alone? Is written Scripture sufficient for all faith and practice? What is the place of tradition, of the teaching authority of the pope and the church? How should we respond to councils, creeds, and confessions if they conflict with the written Word? Is the central teaching of Scripture clear?

The material principle was equally important to the formal. In this the Protestant Reformers followed Paul's teaching in Romans that people are made right with God by Christ alone, through grace alone. The key part of this equation was that Christ and grace were received by faith alone. By this the Reformers stressed that true faith laid hold of Christ and the grace of God without any human merit.

These two principles exposed a number of serious theological differences with Rome that are still the cause of division today.[1]

In the light of these two principles of controversy, we can determine that the Reformation was a titanic struggle to discover what truly constituted the revelation of God to men and the redemption of men to God. To Scripture Rome added tradition and to grace they added works. For Protestants, it was a case of *Sola Scriptura* and *Sola Gratia*. The Bible alone speaks, and God alone saves. That was the cause of division then and still remains a problem today.

In his book *What's the Difference?* Peter Toon, a minister in the Church of England, echoes the historical reality of what John Armstrong just outlined with regard to the formal principle of the Reformation. For Toon, the core of the Reformation was the battle over the Bible.

> Between 1515 and 1530, certain members of the great Church began to read the Scriptures—especially the New Testament—with searching and penetrating eyes. They were able to do this because of the new learning and methods of the Renaissance. As they read, they began to realize that many aspects of the life, worship and teaching of the Church appeared to be contrary to the standards set by Jesus and his apostles. One person who felt this keenly was Martin Luther, whose concern over the practice of selling Indulgences (official remission of punishment for sin) led to his nailing of the ninety-five theses to the church door in Wittenberg, on 31 October 1517. This action can be said to have set the Reformation in motion.
>
> In 1523, Huldreich Zwingli initiated the Protestant Reformation in Switzerland with his Sixty-seven Articles, which were debated in Zurich. These are more comprehensive than the ninety-five theses of Luther. The claim that each of them carries is that they are Scripture-based and in accordance with Scripture. Here are two of them:
>
>> *Article X.* Just as a man is demented whose members operate without his head, lacerating, wounding and harming himself, so also are the

members of Christ demented when they undertake something without Christ, their Head, tormenting and burdening themselves with foolish ordinances.

Article XI. Therefore we perceive that the so-called clerical traditions with their pomp, riches, hierarchy, titles and laws are a cause of all nonsense, because they are not in agreement with Christ, the Head.

Here the claim is that Christ can only be known through the authoritative Scriptures; to listen to Christ clearly involves listening to the pure message of the Bible.[2]

This historical issue is not a theological corpse, but a live debate between Evangelicals and devotees of the Vatican. Even today Rome, just as in the 16th Century, denies the sufficiency of the Bible in matters of faith and morals. Catholicism does not deny the authority or inerrancy of the Bible, but she does deny the Bible's adequacy. According to Roman doctrine God has revealed Himself by the twofold means of written and oral revelation; written revelation being the Bible and oral revelation being the verbal teaching of the apostles handed down to their successors in the bishops of Rome (popes).

"The New Catechism" is unambiguous when it addresses these two distinct modes of transmission concerning God's truth; consider the following:

As a result the Church, to whom the transmission and interpretation of Revelation is entrusted, does not derive her certainty about all revealed truths from the holy Scriptures alone. Both Scripture and Tradition must be accepted and honored with equal sentiments of devotion and reverence.[3]

According to Rome, the Protestant is remiss in his search for God's truth since this search is committed exclusively to the Scriptures. This dedication to written revelation deprives the Evangelical of discovering God's truth as revealed through the traditions of the Church. Furthermore, the Protestant, therefore, remains ignorant to Rome's favored interpretation of it, since she alone serves as the principle disseminator of truth. For both Catholics and Protestants, this is where the battle rages.

Why are there such discrepancies between Rome and Evangelicals? Well, simply stated, Rome has two sources of revelation while Evangelicals have only one. Is it not somewhat unremarkable, therefore, that Catholics have developed doctrines that are alien to Bible-believing Protestants? This doctrinal chasm is a watershed for both Catholics and Protestants. Consider the following passage from Cardinal Wiseman of England, as he lectures on the Doctrine and History of the Roman Catholic Church, addressing what happens when people are given a copy of the Scriptures in their own language.

The history in every case is simply this: that the individual, by some chance or other . . . happened to become possessed of the Word of God and of the Bible; that he perused this Book, that he could not find in it Transubstantiation; that he could not find in it Auricular Confession; that he could not find in it one word of Purgatory; nothing in it of worshipping Images. He perhaps goes to the Priest; he tells him that he cannot find these doctrines; his Priest argues with him, and endeavors to convince him that he should shut up the book that is leading him astray; he perseveres; he abandons the communion of the Church of Rome—that is, as it is commonly expressed, the errors of that Church—and becomes a Protestant. Now in all that the man was a Protestant before he began his inquiry; he started with the principle that whatever is not found in that book is not correct—that is the principle of Protestantism. He took for granted Protestantism, therefore, before he began to examine the Catholic religion. He sets out with the supposition that whatever is not in the Bible is not part of God's truth; he does not find certain things in the Bible; he concludes, therefore, that the religion that holds these is not the true religion of Christ.[4]

In his comments, we should take careful note of two things stated by Cardinal Wiseman. First, the Cardinal states that faith and theological awareness based solely upon the Bible is the governing principle of Protestantism. Second, Cardinal Wiseman, an eminent leader in the Catholic Church in England during the 19th century, issues a written confession that Transubstantiation, Auricular Confession, Purgatory, and the worshipping of images is are not permitted or sanctioned in the Bible, and that the Scriptures are mute in rendering any mention of such doctrines. These practices, exclusive to Catholic dogma, have purportedly been disseminated along the path of apostolic oral tradition into the hands of the bishops of Rome. Therefore, what constitutes truth and authority within the church, an unbridgeable gulf opens between Protestantism and Catholicism. To Catholics, the Protestant in his dependency upon the Bible and the Holy Spirit alone is a fool and voluntarily deprives himself of so much more that God would teach him through the oral traditions of Rome.

The late Cardinal D'Alton, Roman Catholic Bishop of Armagh in Ireland, wrote in his Lenten pastoral, which appeared in the Irish News, that Protestants have been in error since the 16th century concerning doctrines of written and oral revelations.

> In these days, when the question of the reunion of our separated brethren is being widely discussed, we should have some knowledge of how the unity of the Church was disrupted and the issues at stake. . . . The Protestant revolt in the sixteenth century was a more serious affair, bewildering in its complexity owing to the grave difference of views amongst the Reformers themselves. However they disagreed on points of doctrine, they were of one mind in repudiating the authority of the pope. The principle they espoused of allowing each one to interpret for himself the Scriptures, which they regarded as the sole rule of faith, has led inevitably to the multiplicity of religious bodies so much at variance with Christ's ideal of one fold and one shepherd. At the present time we should in all charity pray earnestly for our separated brethren that, enlightened by the Holy Spirit, they may find their way back to the one fold of Christ.[5]

From these citations, it is clear that the doctrine of Scripture provides neither common ground nor opportunity for compromise between Catholics and Protestants. *Sola Scriptura* was a matter of first importance for the Reformers, and their engagement with Rome over this issue ought not to be forsaken in our day either.

When Luther stood before his detractors at Worms he said, "Unless I am convinced by Scripture and plain reason, my conscience is captive to the Word of God."

Speaking at a later date, Luther characterized the Reformation as a movement to rediscover the authority of the Word of God, and he attributed the success of the movement to the sufficiency and power of the Bible itself. He said:

> I did nothing. The Word did it all. I simply taught, preached, wrote God's Word, otherwise I did nothing. And while I slept and drank Wittenburg beer with Philip and Amsdorf, the Word weakened all who opposed me.[6]

Rowland Taylor, Rector of Hadleigh and considered to be the third leading Reformer in England, suffered under Bloody Mary's reign for his faith. When he was led forth to be burned at the stake in Suffolk he said,

> Good people, I have taught you nothing but God's Word and those lessons that I have taken out of the Bible; and I am come hither to seal it with my blood.[7]

This battle over the Bible was the kernel of the issue for the Reformers, and continues to remain so for Evangelicals today. This was and is the reason for the parting of the ways. The doctrine of *Sola Scriptura* is not an academic one, but one written in blood and forged with steel conviction in the furnace of affliction.

Having established the front lines in the doctrinal war over the sufficiency of God's word, I wish to present the following material concerning *Sola Scriptura*, especially in terms of its definition and its defense.

1. The Principle of *Sola Scriptura* Defined

Before considering the error of rejecting this truth, we must clarify *Sola Scriptura* and its centrality to core Protestant beliefs. Apart from some authority to fix and settle beliefs there can be no such thing as unity in churches or anything else in the sphere of religion. Thus, the dream of Evangelicals and Catholics seeking union based on certain commonalties will remain forever incomplete due to the difference concerning *Sola Scriptura*.

For Baptists and Protestants that authority is singularly the Word of God. The doctrine of *Sola Scriptura* refers to the Scriptures of the Old and New Testaments as the primary and absolute source of authority, the final court of appeal for all doctrine and practice (faith and morals). Nothing more, nothing less, and nothing else is necessary for the practice of our faith. The Holy Scriptures contains all that is required for what we are to believe, what we are to be, and what we are to do. In sports, players look to the referee to ensure that there is fair play. In the due process of law, men and women look to the judiciary and courts for justice. So in the church, believers look to the Bible to referee and to become the final court of appeal in determining faith, belief, practice and behavior.

In the New Hampshire Confession of Faith, Article 1, this very point is made:

> The Holy Bible was written by men divinely inspired, and is a perfect treasure of heavenly instruction. (2 Tim. 3:16-17; 2 Pet.1:21; 2 Sam 23:2; Psalm 119:111)

> That it has God for its Author, salvation for its end, and truth without any mixture of error, for its matter. (2 Tim. 3:15; 2 Peter 1:10-12; Prov. 30:5-6)

That it reveals the principles by which God will judge us. (Rom. 2:12; 1 Cor. 4:3-4)

That it, therefore, is, and shall remain to the end of the world, the true center of Christian union. (Phil. 2:1-2; Eph. 4:3-6; 1Peter 4:11)

And the supreme standard by which all human conduct, creeds, and opinions should be tried. (Acts 17:11; Jude 3; Psalm 119:59-60)[8]

In 1528, the City of Berne expressed its newfound Protestantism in the Ten Theses, which affirmed the sufficiency of Scripture.

- The holy, Christian Church, whose only Head is Christ, is born of the Word of God, abides in the same, and does not listen to the voice of a stranger.

- The Church of Christ makes no laws or commandments without God's Word. Hence all human traditions, which are called ecclesiastical commandments, are binding only in so far as they are based on and commanded by God's Word.[9]

The name Roger Williams is well known among seventeenth-century Baptists. Williams is famous for his stand on religious freedom and liberty, especially concerning the separation of Church and State and the persecution which subsequently results from such an alliance. Just as the Reformers that preceded him two centuries before, Williams had only the highest regard for the authority of God's Word; consider the following as Williams defended the principle of *Sola Scriptura*.

I urge that this will of God (for this declaration of what Christ said and did and of all the rest of the

Scripture was a Declaration and Revelation of God's Will to his People and to the whole World) this written and revealed will of God I said was the Judge and Decider of all Questions, the Tryer of all Spirits, all Religions, all Churches, all Doctrines, all Opinions, all Actions.[10]

The second London confession (1688-1689) is one of the most influential Baptist statements of faith. It is the Baptist revision of the famous Westminster confession, which became the founding theological document of the Presbyterian and Reformed Churches. The 1689 Baptist Confession clearly defined the principle of *Sola Scriptura*:

The whole Counsel of God concerning all things necessary for His own Glory, Man's Salvation, Faith and Life is either expressly set down or necessarily contained in the Holy Scripture; unto which nothing at any time is to be added, whether by new Revelation of the Spirit, or traditions of men.[11]

From these quotations we see that Protestants and Baptists collectively hold the conviction that the Bible is the divine revelation of God to man, and is complete, infallible, and the standard of authority in matters of faith and conduct. Protestant affirmation of *Sola Scriptura* has caused an unbridgeable schism with a Roman Catholic theology that clings to its duality of written Scripture with unwritten tradition.

By way of explanation and expansion, I want to share something from James White's book *The Roman Catholic Controversy* concerning what *Sola Scriptura* is not and what it is. Perhaps this will help blow away some of the unnecessary smoke that surrounds this battle.

What *Sola Scriptura* is Not:

+ First and foremost, *Sola Scriptura* is not a claim that the Bible contains all knowledge.

+ *Sola Scriptura* is not a claim that the Bible is an exhaustive catalog of all religious knowledge.

+ *Sola Scriptura* is not a denial of the authority of the Church to teach God's truth.

+ *Sola Scriptura* is not a denial that the Word of God has at times been spoken.

+ *Sola Scriptura* does not entail the denial of every form or kind of tradition.

+ *Sola Scriptura* is not a denial of the role of the Holy Spirit in guiding and enlightening the Church.

What *Sola Scriptura* Is:

+ The doctrine of *Sola Scriptura* simply stated is that the Scriptures alone are sufficient to function as the *regula fidei*, the infallible rule of faith for the Church.

+ All that one must believe to be a Christian is found in the Scripture.

+ That which is not found in Scripture either directly or by necessary implication -is not binding upon the Christian.

+ Scripture reveals those things necessary for salvation.

+ All traditions are subject to the higher authority of Scripture.[12]

The above guidelines and points of clarification act as a safety harness to keep us from falling for the common myths about what *Sola Scriptura* does and does not teach. They also provide a good grip on a positive presentation of this doctrine.

By way of summary and conclusion, the words of Edward Hiscox in *The New Directory of Baptist Churches*, seem appropriate in proclaiming Christ as the only lawgiver in Zion and that His royal law has been exclusively laid down in the Holy Scriptures.

> The Bible is a divine revelation of God to man, and is a complete and infallible guide and standard of authority in all matters of religion and morals; whatever it teaches is to be believed, and whatever it commands is to be obeyed; whatever it commends is to be accepted as both right and useful; whatever it condemns is to be avoided as both wrong and harmful; but what it neither commands nor teaches is not to be imposed upon the conscience as of moral obligation.

> The New Testament is the constitution of Christianity, the charter of the Christian Church, the only authoritative code of ecclesiastical law, and the warrant and justification of all Christian institutions. In it alone is life and immortality brought to light, the way of escape from wrath revealed, and all things necessary to salvation made plain; while its messages are a gospel of peace and of hope to a lost world.[13]

2. The Principle of *Sola Scriptura* Defended

Having established the principle of *Sola Scriptura*, let us now consider the solid pillars of evidence upon which it is supported. Our argument for the authority of the Bible will come from the Bible. Just as black and white declare their color, and bitter and sweet demonstrate their taste, so the Bible bears evidence of its own sole authority. Dr. Martin Lloyd-Jones affirms this when he says, "The most important argument of all is that we should believe in the authority of the Scriptures because the Scriptures themselves claim that authority." It is difficult to dodge the claims of the Bible.

Defending the principle of *Sola Scriptura* from the Scriptures themselves is a crucial issue because Rome denies that possibility. Listen to Karl Keating, a Roman Catholic apologist, in his book, *Catholicism and Fundamentalism*, as he inadvertently underscores the importance of what we are about to do:

> Fundamentalists say the Bible is the sole rule of faith. Everything one needs to believe to be saved is in the Bible, and nothing needs to be added to the Bible. The whole of Christian truth is found within its pages. Anything extraneous to the Bible is simply wrong or hinders rather than helps one toward salvation. Catholics, on the other hand, say the Bible is not the sole rule of faith and that nothing in the Bible suggests it was meant to be. In fact, the Bible indicates it is not to be taken by itself. The true rule of faith is Scripture and Tradition, as manifested in the living teaching authority of the Catholic Church, to which were entrusted the oral teaching of Jesus and the apostles plus the authority to interpret Scripture rightly.[14]

Keating's assertion that the Bible does not consider itself the sole rule of faith throws the gauntlet down at the feet of every Evangelical. In fact, he suggests that the Bible implies the opposite. This claim, therefore, constitutes the true bone of theological contention between Catholics and Protestants. The viewpoint that can best defend its claim to authority shall win the fight and rule the day. That is why my treatment of this issue will be more extended than other areas of conflict; consequently, *Sola Scriptura* must be defended at all costs and with total commitment. Therefore, we shall let the Bible defend itself, as it is most capable of doing.

The Doctrine of *Sola Scriptura* is Based on the Nature of the Scriptures as the Word of God

There can be no understanding of the Bible's sufficiency apart from recognition of the true nature and origin of Scripture. The cornerstone passage in this defense is 2 Timothy 3:14-17. In this passage, a number of statements are asserted which are pivotal to the defense of *Sola Scriptura*.

The Scriptures are described as being inspired by God which literally means, *God-breathed*. The Scriptures are God's very words to man through man, where God is not breathing into man's words, but breathing out His words to man (2 Sam. 23:2; Jer. 1:4-5, 9; Ezek. 3:10-11; Rev. 1:10-11). The Scriptures, therefore, are the very words of God. The means by which this was accomplished was the superintendence of the Holy Spirit upon the author in the production of Scripture, so that they wrote with personality out of their own vocabulary, precisely what God wanted them to write (2 Pet. 1:21). Although God did not dictate every word to them, the end product was just as inerrant as though He had. The measure of that inspiration is to be seen in the use of the word "all". The Greek word *pasa* means all and every; thus in his description of God's influence on Scripture, Paul was unequivocal that the Bible is therefore every bit the Word of God from cover to cover.

By way of footnote, please bear in mind that Paul is centering on the origin and resultant nature of inspiration, not its extent. Although the Old Testament is in view, the New Testament is not to be placed outside the picture. Paul quotes Luke's writings with the standard introduction of "for the Scriptures say . . ." (1 Tim. 5:18 quoting Luke 10:7), and Peter refers to Paul's writings as "Scripture" in 2 Peter 3:16. Hence, the principles concerning the inspiration of the Old Testament hold true for the New Testament.

In his description of Scripture, the Apostle Paul asserts that only Scripture is God-breathed and inspired. The words and writings were inspired, not the writers. In all of Paul's writings he does not refer to any other instruments of authority than the written Word (Gk. *graphe*). This is proof that all Christian authority must be based solely on the written Word (ie., Scritpture).

In addition, the terms used to describe the ability of God's Word in the redemptive purposes of God in the soul of man is also worth highlighting. The use of the word "competent" or "thoroughly" (KJV, NKJV) in connection with the Scriptures ability to save (v.15) and sanctify (vv. 16-17) implies manifestly, the sole authority and complete sufficiency of the Bible for faith and practice.

Finally, the surrounding context of these verses stand in defense of the principle of *Sola Scriptura*, in that Paul repeatedly takes his highlighter and stresses the importance of holding fast to the Word of God (1:13; 2:15; 3:15-16; 4:2). In fact, the lack of a reference to any other authority than the written Word of God is quite conspicuous; nowhere will one find oral church tradition as having any authority assigned by Paul.

The doctrine of *Sola Scriptura* is indeed founded and built upon the very nature and authorship of the Word of God itself. Read again the words of the 1689 Baptist Confession of London:

> The Authority of the holy Scripture for which it ought to be believed dependeth not upon the testi-

mony of any man or Church; but wholly upon God (who is truth itself) the Author thereof; therefore it is to be received, because it is the Word of God.[15]

John Calvin, the father of Presbyterian and Reformed theology, is likewise unambiguous in his statements concerning Scripture:

> In order to uphold the authority of Scripture, he [Paul] declares it to be divinely inspired. For it be so, it is beyond all controversy that men should receive it with reverence ... Whoever, then, wishes to profit in the Scriptures, let him first of all lay down as a settled point this—that the law and the prophecies are not teachings delivered by the will of men, but dictated by the Holy Ghost ... Moses and the prophets did not utter at random what we have from their hand, but since they spoke by divine impulse, they confidently and fearlessly testified, as was actually the case, that it was the mouth of the Lord that spoke ... We owe to the Scripture the same reverence which we owe to God, because it has proceeded from Him alone ...[16]

The Doctrine of *Sola Scriptura* is Reflected in the revealed Attributes and Actions of the Word of God

The Holy Scriptures speak for themselves; they tell us that they are perfect, competent, and able. Consider the following list of names and ministries of the Bible as *prima facie* evidence of its sufficiency and authority:

The Description of The Scriptures:
- Word. James 1:21-23; 1 Peter 2:2

- Word of God. Luke 11:28; Hebrews 4:12
- Word of truth. James 1:18
- Holy Scriptures. Romans 1:2; 2 Timothy 3:15
- Scripture of truth. Daniel 10:21
- Book. Psalm 40:7; Revelation 22:19
- Book of the Lord. Isaiah 34:16
- Book of the law. Nehemiah 8:3; Galatians 3:10
- Law of the Lord. Psalm 1:2; Isaiah 30:9
- Sword of the Spirit. Ephesians 6:17
- Oracles of God. Romans 3:2; 1 Peter 4:11
- Word of the Lord. Acts 13:48; 2 Thessalonians 3:1
- The Word of Life. Philippians 2:15, 17; Acts 5:20
- The Word of Faith. Romans 10:8-9

The Design of The Scriptures:

- By them we are born again. James 1:18; 1 Peter 1:23
- They quicken. Psalm 119:50, 93
- They illuminate. Psalm 119:130
- They convert the soul. Psalm 19:7
- They make wise the simple. Psalm 19:7
- They cleanse. John 15:3; Ephesians 5:25-26; Psalm 119:9
- By them we are built up. Acts 20:32; 1 Peter 2:2
- By them our hearts are made to burn. Luke 24:32, 45
- By them God's will is accomplished. Isaiah 55:10-11; Jeremiah 23:29
- They expose the thoughts of the heart. Hebrews 4:12; Psalm 119:11
- The sinner is to be judged by them. John 12:48; Luke 16:29-31
- They sanctify. John 17:17; Ephesians 5:26
- They keep from destructive paths. Psalm 17:4

- They promote growth in grace. 1 Peter 2:2
- They admonish. Psalm 19;11; 1 Corinthians 10:11
- They comfort. Psalm 119:82; Romans 15:4
- They rejoice the heart. Psalm 19:8; 119:111[17]

Although enough has been said already under this point, I do wish to expand by considering more deeply one attribute and one ability of Scripture that I trust will dispel any remaining doubts about whether the Bible is enough.

First let us consider how David describes the Word of God in Psalm 19:7. "The law of the Lord is perfect." The English word "perfect" is the translation of a common Hebrew word that also bears the meaning "whole," "complete," or "sufficient." It conveys the idea of something that is comprehensive, so as to cover all aspects of an issue. Albert Barnes, writing on this Psalm, said:

> The meaning [of "perfect"] is that [Scripture] lacks nothing [for] its completeness; nothing in order that it might be what it should be. It is complete as a revelation of Divine truth; it is complete as a rule of conduct . . . It is absolutely true; it is adapted with consummate wisdom to the [needs] of man; it is an unerring guide of conduct. There is nothing there which would lead men into error or sin; there is nothing essential for man to know which may not be found there.[18]

Second, note the expressed ability of the Bible in the words of the Apostle Paul in 2 Timothy 3:14-17. The Scriptures are said to make us complete. Regarding the word *complete*, a survey of the best Greek lexical tools will yield such meanings as "fitted," "capable," and "proficient." This is, as we say, able to meet all demands. God's Word is able to qualify us for all matters of faith and practice.

Paul doesn't stop there; rather, he continues under the steam of the Holy Spirit to reveal that God's Word is also able to fully equip us unto every good work. An explanation of this is best given by way of illustration, one afforded to us by James White in his book, *The Roman Catholic Controversy*, in which he wrote:

> We see here, then, that Paul teaches the man of God is thoroughly or completely equipped for every good work. Now, what does it mean that the Scriptures are able to fully equip the man of God if not that they are sufficient for this task? If I am a store owner who can fully equip a hiker to hike the Grand Canyon—if I have the resources and abilities to provide everything he needs in the way of supplies, hiking gear, shoes, maps, food, etc.—does it not follow that I am a sufficient source of supply for the hiker? If he has to go next door to another shop for a few more things, and then to a third shop for some things that neither mine nor the other shop had, then none of us are sufficient to equip the hiker. But if that hiker can come to my shop alone and get everything he needs to accomplish his task, then I can rightly call myself a sufficient equipper of a hiker of the Grand Canyon.[19]

In the exact same way the Scriptures are able to equip the man of God fully so that he is able to do every good work. No true Protestant needs to shop in Rome for another source of truth and equipment. Rome is selling something the Protestant doesn't need because he has been totally outfitted by the Word of God.

The Doctrine of *Sola Scriptura* is Supported in the constant Appeal of Jesus and His Apostles to the Bible as the Final Court of Appeal

Jesus and his Apostles often did this by the introductory phrase, "It is written," which is repeated over 90 times in the New Testament. Jesus was constantly and continually using the authority of the Scriptures, whether disputing with men or the devil, often using the words, "It is written . . ." or "Have you not read?" (Matthew 4:4, 7, 10; 12:3-5; 19:4; 21:16; 21:42; 22:31).

Although the Lord possessed all authority (Mt. 28:18), exercised authority (lk. 4:33-36), and taught with authority (Mt. 7:28-29), He appealed to the authority of the Old Testament Scriptures (Jn. 5:45-47; Mt. 23;23). He also submitted Himself to their authority in His life and work (cp. Mt. 5:17; 26:52; Lk. 18:31-33).

The apostles recognized the authority of the Scriptures, both the Old Testament (II Tim. 3:16; Acts 2:14-36; Rom. 3:9-22) and the New Testament (I Thess. 2:13; II Pet. 3:2).

Of course, Jesus (Matt. 5:22; 28:18) and the apostles (1 Cor. 5:13; 7:12) sometimes referred to their own God-given authority, but their appeal to an authority outside the Bible was due to the fact that God was still giving normative revelation for the faith and morals of believers. But as we know (and Rome agrees) apostolic revelation ceased when apostolic miracles ceased. Therefore, it is pushing the limits of what's reasonable to appeal to any oral revelation in the New Testament times as evidence that non-biblical authority exists today.

The Doctrine of *Sola Scriptura* is Further Defended by the Bible's Warnings Not to Step Outside the Finished Written Truth of the Word of God

The Bible is not a book that requires a leader's guide or an expanded edition. In fact, a severe judgment and sober admonition is given to one and all if they should attempt to add to or subtract from the Bible (1 Cor. 4:6; Deut. 4:2; Prov. 30:5-6; Rev. 22:18-19). Jesus specifically warned about the danger of sometimes adding tradition to the Word of God thereby short-circuiting its effect (Matt. 15:3-6).

The Doctrine of *Sola Scriptura* Finds a Witness for its Case in the Clear Intent of God Communicated From the Beginning That Normative Revelation be Written Down and Preserved for Future Generations

Recalling an observation we made when dealing with 2 Timothy 3:14-17, it was noted that the inspired truth of God encompasses only that which was written down (Greek *graphe*).

Consider the following words from Norman Geisler and Ralph MacKenzie as they address this very issue in their book, *Roman Catholics and Evangelicals.*

> "Moses then wrote down all the words of the Lord" (Ex. 24:4). Indeed, Moses wrote in Deuteronomy, "these are the words of the covenant which the Lord ordered Moses to make with the Israelites" (Deut. 28:69), and Moses' book was preserved in the ark of the covenant (Deut. 31:26). "So Joshua made a covenant with the people that day and made statutes and ordinances for them . . . which he recorded in the book of the law of God" (Josh. 24:25-26) along with Moses' (cf. Josh. 1:7). Likewise, "Samuel next

explained to the people the law of royalty and wrote it in a book, which he placed in the presence of the Lord" (1 Sam. 10:25). Isaiah was commanded by the Lord to "take a large cylinder-seal, and inscribe on it in ordinary letters" (Isa. 8:1) and to ". . . inscribe it in a record: That it may be in future days an eternal witness." (Isa. 30:8) Daniel had a collection of 'the books" of Moses and the prophets right down to his contemporary, Jeremiah (Dan. 9:2). Jesus and the New Testament writers used the phrase "Scripture has it" (cf. Matt. 4:4, 7, 10) over ninety times, stressing the importance of the written Word of God. When Jesus rebuked the Jewish leaders it was not because they did not follow the traditions but because they did not "understand the Scriptures." (Matt. 22:29) The apostles were told by Jesus that the Holy spirit would "guide . . . [them] to all truth." (John 16:13) But Jesus said in the very next chapter "Your word is truth" (John 17:17) and the apostles claimed their writings to the churches were "Scripture . . . inspired of God." (2 Tim. 3:16; cf. 2 Pet. 3:15-16) Clearly God intended from the very beginning that his revelation be preserved in Scripture, not in extra-biblical tradition. To claim that all God's revelation was not written down is to claim that the prophets were not obedient to their commission not to subtract a word from what God revealed to them.[20]

For Catholics, the Bible is not the sole rule of faith but is to be complemented with tradition; and according to the Catholic theologian Karl Keating, there is nothing in the Bible that would even suggest that. Contrary to Catholic dogma, the fact that Scripture without tradition is said to be "God-breathed," and thus its believers are "completed and fully equipped for every good work" demolishes the Roman argument. Paul's assertion flies in the face of the Catholic claim that the Bible is formally insufficient, without the prop of church tradition. The Word of God tells us that it alone is the final court of appeal, and consequently indicts the Roman Church with falsifying and counterfeiting the truth through its additions and appendages.

> A team restoring da Vinci's "Last Supper" in 1981 found original details in the masterpiece that had been hidden or altered through the years. The dark windows behind the figures were actually finely detailed tapestry. Orange slices, unseen for centuries, materialized on the plates, as did a golden thread on the rims of the glasses. Even Simon Peter's beard grew longer with the brush of each restorationist.

A similar masquerade has been perpetrated on the Bible and Christianity across the centuries. Over the centuries, many books, creeds, and traditions have existed proposing to explain the Bible or to be as authoritative as the Bible and many people have mistaken them for the Bible. In Christendom today, there exists many practices and beliefs that were conspicuously absent in the beginning. Whatever the intent, these additions can mask the glory and cloak the blinding luminosity of Scripture and biblical Christianity. God's promise of power comes only through his Word, not through human additions to it.

As we shall see in the next chapter, Rome is the chief culprit in this masquerade. It is one thing to lengthen Peter's beard, but quite another to add to the Word of God. It's one thing to touch up the work of men, but another thing to improve upon the Word of God. This is Rome's claim, and this is Rome's crime, and she stands exposed to the marksmanship of God's judgment (Rev. 22:18-19).

By way of positive application and conclusion, may God lead every true child of His to a renewed appreciation for the Holy Scriptures as our sufficient and authoritative guide concerning our worship of and walk with God. We must not only expose error but also embrace truth. It is one thing to give theological assent to the position of *Sola Scriptura*, but it is another thing to express practical compliance (Luke 6:46-49). That which is our creed must be part of our conduct. Let us therefore be diligent to recognize the Bible's value and authority over our lives.

Many Protestants need to be reminded that at the end of the day their neglect of the Bible in practical terms leaves them no better off than the Roman Catholic and his tradition, because neither manifests a dependence upon the Scriptures. In this context, neglect is as much an attack upon the doctrine of *Sola Scriptura* as is the addition of Catholic tradition. Through tradition, the Catholic says the Bible is not enough; while through neglect, the Protestant says the Bible is not necessary. The Protestant's slothfulness is perhaps the greater sin since he should know better and do better. How quick we are to nod with approval concerning the theology of this chapter, but how slow we are to prove the genuineness of the nod. Too often ours is but lip service and not life service to the Word of God. More often than we might care to acknowledge, the average Evangelical carries his or her Bible to church, but leaves it far behind in work, rest, and play.

This shouts for repentance and calls for renewal in the heart of Evangelicals towards the Word of God. It seeks a commitment to the Scriptures that will manifest itself in greater study, wider obedience, higher reverence, and deeper devotion to the Book and it's Author. This is the need of the hour. As I heard Dick Mayhue share in a class at the Master's Seminary:

- We need to receive God's Word like the Thessalonians (1 Thess. 2:13).
- We need to feed upon God's Word like Job (Job 23:12).
- We need to obey God's Word like Caleb (Num. 14:24).
- We need to honor God's Word like the Jew (Neh. 8:4-6).
- We need to study God's Word like Ezra (Ezra 7:10).
- We need to know God's Word like Apollos (Acts 18:24-28).
- We need to preach God's Word like Christ (Matt. 7:28-29).
- We need to commit God's Word like Paul (2 Tim. 2:2).
- We need to value God's Word like David (Ps. 19:10).
- We need to publish God's Word like the runner (Ps. 68:11).

In John Richard Green's *A Short History of the English People*, he states:

> No greater moral change ever passed over a nation than passed over England during the years which parted the middle of the reign of Elizabeth from the Long Parliament. *England became a people of the book, and that book was the Bible.* It was read at churches and read at home, and everywhere its words kindled a startling enthusiasm. As a mere literary monument, the English version of the Bible remains the noblest example of English tongue. But far greater was the effect of the Bible on the character of the people. The whole temper of the nation felt the change. A

new conception of life and of man superseded the old. A new moral and religious impulse spread through every class.[21]

May God make us like England of old, a community of believers who live obediently under the reign of the the royal law of King Jesus. A people of the Book. May God brand upon our souls the words of the Psalmist: *"I will delight myself in your statues. I will not forget your Word"* (Ps. 119:16).

---

1. John H. Armstrong, *A View of Rome*, (Chicago: Moody Press, 1995) 49.
2. Peter Toon, *What's the Difference?*, (Basingstoke: Marshall Paperbacks, 1983) 39-40.
3. *The Catechism of The Catholic Church*, (Missouri: Liguori Publications, 1994) para. 82.
4. Wendell Holmes Rone, *The Baptist Faith and Roman Catholicism*, (Wisconsin: Baptist Heritage Press, 1989) 9.
5. Donald Gillies, *Unity in the Dark*, (London: Banner of Truth Trust, 1964) 28.
6. David Roper, *Seeing Through*, (Oregon: Multnomah Books, 1995) 55.
7. J. C. Ryle, *English Reformers*, (London: The Banner of Truth Trust, 1960) 18.
8. Rone, 4.
9. Toon, 40.
10. Dr. James Draper, *Authority: The Critical Issue for Southern Baptists*, (New Jersey: Revell, 1984) 57.
11. Ibid., 56-57.
12. James White, *The Roman Catholic Controversy*, (Minnesota: Bethany House Publishers, 1996) 56-62.
13. Rone, 5-6.
14. Karl Keating, *Catholicism and Fundamentalism*, (San Francisco: Ignatius Press, 1988) 134.
15. Draper, 57.
16. Ibid., 51-52.
17. Rone, 4-5.
18. Albert Barnes, *Notes on the Old Testament: Psalms, Volume 1*, (Grand Rapids: Baker, 1974) 171.
19. White, 66.

20. Norman Geisler and Ralph McKenzie, *Roman Catholics and Evangelicals,* (Grand Rapids: Baker, 1995) 189.

21. Steve Lawson, *Faith Under Fire,* (Illinois: Crossway Books, 1995) 144.

CHAPTER 4

BY WHAT AUTHORITY?
PART II

2 Timothy 3:14-17

In the previous chapter our eyes were opened to Rome's self-inflicted blindness concerning the sole sufficiency and singular authority of God's Word. The Bible has a place in the faith of the Vatican but it is not one of preeminence. The Bible is the Word of God, but it is only part of God's Word. According to Rome, church tradition is to be set alongside the Bible as a equal partner in the communication of revelation and truth. However, this position is a contradiction of the self-revelation of God as found in Scripture. The Bible itself speaks of its own sufficiency and is its own best witness, is it not? Not according to Rome, which continues to deny what we sought to defend in the previous chapter.

Why this denial? Rome's denial of the principle of *Sola Scriptura* is based in large part upon a desire for self-preservation. Stated bluntly, the faith of the Vatican practices many things, as we shall see, that cannot be grounded in the Word of God. Therefore it must preach from another standard apart from the Word of God. Roman Catholicism is a system with major theological beliefs that cannot be found inside the Bible and therefore it must have an authority outside of the Bible. The same holds true for Mormonism and other aberrant man-made systems of belief. When man cannot find what he wants to believe in the Bible, he will either change the Bible or add to it.

Charles Haddon Spurgeon in his autobiography addressed this very point:

> The Church of Rome is afraid to trust the Bible alone, because it destroys the foundations of its religion. If the Scriptures were given to the people simply as they are, Romanism would never be able to stand against them: it would soon be known that Rome is the very Antichrist. She therefore mystifies the Word of God by means of the words of men: she puts her own perversions side by side with Scriptures and declares that, as she alone can interpret them, whatever is said to be the meaning of them must really be so.[1]

With these words Charles Haddon Spurgeon, a great and articulate advocate of the Protestant faith, unmasks the Bible denying nature of Catholicism. His indictment of the Roman Catholic Church is based on three counts with regards to her treatment of the Bible. These counts involve imprisonment, assault, and deception. For Spurgeon, Rome's denial of the principle of *Sola Scriptura* was, and is, manifest in her prohibiting of the free distribution of the Bible; in her defacing the Word of God by the addition of tradition; and in her deception by claiming to be the one and true interpreter of the Bible.

Spurgeon's criticism of Rome's aversion to *Sola Scriptura* cuts to the very bone of contention between Romanism and biblical Protestantism. Throughout the centuries, Rome has denied access to the Bible, denied the sole authority and complete sufficiency of the Bible, and denied the perspicuity of the Bible, claiming its meaning cannot be clear without the church's help. Such denials and distortions continue to be at the heart of our disagreement and diversity with the faith of the Vatican. Thus, the Protestant war with Rome is a battle over the Bible. The Reformation was a recovery of the Bible, elevating its place and power within the church. The Reformers realized that the message of the Bible was clear and its truth sufficient. They understood the need and importance for putting the Bible into the common vernacular. For this reason, John Wycliffe and William Tyndale worked to translate the Bible into the language of the people, and Martin Luther and John Calvin sought to preach it to the masses.

During the hearing of the British Royal Commission on Palestine in 1937, David Ben Gurion, chairman of the executive committee of the Jewish agency for Palestine, affirmed: *"The Bible is our mandate. The mandate of the League is only a recognition of this right and does not establish new things."* To draw an analogy from the Jewish struggle for independence, the Protestant struggle for freedom from Rome's bondage and unbelief had as its mandate, the Bible alone. The Reformation, and its subsequent radical reformation in the Baptist movement, was not the act of establishing a new religion but simply the calling forth of a recognition of the *faith once delivered to the saints* through the Scriptures. Singularly, the Bible was its mandate for doing so. This recognition of Scripture's sufficiency was, and is, sadly lacking by Rome. This whole issue of the Bible's availability, sufficiency, and perspicuity is still smoking, and the heat of the debate has never relented.

For instance, in the ECT document there is an admission that theological differences still exist between Evangelicalism and Romanism, and that the outstanding differences include the authority of the Bible. ECT notes a difference over, "The sole authority of Scripture [*Sola Scriptura*] or Scripture as authoritatively interpreted in the church [the Roman Church]."[2]

By way of footnote, please underscore the fallacy of the ECT document in that unity is declared apart from and without the stated recognition of the Bible's sole authority and complete sufficiency. Here is an admission that faith among brothers and sisters in Christ is not regulated by the Word of God itself. From this we see that the principle of *Sola Scriptura* remains an unresolved issue and continues to be a point of contention. Even Roman Catholics themselves agree that *Sola Scriptura* remains a divisive issue. Speaking of Thomas Howard's conversion to Catholicism, the 1985 September edition of *Christianity Today* relates:

> When Thomas Howard, brother of Elizabeth Elliot (wife of martyred missionary Jim Elliot), became a Catholic, Gordon College removed him from its faculty. Among the reasons given was the fact that the statement of faith which all faculty had to sign affirmed the Bible as "the only infallible guide in faith and practice"—impossible for a Catholic to sign. Howard acknowledged that "the sole authority of Scripture is a principle unique to Protestantism, and that he, as a Catholic, could not subscribe to it."

Therefore, in this complementary chapter to the previous one, I wish to join the case for the prosecution along with Spurgeon and prove Rome's denial of *Sola Scriptura*. Rome is criminally negligent in her handling of God's Word and has viciously assaulted the truth of the Bible's perspicuity and sufficiency. It must be recognized that Rome is no guardian of truth. She is a vandal and thief of the treasure of Scripture, and three historical and theological facts will give evidence of her unlawful behavior.

The Principle of *Sola Scriptura* Denied

Denied by Rome's Record of Prohibition

The history of Protestantism is one marked by a desire to preach and print the Word of God in the belief that faith comes by hearing and hearing by the Word of God (Rom. 10:17; 2 Tim. 3:15; James 1:21). During the Reformation, the combined forces of Protestant preachers and printers led the attack for the cause of truth in the sixteenth century and following. The availability of the Word of God, coupled with the powerful declaration of the Gospel, shook the culture and the church of that day to its very foundation (Acts 17:6; 1 Thess. 1:5-8).

The Protestant desire to put the Scriptures into the hands of the laity was evidenced by the example of William Tyndale. As the father of the English Bible and a true Evangelical, Tyndale is reported to have on one occasion ruffled the feathers of a certain church dignitary by his method of quoting the Bible as God's law. The man exclaimed:"We would better be without God's law than the pope's!" To which Tyndale replied,"I defy the pope and all his laws, if God spare my life, ere many years, I will cause a boy that drives a plow to know more of the Scripture than you do."[3] These words of Tyndale exemplify the heart and soul of the Protestant effort. The Bible was considered to be sufficient and clear, and therefore ought to have been the proclamation of every minister and the possession of every plowboy. From its very conception, Protestantism sought to facilitate the free distribution and full proclamation of the Bible.

The history of Roman Catholicism sadly demonstrates contempt for placing God's Word into the hands of its parishioners. The faith of the Vatican has to its eternal shame, a record of choking the distribution of the Bible and murdering those who attempted to do so. The aforementioned William Tyndale was strangled by the Roman religion for the crime of translating the Word of God into the language of the English people. In England during the reign of Bloody Queen Mary, heaps of Bibles were used to provide fuel with which to burn the martyrs and it was said that no burnt offerings could be more pleasing to Almighty God.

Over the centuries, the papacy has considered the possession of a Bible as tantamount to signing one's death warrant. Rome sought to make the Bible a hidden book, to be handled and decoded by church experts only; ordinary people could not be trusted with the Bible. The Bible during the dark ages wore a papal muzzle and could only speak as the church permitted. Historically, one of the dominant characteristics of Catholic lands and legacy is an appalling ignorance of the Word of God, and that is still in large part the case even today.

In his classic work, *Roman Catholicism*, Lorraine Boettner elucidates this very point:

> The Bible was first officially forbidden to the people by the Church of Rome and placed on the Index of Forbidden Books by the Council of Valencia (a cathedral city in southeastern Spain) in the year 1229, with the following decree:
>
>> "We prohibit also the permitting of the laity to have the books of the Old and New Testament, unless any one should wish, from a feeling of devotion, to have a Psalter or breviary for divine service, or the hours of blessed Mary. But we strictly forbid them to have the above mentioned books in the vulgar tongue".

Here we see that the Bible was forbidden to the laity, except for the Psalms or breviary (book of devotion), and even then it could be only in Latin—which of course, placed it beyond the reach of the common people. That decree was passed at the time the Waldensians were gaining strength, and it was enforced with bitter persecutions.

The Council of Trent reaffirmed that decree and prohibited the use of the Scriptures by any member of the church unless he obtained permission from his superior. The decree read as follows:

> "Inasmuch as it is manifest, from experience, that if the Holy Bible, translated into the vulgar tongue, be indiscriminately allowed to everyone, the temerity of men *will cause more evil than good* to arise from it; it is, on this point, referred to the judgment of the bishops, or inquisitors, who may, by the advice of the priest or confessor, permit the reading of the Bible translated into the vulgar tongue by Catholic authors, to those persons who faith and piety, they apprehend, will be augmented, and not injured by it; and this permission they must have in writing."

To this decree, as to more than a hundred others passed by this council, was attached an anathema against anyone who should dare to violate it, and penalties were also fixed against the illegal possessor or seller of those books. Here we observe particularly the statement that the reading of the Bible in the native tongue will do "more evil than good"! Imagine that, as the deliberate teaching of a church professing to be Christian! How insulting to God is such teaching, that His Word as read by the people will do more evil than good! That attitude toward the Word of God is the mark, not of a true church, but of a false church.[4]

As if the above were not enough to convict Catholicism, let me produce further incriminating evidence of Rome's imprisonment of the Bible, by citing their own commentary and condemnation of the work of John Wycliffe. Having been described as the Morning Star of the Reformation, John Wycliffe pioneered the translation of the Bible into English. Unlike Tyndale, who translated from the Greek, Wycliffe translated from the Latin. Articulating the Catholic bias against distribution of the Bible, Pope Gregory XIII, in a papal bull to the University of Oxford in 1378, stated he had "run into a detestable kind of wickedness." This he spoke regarding Wycliffe's work. For committing this supposed wickedness, namely translating the Bible into the language of the day, Wycliffe was never to be forgiven and long after his death, the Catholic Church had the bones of John Wycliffe exhumed and burned, whereupon his ashes were scattered upon the river Swift in England.

In Anderson's book *The Annals of the English Bible*, there is a quotation that both summarizes and unmasks Rome's disdain for the work of Wycliffe and manifests Catholicism's fear of Bible distribution in general:

> Master John Wycliffe has translated the gospel out
> of Latin into English, which Christ has entrusted to
> the clergy and doctors of the Church, that they

might minister it to the laity and the weaker sort, according to the state of the times and the wants of man. So that by this means the gospel is made vulgar (common) and laid more open to the laity, and even the women who can read, that it used to be to the most learned of the clergy and those of the best understanding. And what was before the chief gift of the clergy and doctors of the Church is made forever common to the laity.[5]

Surely, critics shall scoff and aver that this was the Rome of yesteryear, but what about today? Has Vatican II not changed all that? The latter half of the twentieth century has indeed seen remarkable change in the attitude toward Scripture among Roman Catholics. The Bible is no longer strictly the prerogative of the priest. Possession of the Scriptures and personal Bible study is on the increase and for that we are grateful to God. Vatican II and the New Catechism exhorts the free access of the faithful to the sacred Scripture and condemns ignorance of the Bible as ignorance of Christ.[6]

Is not this exemplary and commendable? Yes, as far as it goes. The reality is that the Roman Catholic Bible is still not a book of the people, but a book of the church. Catholics may be encouraged to read their Bibles but they are still not free to determine what it means.[7] The true interpretation of the Scriptures remains the sole right of the Church Magisterium.[8] To ensure that Catholics reading the Bible come to the pre-approved conclusions, Vatican II ordered that Bibles with "suitable notes" be equipped with necessary and sufficient explanations. Therefore, the end result of Catholic Bible study is not to understand the Scriptures in the original sense in which they were written, but to understand them in the sense by which they are understood by the church.

Vatican II may have been the dawning of a new day, but it has not changed the old ways of Rome. As in Wycliffe's day, the Bible remains a book truly for the "clergy and good doctors" of the church.

The vast majority of Catholics remain blind to the Bible and the glorious Gospel, because God's Word is to be read through the eyes of the church, resulting in the blind leading the blind (Matt. 23:16,17,24). The window dressing of Vatican II cannot change the facts of history, nor does the placement of the Bible in the hands of a false church produce truth. It is extremely difficult to see how a church, which has manifested such hostility to the Bible, can be the church which Jesus promised to build and sanctify by His truth. Rome believes that the Bible in the hands of the people without some safeguards does "more evil than good." In these words, the evil heart of the Roman Catholic system is laid bare.

John Wesley, the great Anglican preacher who founded the Methodist Church, wrote these words in the preface to a volume of his sermons which was published in 1746:

> I am a creature of a day, passing through life as an arrow through the air. I am a spirit, come from God and returning to God: just hovering over the great gulf. I want to know one thing—the way to heaven; how to land safe on that happy shore. God Himself has condescended to teach the way. He hath written it in a Book. O! Give me that Book![9]

God wrote a book and desired that men should have it. The very fact that the Bible was written for the common people is testimony enough. The language of the Old Testament was the language spoken in the homes and marketplaces by the Hebrews. New Testament Greek was not the classical Greek of an earlier period, but the Greek uttered by the common people. It was Koine Greek, so called because it was the common language, what today we would call newspaper talk. This all goes to prove that God intended the common people to understand the Bible.

God's Word is not a dark and mysterious book, but as Peter says, "a light shining in a dark place" (2 Peter 1:19). God intended mothers and fathers to teach it to their children (Deut. 6:7-9). It's message is so plain a child can find the path to Christ through it (2 Tim. 3:15). How wrong can the Catholic Church be?

Denied by Rome's Reverence of Tradition

Roman Catholicism has not only denied the principle of *Sola Scriptura* by restricting the Bible's availability, but also by limiting the Bible's authority. Like the Rome of old, its present-day successor continues to propagate the message that God's truth is not singularly found within the perimeters of the Old and New Testaments. Thus, Rome has added to a compact Bible a vast and developing library of tradition.

As James McCarthy points out, Roman Catholic theologians picture divine revelation as a pool. They postulate that transmission of God's revealed truth to the modern church takes place by means of two streams flowing from the one pool. One stream represents Scripture, the other tradition and together they comprise the preserved and transmitted revelation of Christ, entrusted by Christ to His apostles.[10] Upon this premise, the Catholic Church defines the Word of God as being both Scripture and tradition. It is a fair assumption that when a Catholic priest speaks about the Word of God, he is likely referring to Scripture and tradition together. To put it another way, according to the Catholic Church, the Bible alone is not the complete Word of God. For Rome, there is vital and essential truth preserved in tradition not clearly taught in the Bible. When the Bible speaks, it tells the truth and nothing but the truth, but for Catholics, it fails to encompass the whole truth. The Vatican has decreed that the Scriptures need to rest upon the shoulders of tradition.

The New Catholic Catechism articulates this position with the following statements:

In keeping with the Lord's command, the Gospel was handed on in two ways:

> *Orally* "by the apostles who handed on, by the spoken word of their preaching, by the example they gave, by the institutions they established, what they themselves had received—whether from the lips of Christ, from his way of life and his works, or whether they had learned it at the prompting of the Holy spirit."

> *In writing* "by those apostles and other men associated with the apostles who, under the inspiration of the same Holy Spirit, committed the message of salvation to writing."[11]

> "Sacred Tradition and Sacred Scripture, then, are bound closely together and communicate one with the other. For both of them, flowing out from the same divine well-spring, come together in some fashion to form one thing and move towards the same goal." Each of them makes present and fruitful in the Church the mystery of Christ, who promised to remain with his own "always, to the close of the age."

"Sacred Scripture is the speech of God as it is put down in writing under the breath of the Holy Spirit."

"And [Holy] Tradition transmits in its entirety the Word of God which has been entrusted to the apostles by Christ the Lord and the Holy Spirit. It transmits it to the successors of the apostles so that, enlightened by the Spirit of truth, they may faithfully preserve, expound, and spread it abroad by their preaching."

As a result the Church, to whom the transmission and interpretation of Revelation is entrusted, *does not derive her certainty about all revealed truths from the holy Scriptures alone. Both Scripture and Tradition must be accepted and honored with equal senti-ments of devotion and reverence.*"[12]

Revelation disseminated through Scripture and Tradition is the present position of the modern Catholic Church, and is a reflection of her position throughout the ages. Hitched to the vehicle of Scripture is the trailer of tradition. Added to the Words of God are the traditions of men. Neither do Catholics derive certainty about their relationship with God nor future security from the Bible alone, they never have.

Since the Council of Trent, for whom Luther was a heretic, the Catholic Church has articulated this article of her faith. In its fourth session, it made clear that it accepted a twofold source of truth: Scripture and Tradition—a position subsequently reiter-ated in both Vatican I and Vatican II, and encased in the New Catechism as just noted. The Council of Trent stated in the Decree Concerning the Canonical Scriptures:

It also clearly perceives that these truths and rules are contained in the written books and in the unwritten traditions which, received by the Apostles, from the mouth of Christ himself, or from the Apostles themselves, the Holy Ghost dictating, have come down to us, transmitted as it were from hand to hand. Following then, the examples of the orthodox fathers, it receives and venerates with a feeling of piety and reverence all the books both of the Old and New Testaments, since one God is the author of both; also the traditions, whether they relate to faith or to morals, as having been dictated either orally by Christ or by the Holy Ghost, and preserved in the Catholic Church in unbroken succession.[13]

Is that true? Has God intended for His truth to be preserved and transmitted in two forms, one oral and the other written, but both forming an equal authority? Does the Catholic have an advantage over the Protestant in that he has more revelation? My answer to all three questions is an emphatic No! Let me reason this negative response out for you.

I Refuse to Accept the Catholic Position on Tradition Because of the Practical Facts

The proof of the pudding is in the eating we say. How then has Roman tradition served the church over the centuries? Well let's taste and sample from the menu of Catholic belief cooked up by Catholic tradition:

Prayer for the dead commenced . . . . circa 310

Wax candles introduced into churches . . . . circa 320

Worship of the saints and angels . . . . circa 375

Mass first adopted . . . . circa 394

Worship of Mary began to develop 431

Priests began to dress differently from laity 500

The doctrine of purgatory taught 593

Worship in an unknown tongue. 600

The pretensions of the pope to universal supremacy. 606

Feasts in honor of the virgin Mary began . . . . circa 650

Worship of images and relics authorized 788

Holy water invented, circa 850

Worship of St. Joseph began, circa. 890

Baptism of bells 965

Canonization of saints 993

Feasts of the dead instituted, circa. 1003

Celibacy of priesthood decreed 1074

The doctrine of the infallibility of church 1076

Prayer beads invented. 1090

Doctrine that seven sacraments are taught 1140

Origin of Inquisition 1184

Sale of indulgences 1190

Wafer substituted for bread in Lord's Supper 1200

Transubstantiation adopted 1215

Confession instituted 1215

The Inquisition introduced into France 1216

Adoration of the wafer (Host) 1220

Hand bell used during mass 1227

Cardinals ordered to wear red hats 1245

Feast of Corpus Christi instituted. 1264

The scapular invented, circa 1287

Sprinkling for immersion decreed.................. 1311

The Ave Maria.................................. 1316

The procession of the Holy Sacrament 1336

Communion in one kind; cup taken from laity 1415

Purgatory decreed................................ 1439

The Inquisition introduced into Spain............. 1478

Roman tradition placed on same level as Scriptures . 1546

Apocryphal books received into sacred canon....... 1546

Immaculate conception of virgin Mary 1854

Doctrine of temporal power of pope proclaimed 1864

Proclamation by Pius IX's "Syllabus"
condemning modern liberties...................... 1864

Pius IX's "Syllabus" ratified by Vatican Council 1870

Infallibility of pope decreed 1870

Pius X's Encyclical on mixed marriages,
condemning as null and void all marriages
between two Catholics, or a Catholic and
a Protestant if not celebrated by priest 1908

The Assumption of Mary, i.e., she bodily ascended
into Heaven without ever experiencing death....... 1950

If that's what's being served off the plate of church tradition, then I can do without. My theological appetite finds no savor in Roman church tradition. The practical facts are clear in that these objections have in no way emerged from the uncontaminated pool of the Scripture, but has come from the poisoned well of error.

I Refuse to Accept the Catholic Position on Tradition Because of the Biblical Facts

As we saw in the previous chapter, the biblical facts speak for themselves in defending the principle of *Sola Scriptura*. The Bible itself advocates the certainty and sufficiency of the Scriptures alone on a number of fronts:

+ The nature of Scripture itself due to the act of inspiration.

+ The revealed actions and attributes of Scripture.

+ Christ and his apostles appeal to Scripture as the final court of appeal.

+ The warnings about adding to the Scriptures.

+ God's intention that revelation be written down.

By way of further expansion, it is important to address the verse of Scripture that Catholic apologists use to support the supposed insufficiency of Scripture and the necessity of tradition. Paul's reference in 2 Thessalonians 2:15 to the oral and written communication of biblical tradition is held up by Catholic apologists as proof for their case. Thus, from one pool of revelation flow two streams, written Scripture and oral tradition, which are equally true and authoritative. For Catholics, the underlying assumption is that oral tradition is somehow different or separate from the written tradition. But does Paul defend this in the passage? A careful study of the context does not support the assertion made by Catholic apologists.

First, the believers whom Paul addressed himself were called to hold fast to a single body of traditions already delivered to them. Paul offers no pretense for future understanding in relation to tradition. The traditions were already given to the assembly and were given to the whole Church. Second, the content of the oral teaching was the gospel (vv. 13-15). The Thessalonians, much like the Corinthians, were being called to stand up for Jesus as soldiers of the cross (1 Cor. 16:13; 2 Thess. 2:15).

This is a far cry from traditions yet undeveloped and contrary to the gospel of Jesus Christ that are central to the Catholic Church. Tradition, as Paul defines it in this letter, is nothing like the future departures from the gospel of the Roman System. The apostle Paul is speaking of doctrines that he personally had delivered to the Thessalonians. They were direct revelation from God and in perfect harmony with the Word of God. The Church of Rome would have us compare apples with oranges.

I Refuse to Accept the Catholic Position on Tradition Because of the Historical Facts

History serves as an ally to the principle of *Sola Scriptura* as set against the falsity of Roman Catholic tradition. Rome's embrace of tradition is not the only time human tradition has pitched itself against divine revelation. In his book, *Faith of the Vatican*, Herbert Carson expands on the point at hand:

> This matter of Scripture and tradition did not emerge as a new controversy in the sixteenth century. It was a live issue in the days of Jesus. Again and again he encountered the appeal of the Pharisees to their traditions. Of course, they wholeheartedly accepted the Scriptures of the Old Testament as the Word of God to which they must submit. They recognized the threefold division into the Law, the Prophets, and the Writings, but that recognition in no way modified or negated acceptance of the unity of the Old Testament. Yet at the same time they would make their appeal to the traditions which they had received from

their fathers and which, for them, were also authoritative. The great rabbinical teachers had commented on the Scriptures and had endeavored to apply their teaching to the pattern of worship and to the daily lives of their people. This mass of writings and the developed norms of conduct had an authority which stood alongside that of the Scriptures and at times qualified, or even violated, the law.[14]

Protestants have historical precedence when it comes to this problem of tradition versus Scripture. The Scriptures possess an infallible rule in the example of Christ and His reaction to such additions to the Scriptures by means of clerical tradition. Christ made several condemnatory statements against such dualism, which will provide clarity to this point.

It is a matter of sinning (Matt. 15:3).

It short-circuits the power of God's Word (Matt. 15:6; Mark 7:13).

It desecrates our worship of God (Matt. 15:9; Mark 7:7).

It turns us from the Bible (Mark 7:8).

If we learn anything from history, it is that we have learned little from history. Rome perpetuates the error of the Pharisees in creating a duality of authority which was condemned by Christ, and therefore must be rejected by us (Col. 2:8; Gal. 1:14-16; Phil. 3:7; 2 Peter 1:16-21).

Addressing the Council of Trent's claim that certain traditions of the Church could be traced back to oral instruction from the first apostles, this Swiss Confession counters:

Likewise we reject human traditions, even if they be adorned with high-sounding titles, as though they were divine and apostolic, delivered to the Church by the living voice of the apostles, and, as it were, through the hands of apostolic men to succeeding bishops which, when compared with the Scriptures, disagree with them; and by their disagreement show that they are not apostolic at all. For as the apostles did not contradict themselves in doctrine, so the apostolic men did not set forth things contrary to the apostles. On the contrary, it would be wicked to assert that the apostles by a living voice delivered anything contrary to their writings. Paul affirms expressly that he taught the same things in all churches (1 Cor. 4:17). And, again "For we write you nothing but what you can read and understand" (2 Cor. 1:13). Also, in another place, he testifies that he and his disciples—that is, apostolic men—walked in the same way, and jointly by the same Spirit did all things (2 Cor. 12:18). Moreover, the Jews in former times had the traditions of their elders; but these traditions were severely rejected by the Lord, indicating that the keeping of them hinders God's law and that God is worshiped in vain by such traditions (Matt. 15:1ff; Mark 7:1ff).[15]

Surely the biblical and historical facts direct us away from the theological proposition of the Roman Church, that the Bible is the truth and nothing but the truth, but not the whole truth. Rome's recognition and promulgation that tradition is as vital to obtaining God's revelation as Scripture has taken away from the uniqueness of the Bible. Through the addition of tradition, the Vatican has therefore multiplied God's anger toward her (Prov. 30:5-6). Rome denies the principle of *Sola Scriptura* not only by the prohibition of what is true but also by the addition of what is false.

Denied by Rome's Right of Interpretation

In presenting a third aspect to Rome's denial of *Sola Scriptura*, I wish to reiterate the point that the average Catholic, although presently encouraged to read his or her Bible, is not free to determine its true meaning. Proper and accurate interpretation of the Bible remains the sole right of the Church through the channel of the Magisterium. Therefore, based on Catholic dogma, it is possible to conclude that without the tradition of Rome, the Bible is not the whole truth, and without the interpretation of Rome we lack a clear and understandable Bible.

In his book *The Gospel According to Rome*, James McCarthy frames for us the very picture that has just been presented.

> The teaching authority of the Church resides in the bishops and is called the Magisterium, from the Latin word for master. Only the bishops of the Church have the right to judge the true meaning of revelation and to teach it with authority (NCC para. 85, 100, 939):

> > The task of giving an authentic interpretation of the Word of God, whether in its written form or in the form of Tradition, has been entrusted to the living teaching office of the Church alone. Its authority in this matter is exercised in the name of Jesus Christ.
> >
> > Second Vatican Council

> Catholics, therefore, are to obey the bishops even as they would Christ Himself (NCC para. 87, 862):

> > . . . the bishops have by divine institution taken the place of the apostles as pastors of the Church, in such wise that whoever listens to

117

them is listening to Christ and whoever
despises them despises Christ and him who
sent Christ (cf. Luke 10:16).

Second Vatican Council

Consequently (NCC para. 891, 2034, 2037, 2041,
2050):

. . . the faithful, for their part, are obliged to
submit to their bishops' decision, made in the
name of Christ, in matters of faith and morals,
and to adhere to it with a ready and respectful
allegiance of mind.

Second Vatican Council

Matters of faith here refers to the doctrinal beliefs of
the Roman Catholic religion, such as the real presence of Christ in the Eucharist and the Immaculate
Conception of Mary. Matters of morals refers to
proper conduct, such as loving one's neighbor and
obedience to the commandments.[16]

The unequivocal message taken from the above statements is that Catholicism presents the Bible as a book of the
Church not of the people. Although professing to be servants of
the Bible, the bishops of Rome, along with the supposed successor of St Peter, have for all intents and purposes become the
Bible's master. Without pontifical authority, the Bible can neither teach nor instruct. The light of the gospel must be filtered
through them, and the keys to biblical knowledge have been
entrusted to them. The pope maintains the status of the Bible's
sole legitimate interpreter. Thus if there is but one interpretation, which would be Rome's interpretation, then there can but
one Church, the Church of Rome.

Do all theological roads lead to Rome for an answer? Is Biblical interpretation the rightful mandate of the pope? I don't think so, and I will tell you why.

In the New Testament, the Standard of Measurement for Examining Teaching in the Church was Not Peter, nor the Apostles, But the Bible Itself

Paul exhorted the believers at Galatia to test that which was preached to them, even by an apostle, against that which had already been preached and received as the Gospel (Gal. 1:6-9). In other words, they were to test those who purport to preach the Gospel by the very words contained in the Gospel. By implication, the New Testament considers the messenger to receive his authority from the message he preaches not vice versa. The Bible is the measure of a man and the truthfulness of his ministry, not the other way around.

Another example of this principle is found in Luke's account of the Jerusalem Council. Regarding the controversy of Gentile circumcision, we see Peter rise to give his opinion (Acts 15:7-11). What is of note, in reading the historical account, is that Peter's perspective was received, not because Peter said it, but because Amos agreed with it. Only then was James prepared to state his conclusion and let the business proceed (Acts 15:15-19; Amos 9:11-12). Again we see that the measurement for examining teaching in the church was not Peter nor the apostles, but the Bible itself.

Related to this matter John Calvin wrote:

> Paul testifies that the Church "is built on the foundation of the apostles and the prophets" (Eph. 2:20). If the doctrine of the apostles and prophets is the foundation of the Church, the former must have had its

119

certainty before the latter began to exist . . . Nothing therefore can be more absurd than the fiction that the power of judging Scripture is in the Church, and that on her nod its certainty depends. When the Church receives it and gives it the stamp of her authority, she does not make that authentic which was otherwise doubtful or controverted, but acknowledging it as the truth of God, she as in duty bound, shows her reverence by an unhesitating assent.[17]

The substance of Calvin's statement is that the apostles built their doctrine upon the Word of God and the Church is built upon the foundation of the apostle's doctrine, thus the Church is a product of the Scriptures, not its proprietor. Rome errs greatly when she makes the Church, and not the Bible, the immediate and sufficient source of religious knowledge. The soteriological consequence is frightening in that Catholicism makes the relationship of the individual to Christ dependant upon his relation to the Church. The Bible, however, makes the relationship of the individual to the Church dependent upon his relation to Christ. This is the position of Evangelicals relative to a regenerated Church membership.

Rome's Protected Position as the Sole and Safe Interpreter of Holy Scripture is Further Damaged When One Grasps the Right and Ability of Each Believer, Under the Supervision of the Holy Spirit to Interpret Scripture

This is the united testimony of the New Testament writers themselves (Acts 17:11; 1 Cor. 2:12-16; 1 John 2:26-27). These verses are not a denial of the role given by the Holy Spirit to the teaching pastor within the Church (Eph. 4:11-12), but they are a denial of the saint's supposed inability to understand and interpret the Bible by himself apart from the Church. These verses betray the lie of an elite group of decoders of Scripture, infallible and indispensable to God's people for knowledge of God's Word.

In the above reference taken from 1 John, the apostle writes in a context of false teachers and erroneous doctrine plaguing the Church, and warns against blind obedience and unquestioning dependence upon any man as our teacher. Through a possessed anointing by the Holy Spirit, every believer can test for himself claims to truth, and contest claims to truth, through a personal knowledge of the Bible. The child of God must never allow any man or men to take the place of God the Holy Spirit in leading them into all truth (1 John 2:26-27; John 14:26). Blind faith is a spiritual illness that we must open our eyes to, and it is especially found in Roman Catholicism.

In his book, *The Woman that Rides the Beast*, Dave Hunt gives us a classic example of this very disease when he writes:

> Cardinal Ratzinger, watchdog of orthodoxy, exemplifies this blind faith in Catholicism. He tells of a theology professor who admitted that the Assumption of the Virgin Mary, declared a Roman Catholic dogma in 1950 by Pope Pius XII could not be supported by Scripture, yet decided to believe it because "the Church is wiser than I." Sadly, he is actually acknowledging the Church to be wiser than the Bible and thus capable of contradicting it![18]

By way of countermeasure, Catholic apologists will point to 2 Peter 1:20-21 and claim that Scripture, as Peter wrote, is not subject to any private interpretation, and therefore the child of God does not have the wherewithal to pick the fruit of Bible interpretation. The Church alone holds the key to unlocking the treasury of biblical knowledge. In my estimation, this is plainly a misrepresentation of the issue of private interpretation. This is a text ripped from its context and has become in the hands of Rome a pretext to error concerning the Magesterium.

James White, whom we noted in a previous study, is again helpful on this matter as he writes concerning this verse.

> This text is frequently used by Roman Catholics to insist that Scripture is of no "private interpretation," the point being that one must have the Roman hierarchy to interpret the text—the individual is incapable of such a momentous task. But this is not the point of Peter at all. The text, taken as a whole, makes it clear that the concern of Peter is not with "interpretation" of the text but rather with the origin and resultant surety of the text. Immediately before, Peter refers to his experience of hearing the voice of the Father speak to the Son on the Mount of Transfiguration (Matthew 17). But despite this personal experience, Peter insists that we have the "more sure" word of prophecy. Why is this written revelation more "sure" than his own personal experience? Because of the nature of that revelation.[19]

Underline clearly in your thinking that the nature of revelation, and not the right of interpretation, was foremost in Peter's thinking at this point.

The Moral Necessity of the Magisterium is a Plain Denial of the Perspicuity of the Scriptures

The perspicuity of the Scriptures does not mean that everything in the Bible is perfectly clear (2 Peter 3:15-16), but rather that the essential teachings are. To put it simply, in the Bible the main things are the plain things and the plain things are the main things.

Mark Twain once said, "Most people are bothered by those passages of Scripture which they cannot understand; but as for me, I have always noticed that the passages in Scripture which trouble me most are those which I do understand."

Indeed, our greatest problem lies not in understanding the Bible, but in obeying it. The Bible is lucid, clear and plain, lending itself to the fruits of reading even by the simplest mind.

In his admirable book, *Systematic Theology*, Wayne Grudem explained these very points:

> The character of Scripture is said to be such that even the "simple" can understand it rightly and be made wise by it. "The testimony of the Lord is sure, making wise the simple" (Ps. 19:7). Again we read, "The unfolding of your words gives light; it imparts understanding to the simple" (Ps. 119:130). Here the "simple" person (Heb. peti) is not merely one who lacks intellectual ability, but one who lacks sound judgment, who is prone to making mistakes, and who is easily led astray. God's Word is so understandable, so clear, that even this kind of person is made wise by it. This should be a great encouragement to all believers: no believer should think himself or herself too foolish to read Scripture and understand it sufficiently to be made wise by it.

There is a similar emphasis in the New Testament. Jesus himself, in his teachings, his conversations, and his disputes, never responds to any questions with a hint of blaming the Old Testament Scriptures for being unclear. Even while speaking to first-century people who were removed from David by 1,000 years, from Moses by about 1,500 years, and from Abraham by about 2,000 years, Jesus still assumes that such people are able to read and rightly to understand the Old Testament Scriptures.

In a day when it is common for people to tell us how hard it is to interpret Scripture rightly, we would do well to remember that not once in the Gospels do we ever hear Jesus saying anything like this: "I see how your problem arose—the Scriptures are not very clear on that subject." Instead, whether he is speaking to scholars or untrained common people, his responses always assume that the blame for misunderstanding any teaching of Scripture is not to be placed on the Scriptures themselves, but on those who misunderstand or fail to accept what is written. Again and again he answers questions with statements like, "Have you not read . . ." (Matt. 12:3,5; 19:14; 22:31), "Have you never read in the Scriptures . . ." (Matt. 21:42), or even, "You are wrong because you know neither the Scriptures nor the power of God" (Matt. 22:29; cf. Matt. 9:13; 12:7; 15:3; 21:13; John 3:10; et at.).[20]

The Theological Implications of This View as Espoused by Rome is to Claim the Ability to Fill the Shoes of the Holy Spirit and to Become God to the Seeker

By her claim to be the sole and authentic interpreter of Scripture, Rome is for all intents and purposes seeking to compete with the Holy Spirit. Yet according to the New Testament, only the Holy Spirit, not the pope or his henchmen, can serve as a sufficient teacher and guide to the Church of Christ.

For example, a scanning of the verbs contained in John 14:26, John 16:12-15, and 1 Cor. 2:10-13 reveals that the Holy Spirit instructs, brings to remembrance, guides, declares, and reveals directly and sufficiently to the flock of Christ. These promises of divine instruction pertain to several areas: (1) Instruction in "all things" (John 14:26); (2) Recollection of past utterances of Christ (14:26); (3) Guidance into "all truth" (16:13); (4) Declaration of future events (16:13); and (5) Revelation of "the deep things" of God (1 Cor. 2:10).

By God Himself in the person and work of the Holy Spirit, His people have ample provision. Why bow to the pope and seek his help when as a Christian one can kneel before the Holy Spirit and have His help?

From the Greater Arguments to the Lesser, it Must be Noted that in Practice, the Theory of the Moral Necessity of a Magisterium is a Complete Failure

A single infallible authoritative teaching body has not produced a distinct harmonious Catholic Church. The Roman sea may look placid on the surface, but beneath the surface, crosscurrents of division and dispute rage. Catholic apologists love to poke fun at the proliferation of Protestant denominations as proof for the Magisterium, but they are diligent in keeping the gate closed to their own back yard and the family feuding that goes on there.

In *The Gospel According to Rome*, James MacCarthy explodes the myth of the Magisterium's profitability with these words:

> Furthermore, even with its Magisterium, the Roman Catholic Church is hardly an oasis of doctrinal harmony in a theologically troubled world. Indeed, the very purpose of the new Catechism of the Catholic Church is to quell ever-increasing dissent within the Church. In a book explaining the need for the Catechism, Monsignor Michael J. Wrenn, special consultant for religious education to Cardinal John O'Connor, listed just some of the doctrinal areas in which independent-minded Roman Catholic priests and theologians are challenging the Church's official teaching: the existence of angels, the direct creation of the human soul, the fall of man in Adam, the virgin birth of Christ, the atoning sacrifice of Christ, the perpetuation of the cross in the Mass, the real presence of Christ in the Eucharist, the infallibility of the Magisterium, the hierarchical authority of the pope and bishops, the efficacy of the sacraments, the Trinity, purgatory, and sexual ethics.
>
> The Magisterium has also failed to produce a common faith among the laity. Many Catholics are opposed to the Church's ban on contraceptives and its exclusion of women from ordination to the priesthood. They sympathize with a growing number of clergy who believe that mandatory priestly celibacy is doing more harm than good. Some Catholics have stopped listening to the Magisterium altogether.[21]

By now you should agree that there is a strong case for prosecuting Rome for treason regarding the matter of *Sola Scriptura*. Through prohibition Rome has denied the necessity of the Bible, through tradition Rome casts doubt upon the sufficiency of the Bible, and through restricted interpretation Rome shrugs her shoulders at the Scripture's perspicuity. The faith of the Vatican is not an ally but an enemy of true biblical Christianity. She teaches that the Bible is not enough and the Holy Spirit is not enough. That is high treason against God, the author and sender of each.

By way of conclusion, let me share with you a light-hearted story with a rather serious twist to it:

A book collector ran into an unbookish acquaintance who soon revealed that old books didn't mean anything to him. In fact, he observed he had just thrown away a big old Bible which had been packed away in the attic of his ancestral home for generations. He was describing it and said, "Somebody named Guten-some-thing had printed it." The bibliophile gasped. "Not Guttenberg! You idiot! You've just thrown away one of the first books ever printed. A copy sold recently at an auction for over a million dollars!" But the other man was unmoved. He responded, "No, not my copy. It wouldn't have brought a dime. Some fellow named Martin Luther had scribbled notes all through it!"

This book collector's horror over the stupidity and ignorance of his friend is a parable of the shocking plight of Protestantism today. In bringing the lesson of this chapter a little nearer home, it would have to be admitted that many Evangelicals fail to grasp the history and value of their own English Bibles. The heroes and issues of that history are little known. We pay lip service to the centrality of the Bible for Evangelicals but we will marginalize its authority for the sake of a non-biblical unity with those who undermine that very authority. In fact in today's ecumenical climate as ECT demonstrates, we have packed the principle of *Sola Scriptura* away so that Romanist can feel more comfortable in the Evangelical house of faith.

My prayer is that these two chapters will call the Evangelical church back behind the battle lines of the Reformation drawn by our fathers in defense of the Bible's sufficiency, authority, and profitability. May the household of Evangelicalism build once again and only upon the granite rock of divine revelation as contained in the Old and New Testaments and not give credence to the sand of popish tradition. Let us be wise builders in a day of foolish plans (Matt. 7:24-27).

1. Source Unknown.

2. Charles Colson and Richard Neuhaus, *Evangelicals and Catholics Together*, (Dallas: Word, 1995) xxi.

3. John Legg, *The Footsteps of God*, (England: Evangelical Press, 1986) 131.

4. Lorraine Boettner, *Roman Catholicism*, (New Jersey: Presbyterian and Reformed, 1962) 97-98.

5. Wendell Holmes Rone, *The Baptist Faith and Roman Catholicism*, (Wisconsin: Baptist Heritage Press, 1989) 10-11.

6. *Catechism of the Catholic Church*, (Missouri: Ligouri Publications, 1994) para. 131- 133.

7. Ibid., para. 113, 119.

8. Ibid., para. 85, 100, 890.

9. Ian Macpherson, *Live Sermon Outlines*, (Grand Rapids: Baker, 1974) 13.

10. James McCarthy, *The Gospel According to Rome*, (Oregon: Harvest House, 1995) 285.

11. *Catechism of the Catholic Church*, para. 76.

12. Ibid., para. 80-82.

13. James White, *The Roman Catholic Controversy*, (Minnesota: Bethany House Publisher, 1996) 72-73.

14. Herbert Carson, *The Faith of the Vatican*, (England: Evangelical Press, 1996) 41.

15. Peter Toon, *What's the Difference?*, (Basingstoke: Marshall Paperbacks, 1983) 49.

16. James MacCarthy, 265-266.

17. Institutes, 1.7.2

18. Dave Hunt, *A Woman Rides the Beast*, (Oregon: Harvest House, 1994) 332.

19. James White, 238.

20. Wayne Grudem, *Systematic Theology*, (Grand Rapids: Zondervan, 1994) 106.

21. James MacCarthy, 274-275.

CHAPTER 5

ONCE IS ENOUGH

Hebrews 9:23-28

A study of the life of John Knox will show him to be an unapologetic Protestant who pursued the cause of the Reformed Faith in Scotland with vigor and bravery. His favorite characterization of his own work was "to blow his Master's trumpet." John Knox was not one for saving Rome any embarrassment in his sermons. In fact, those who heard him said this of his public ministry: "While others lopped off the branches of papistry, John Knox struck at the roots to destroy the whole."

Taking my cue from such a great Protestant, I wish in this study to strike at the very roots of Roman Catholic piety and practice. In the spirit of Knox, I want to cut to the heart of Catholic life and liturgy in the hope of destroying the whole. I speak concerning the Eucharist and Roman Mass, which is the hub of Roman piety and the cornerstone of Catholic worship. By their own admission the Sacrament of the Mass constitutes the heart of their faith. It is the crown jewel of Roman Catholic ministry and activity.

The centrality of the Mass is confirmed in the following quotes:

> The Second Vatican Council called it "the fount and apex of the whole Christian life."

Pope Pius XII described the Mass as "the culmination and center of the Christian religion; it is the crowning act."

Pope Paul VI affirmed that it is "first in intrinsic worth and implications for the life of the Church.[1]

The Second Vatican Council recognized how central and vital the Mass was to Roman Catholics by making its "constitution on the sacred liturgy" its first completed work. Recognizing the importance of the Mass, one commentator on the Second Vatican Council stated, "While many of the issues discussed in the Council have only indirect bearing on the everyday life of the faithful, the liturgy touches everyone immediately and vitally. Nothing is more evidently at the core of the Christian life than our public worship."

Please note the importance and prominence attached to the Mass within the life and liturgy of popery. It is the "apex, center and crowning act" of Catholic piety and practice. It is the touchstone of their dogma and the cornerstone of their faith. This doctrine goes down to the very roots of Catholicism. This is, therefore, where every true Protestant ought to aim his ax.

Added to the example of John Knox consider the exhortation of Archbishop Cranmer as he warns the Protestants of Great Britain concerning the Mass:

What availeth it to take away beads, pardons, pilgrimages and such other like popery, so long as the two chief roots remain unpulled up? So long as they remain, there will spring up the former impediments of the Lord's harvest, and corruption of the flock. The rest is but branches and leaves, the cutting away whereof is like topping and lopping of a tree, or cutting down the weeds, leaving the body standing and the roots in the ground. But the very body of the tree, or rather the roots of the weeds is the popish doctrine of Transubstantiation, of the real presence of Christ's flesh and blood in the sacrament of the altar (as they call it) and of the sacrifice and oblation of Christ made by the priest for the salvation of the quick and the dead. Which roots, if they be suffered to grow in the Lord's vineyard, will over spread all the ground again with the old errors and superstitions.[2]

With such exhortation and example, let us take the sword of the Spirit, being the Word of God, and begin attacking the diabolical doctrine of the Roman Mass, which reduces Christ to but a thin wafer of bread, and redefines the Gospel of Christ's finished work upon the cross for sinners. What we shall see is incriminating evidence in proving Rome's criminal behavior toward the truth of God's most holy Word. The Catholic understanding of the Eucharist sacrament drives a stake through the heart of the New Testament message concerning Christ, His person, and work.

Luther, a former priest of the Church of Rome, described the Mass as "an unspeakable abomination, quite contrary to the principal article of justification by faith alone." Calvin, the Swiss Reformer and theological stalwart of the Reformed movement, called it "Satan's attempt to adulterate and envelop the sacred supper of Christ as with thick darkness."[3]

Considering the last statement, let us take the light of God's Word and shine it upon the thick darkness of Rome's erroneous teaching concerning the Mass, in the hope of exposing error and lighting up a path for dear Roman Catholics to find present and perfect peace in the sufficiency and singularity of Christ's death for sinners.

The Significance of the Roman Mass

The significance of the Mass within Catholicism cannot be overstated. It is as we have already noted in the words of Vatican II, "the fount and apex of the whole Christian life" to the Catholic mind and worshiper. It is the sacrament of sacraments. It is the chief means of grace to the soul of the sincere Catholic.[4]

Remember that Catholicism is founded upon the belief that Christ has deposited His grace into the treasury of the Catholic Church, and like the windows of a bank teller, Rome dispenses the riches of Christ's grace through the seven windows of the sacraments, the chief of these being the Mass. Grace, according to the Vatican, comes to the soul not directly, but in a mediated manner, in this case brokered through the Roman priesthood and sacraments. We will deal with this more fully when we engage the concept of clerical priesthood. Suffice to say, the role and place of the Eucharist is one of primary importance.

The efficacy of the sacraments and especially the Mass was stated most clearly by Pope Paul VI when he said, "Let no one deny that the sacraments are acts of Christ, who administers them through the agency of men. Therefore they are holy of themselves, and owing to the virtue of Christ, they confer grace to the soul as they touch the body."[5]

The following statements from the 1994 Catechism will show you to what extent grace is conferred when the consecrated wafer touches the lips of the worshiper. Please mark the great significance of this act within Catholicism.

When the Church celebrates the Eucharist . . . the sacrifice Christ offered once for all on the cross remains ever present. "As often as the sacrifice of the Cross is celebrated on the altar, the work of our redemption is carried out."[6]

The Eucharist is thus a sacrifice because it re-presents (makes present) the sacrifice at the cross, because it is its memorial and because it applies its fruit . . . [e.g.,] its salutary power [is] applied to the forgiveness of the sins we daily commit.[7]

The sacrifice of Christ and the sacrifice of the Eucharist are one single sacrifice . . . "In this divine sacrifice which is celebrated in the Mass, the same Christ who offered himself once in a bloody manner on the altar of the cross is contained and is offered in an un-bloody manner."[8]

The Eucharistic sacrifice is also offered for the faithful departed [in purgatory] who "have died in Christ but are not yet wholly purified," so that they may be able to enter into the light and peace of Christ . . . Holy Communion . . . preserves, increases, and renews the life of grace received at Baptism . . . The Eucharist cannot unite us to Christ without at the same time cleansing us from past sins and preserving us from future sins . . . [It] wipes away venial sins . . . [And] the Eucharist preserves us from future mortal sins.[9]

By this sacrifice he pours out the graces of salvation on his Body which is the Church.[10]

When you piece together Catholic teachings on this subject there is nothing left to wonder as to why Catholics refer to the celebration of the Eucharist as the most blessed sacrament. This act procures and preserves salvation. It helps purify those in purgatory. Through the Eucharist, sin is forgiven, the life of grace received at baptism increased, and the whole Church is awash with the graces of salvation.

Since Roman Catholicism holds that the Eucharist helps one to attain to eternal life, the Church encourages the faithful to receive it daily.[11] For this same reason Church law requires Catholics to attend Mass each Sunday and on certain feast days of the Church.[12] Catholics must also receive Holy Communion at least once a year during the Easter Season.[13] It is considered a mortal sin to do otherwise in disobeying the dictates of the Catholic Church.[14]

As for those Protestants who deny the significance of the Mass as authored by Rome, there remains nothing but the anathema of Catholicism upon them.

In the Canon 2 of the Most Holy Sacrament of the Eucharist, a decree belonging to the 13th session of the Council of Trent, 1551, and in the Canon 3 of the Doctrine Concerning the Sacrifice of the Mass, a decree belonging to the twenty-second session of the Council of Trent, 1562, Catholic dogma is explicit in its condemnation of those who denies their Eucharistic doctrine.

> (Canon 2) If anyone says that in the sacred and holy sacrament of the Eucharist the substance of the bread and wine remains conjointly with the body and blood of our Lord Jesus Christ, and denies that wonderful and singular change of the whole substance of the bread into the body and the whole sub-

stance of the wine into the blood, the appearances only of bread and wine remaining, which change the Catholic Church most aptly calls transubstantiation, let him be anathema.

(Canon 3) If anyone says that the sacrifice of the mass is one only of praise and thanksgiving; or that it is a mere commemoration of the sacrifice consummated on the cross but not a propitiatory one; or that it profits him only who receives, and ought not to be offered for the living and the dead, for sins, punishments, satisfactions, and other necessities, let him be anathema.

These decrees and canons are still part of the official dogma of the present Catholic Church and therefore this study alone invites the condemnation of Romanism upon us. As stated earlier, Rome has shown her teeth in defense of this erroneous doctrine by martyring many of God's choice men over this very issue. For example:

Nineteen- year-old William Hunter refused an edict to attend Mass and receive the Communion because 'it would be sin against God to countenance such idolatries.' His confession was that 'he was in heart and soul a Protestant and dared not in conscience attend the mass.' He was encouraged to persevere in his stand by his parents; 'I am glad my son,' said his mother, 'that God has given me such a child, who can find it in his heart to lose his life for Christ's sake.' Hunter died in the fire at Brentwood in Essex in March 1555.[15]

Listen to the words of condemnation and sentence read by the detractors of the Martyred Bishop Ridley:

> "The said Nicholas Ridley affirms, maintains, and stubbornly defends certain opinions, assertions, and heresies, contrary to the Word of God and the received faith of the Church, as in denying the true and natural body and blood of Christ to be in the sacrament of the altar, and secondarily, in affirming the substance of bread and wine to remain after the words of consecration."[16]

We have to some degree, ascertained the significance of the sacrament of the altar by measurement of what it does on behalf of the worshiping Catholic, and what Rome has done in the past to those who have denied the validity of the real presence of Christ in the sacrament. The Eucharist is the sum and summit of Catholic sacramental religion.

By way of response initially to the Catholic view of the Lord's Supper, I would borrow the words of J. C. Ryle as he writes them in *Knots Untied* to challenge and refute the imbalance and excessive importance placed upon this action by the Church of Rome. These words echo my own condemnation and that of every true Evangelical to the place and efficacy given to the sacrament by Rome past and present. Ryle's words are as follows:

> The Lord's Supper is not in its right place when it is made the first, foremost, principal, and most important thing in Christian worship. That it is so in many quarters, we all must know. The sermon, the mode of conducting prayer, the reading of "Holy Scripture", in many churches are made second to this one thing—the administration of the Lord's Supper. We may well ask,

"What warrant of Scripture is there for this extravagant honor?" but we shall get no answer. There are at most but five books in the whole canon of the New Testament in which the Lord's Super is even mentioned. About grace, faith and redemption, about the work of Christ, the work of the Spirit, and the love of the Father; about man's ruin, weakness and spiritual poverty; about justification, sanctification and holy living—about all these mighty subjects we find the inspired writers giving us line upon line, and precept upon precept. About the Lord's Supper, on the contrary, we may observe in the great bulk of the New Testament a speaking silence. Even the Epistles to Timothy and Titus, containing much instruction about a minister's duties, do not contain a word about it. This fact alone surely speaks volumes! To thrust the Lord's Supper forward, till it towers over and overrides everything else in religion is giving it a position for which there is no authority in God's Word. . . . The Lord's Supper is not in its right place, when it is pressed upon all worshiper's indiscriminately, as a means of grace which all, as a matter of course, ought to use. Once more I ask that no one will misunderstand me. I feel as strongly as anyone, that to go to church as a worshiper, and yet not be a communicant, is to be a most inconsistent Christian, and that to be unfit for the Lord's Table is to be unfit to die. But it is one thing to teach this, and quite another to urge all men to receive the Sacrament as a matter of course, whether they are qualified to receive it or not. I should be sorry to raise a false accusation. I do not for a moment suppose that any High Church clergyman recommends, in naked language, wicked people to come to the Lord's Supper that they may be made good. But I cannot forget that from many pulpits people are constantly taught that they are born again, and have grace, by virtue of their baptism; and if they want to stir up the grace within them, and get more religion, they must use all means of grace, and specially the Lord's Supper! . . . My own firm conviction is that the Lord's Supper should on no account be placed before Christ, and that men should always be taught to come to Christ by faith before they draw near to the Lord's Table.[17]

The Substance of the Roman Mass

Central to the idea of the Roman Mass is the doctrine of Transubstantiation, which means a change in substance. Contained in this doctrine is the belief that upon the priest repeating the words that Christ spoke at the Lord's Supper, the bread and the wine mystically and miraculously change into the Body and Blood of Jesus Christ by the power of the Holy Spirit. To put it crudely, Christ is to be found in the form of a wafer in the hand of a Roman priest.

The Catholic concept of the sacrament of the Eucharist is best illustrated in the description given by Mother Teresa of Calcutta in one of her meditations.

It is beautiful to see the humility of Christ . . . in His permanent state of humility in the tabernacle, where He has reduced Himself to a small piece of bread that the priest can hold Him with two fingers.[18]

As shown in this shocking statement, transubstantiation is the view that Christ is uniquely, substantively, wholly and continuously present in the elements of the sacrament. Christ is really present in the bread and wine. When you hold the wafer, you hold Christ. It is the reduction of Christ to a small piece of bread to quote Mother Teresa. The Roman Catholic takes the 6th chapter of John literally and believes he is therefore eating and drinking the flesh and blood of Christ in a real sense.

Listen to the articulation of this in Catholic decrees and councils. At the Fourth Lateran Council (1215) the famous doctrine of Transubstantiation was officially accepted and set forth in this manner:

> There is indeed one universal Church of the faithful outside which no one at all is saved, and in which the priest himself, Jesus Christ, is also the sacrifice. His body and blood are truly contained in the sacrament of the altar under the appearance of bread and wine, the bread being transubstantiated into the body by the divine power and the wine into the blood, to the effect that we receive from what is His in what He has received from what is our [i.e. our humanity] in order that the mystery of unity may be accomplished.

The Council of Trent set forth the essence of the medieval doctrines in its decree concerning the most holy Sacrament of the Eucharist of 11 October 1551. This contained these three canons, one of which we mentioned earlier:

> Canon I.—If any one denieth, that, in the sacrament of the most holy Eucharist, are contained truly, really, and substantially, the body and blood together with the soul and divinity of our Lord Jesus Christ, and consequently the whole Christ; but said that he is only therein as in a sign, or in figure, or virtue: let him be anathema.

Canon II.—If any one saith, that, in the sacred and holy sacrament of the Eucharist, the substance of the bread and wine remains conjointly with the body and blood of our Lord Jesus Christ, and denieth that wonderful and singular conversion of the whole substance of the bread into the body, and of the whole substance of the wine into the blood—the species only of the bread and wine remaining—which conversion indeed the Catholic Church most aptly calls Transubstantiation: let him be anathema.

Canon III.—If any one denieth, that, in the venerable sacrament of the Eucharist, the whole Christ is contained under each species, and under every part of each species, when separated: let him be anathema.

Vatican II may have given Rome a new coat of paint, but the Trentine structure remained underneath and while the form of the liturgy changed somewhat, the essence remained the same as old.

> ... in the sacrament of the Eucharist Christ is present, in a manner altogether unique, God and man, whole and entire, substantially and continuously.

The New Catholic Catechism is not a new breed of Catholicism but follows in the historical and theological groove of past decrees and statements.[19]

Given this significance concerning the Mass, it is not surprising to find within Catholicism various forms of Eucharistic worship, which include kneeling before the sacrament and Eucharistic processions. The acts affirm that the Eucharist is to be held in highest honor and is to be given the same worship that we offer God.

Consider the New Catholic Catechism as it speaks to the issue of Eucharistic worship:

> In the liturgy of the Mass we express our faith in the real presence of Christ under the species of bread and wine by, among other ways, genuflecting or bowing deeply as a sign of adoration of the Lord. "The Catholic Church has always offered and still offers to the sacrament of the Eucharist the cult of adoration, not only during Mass, but also outside of it, reserving the consecrated hosts with the utmost care, exposing them to the solemn veneration of the faithful, and carrying them in procession."[20]

No wonder the priest takes great care to place the wafer into the mouth of the communicant, after all we don't want Jesus falling to the floor. It would be laughable if it wasn't so abominable to teach the worship of God in the form of a piece of bread. This is the substance built upon the significance of the Roman Catholic Mass. "Thick darkness", indeed, as Calvin put it.

What might be our response? Where and how might we lay the ax of sound theology and proper exegesis to the roots of this popish nonsense? Let me suggest a few reasons why we would throw out of hand this fanciful and horrendous view of the Lord's Supper.

The Doctrine of Transubsantiation Finds its Roots in Greek Philosophy, Not Biblical Theology

This supposed change in substance assumes the distinction made by Aristotle between substance and accidents.

According to this philosopher everything consists of substance and accidents. A dog, for example, may have certain "accidents"—it may be white, have four legs, two eyes, a certain weight, and so forth. These characteristics are called "accidents" because the animal would still be a dog even if it lost one eye or one leg, or were dyed a different color, or changed its weight. But in addition to these accidents a dog has a "substance"—its "dogness," so to speak. If this changes, it would no longer be a dog, but something else. Now according to Aristotle the same could be said about an apple or a watch—or any other object. All have accidents and substance. For example, an apple may be red, but if it were yellow it would still be an apple. Chalk may be white and round, but, if it were blue and square, it would still be chalk. But what has all this to do with the doctrine of transubstantiation? Simply this: It teaches that after the consecration of the elements, the accidents of the wine and the bread remain. (In other words, the wine still looks like wine and smells like wine and tastes like wine, for these are accidents.) But the substance has changed. Instead of the substance of wine, it is now the substance of blood, and instead of the substance of bread, the bread is now the substance of flesh. This is the meaning of the doctrine of transubstantiation.

Had the medieval theologians stayed with the Scripture they would have continued to hold to Augustine's position where the Lord's Supper is the "visible Word." Sadly, they tried to compress biblical truth within the confines of transitory philosophical theory.

The Doctrine of Transubstantiation is Based Upon Wooden Literalism That Reshapes the Whole Meaning of the Text and Loses the Force of the Passage

Catholic writers frequently borrow the phrase, "This is my body," as used by Christ in referring to the breaded element of the Lord's Supper. But is it necessary to take these phrases literally?

Herbert Carson responded to this very issue in the following statement:

> But surely such harsh literalism makes nonsense of the Lord's words. One thinks of other occasions when he used figurative language to powerful effect. "I am the door," he claimed (John 10:7). It would be a nonsensical conclusion to draw to infer that he literally became a door. It would be equally absurd to apply bald literalism to his other claim: "I am the true vine" (John 15:1). Only a fool would argue that he had changed the substance of the vine to substitute himself. Of course he was using the words figuratively.

> To take his words at the Passover meal and to try to force them into a rigid mold is not only to distort what Jesus said, but in fact to open the way for one of the earliest heresies in Christian history. Already within the New Testament we see evidence of the emerging conflict as John insists that we must maintain that "Jesus Christ has come in the flesh" (1 John 4:2).

> Clearly he was facing the kind of teaching, which would later develop, that rejected the orthodox doctrine of the incarnation. The early Christians recog-

nized that it was vital to maintain that the doctrine of the incarnation was not some illusory idea, but was in fact a solid affirmation of the truth that the Son of God had truly become one of us. He who was fully God was also fully man.

That means that at the Last Supper Jesus was present in his incarnate perfection. It was a human voice, which the disciples heard. The action of setting apart the bread and the wine was performed by human hands. To accept a literal interpretation of the words of institution is to claim that he who reclined at the table held his body and blood in his own hands. This surely is not only an affront to common sense but also, more seriously, a denial of the essential integrity of his humanity.[21]

The closing words by Herbert Carson remind us that Jesus was in His body and His blood flowed within His body at the very moment of speaking these words. The literalist's approach produces two Christs, one on the seat and one on the table. That is both logically absurd and christologically dangerous.

Another Line of Defense That We Must Strongly Attack is the Catholic Misrepresentation of the Eating and Drinking Concepts of John 6, Matthew 26, and I Corinthians 11

As dogma, Transubstantiation demands that Catholics, when partaking in the bread and wine of the Eucharist, recognize that they are eating Christ's flesh and drinking His blood.

By way of rebuttal, let me employ the words of Walter Martin as found in a publication of the Christian Research Institute entitled *The Roman Catholic Church in History.*

> Catholic theologians make much of such passages as John 6:48-58, Matthew 26:26, and 1 Corinthians 11:23-30 in an attempt to teach that Christ and the apostles taught this doctrine. But the evidence is not as one-sided as might first appear.... That our Lord was using highly figurative language is evident from the fact that both the Jews and His disciples were interpreting His words literally (6th chapter of John, verses 52, 60, and 61) and He deliberately went out of His way to contradict such a literal interpretation: "The words that I am speaking to you are spirit and they are life: the flesh does not profit anything" (John 6:63).

> Our Lord clearly taught that belief in Him was the metaphorical equivalent of "eating" His flesh and blood (John 6:35,36). And as we have seen, He expressly stated that the words "bread," and "flesh," "blood," and "eat," in a fleshly or literal interpretation, profited nothing.

Fortifying the comments that demolish the idea of a literal eating and drinking of Christ, is the biblical command to refrain from the partaking of blood. Such an admonition straddles both the Old and New Testaments (Lev. 7:26, 17:10-11; Acts 15:28-29). Because Christ would never contradict Scripture, it is not possible that He would call upon men to either drink His physical blood or commit a cannibalistic act of eating His flesh. Christ would not approve of, much less advocate such an act. That Christ was referring to believing on Him and illustrating it by the symbol of eating and drinking is the clear thrust of John in his gospel (John 6:35-36, 47-48, 51, 53-54).

In Addressing Again the Issue of Substance and Accidents Which Lies at the Heart of This Doctrine of Rome, the Fact Remains That There is No Proof Whatsoever That a Miracle Has Been Performed After the Priest Consecrates the Wafer. It is Still a Wafer to All the Senses Man Possesses

Bear in mind that every miracle Jesus performed gave evidence to the onlookers' senses that it was a miracle. The supposed miracle of the Eucharist is totally lacking such evidence. Since the wafer and wine remain unchanged, the alleged miracle remains unseen.

Targeting this very notion, Dave Hunt states:

There is no such "miracle" in the Bible. The opening of the Red Sea so that the Israelites could walk through it on dry land was a feat that both Jews and Egyptians observed and that both understood had occurred by God's power. Suppose it had been a "transubstantiation kind of miracle"—the Red Sea "opened" under the appearance of remaining closed and the Israelites had "walked" across on dry land "under the appearance" of having to swim across. Suppose Christ healed a blind man "under the appearance" of his not being able to see, or raised the dead "under the appearance" of lifelessness. Such suppositions are ludicrous, yet that is exactly the nature of the "transubstantiation miracle."

Let's take the miracle of the water turned to wine at Cana of Galilee. When the governor of the feast tasted it he exclaimed to the groom, "Thou hast kept the good [best] wine until now" (John 2:10). Suppose instead he had said, "This isn't wine, it's water!" The servants reply sincerely, "No, sir, it's wine." The governor's voice rises in anger: "Don't mock me! It looks like water, it tastes like water, it is water!" The servants insist, "Sir, it is wine. Jesus miraculously turned water into wine under the appearance of it remaining water." There is no such "miracle" in the Bible, and for Rome to make such a claim is a lame attempt to cover obvious fraud.[22]

Not to Be Overlooked is the Plain Significance That Christ Continued to Speak of the Bread and Wine in Terms of Their Continuing in Their Natural State and Thus Remaining What They Were Before He Spoke

Compare Matthew 26:29 and Luke 22:18. Paul, under the Holy Spirit's inspiration, expands upon the words of the Lord Jesus, but likewise refers to the elements of the supper in their natural condition (1 Cor. 11:26). Paul expected the Church at Corinth to eat bread, not munch upon God Himself. The body of Christ was not on earth, but in heaven and would remain there until He comes again to establish the Kingdom of God on earth (Luke 22:18; 1 Cor. 11:26; Acts 1:11).

The Doctrine of Transubstantiation is Logically Absurd and Christologically Dangerous

For a body to be more than one place at a time is a contradiction. The New Testament record brings us to see that Christ in bodily form is in heaven at the right hand of the Father (Heb. 1:3; Rev. 19:14-16), but is everywhere in His spiritual presence through the ministry of the Holy Spirit. For Rome to claim that Christ is here or there, God and Man in His entirety in the wafer is preposterous. There must be a million Saviors if Christ is present fully in every wafer. We would do well to heed the words of our Lord Jesus as He spoke them in Matthew 24:24-26.

The Teachings of the New Testament Do Not Advocate the Idea That a Ritual Becomes the Primary Channel for the Dispensing of God's Grace

Rome makes the receiving of Christ and the receiving of Sacraments inseparable. God, however, nowhere binds His grace and His Son to the use of certain external forms. Consider the following biblical verses in this light: Luke 18:14 and John 4:21-23. Furthermore, the New Testament has a strong anti-ritualistic flavor that can be tested and tasted again and again (see Matt. 15; Rom. 14:17; 1 Cor. 1:17; 8:8; Col. 2:16-23; Heb. 9:1; 13:9-16; and 1 Peter 3:21).

Placing the Lord's Table into a biblical context in opposition to the erroneous views of Rome, the words of Charles Haddon Spurgeon will help bring this section of our discussion to a positive close:

Christians are to remember Christ at the Supper
with gratitude as their Savior; with reverence as their
living example and Lord; with confidence as their
Strength; as their great Representative before the
throne; and lastly as soon to come . . . their chief
point of remembrance is our Lord Jesus in his death."

"You come to the Communion Table to remember
your absent Friend . . . the Supper is also an exhibi-
tion of the life-giving sacrifice of Jesus. It is a "communion" with Christ so real that . . . symbolically we
feast upon him . . . I believe in the real presence of
Christ; I do not believe in the carnal presence of the
Romanist. I believe in the real presence to the
believer; but that reality is none the less real because
it is spiritual . . . communion also means that we are
one with each other."

Like Spurgeon, we believe the real presence of Christ
mystically as the Head of the Church, not in the carnal presence of the Romanist who places Christ under the power of the
Roman priest. Indeed, Christ's presence is no less real because
it is spiritual.

The Sacrifice of the Roman Mass

Ideas have consequences. Once the premise was accepted
that the component parts of the Lord's Supper were actually
and literally changed into the Body and Blood of Christ, other
traditions grew around the Mass at various epochs of history.
Of all the traditions incorporated by Rome, perhaps there is
none more tragic and significant than the notion that the table
of remembrance is made into an altar of sacrifice.

The doctrine of the mass, as it pertains to Christ's sacrifice, developed over the centuries. Rome's myriad theologians have developed the doctrine that since the Body of Christ was a sacrifice on the cross, it was possible, in their estimation, that Christ was now re-sacrificed in the Mass. After all, if the elements are literal, the incarnation takes place again and again. It therefore seemed a reasonable assumption that He should also be sacrificed over and over. In Catholic theology the Mass continues the sacrifice of the cross. Each time the Mass is offered, the sacrifice of Christ is reenacted and repeated. A new sacrifice is not offered and Catholics will be quick to point out that Jesus is not re-crucified, but by divine power, one and the same sacrifice is repeated. The Mass for them repeats that moment of Christ's death in reality, allowing time and space to encompass once again what is eternally happening—the redemptive act of Jesus giving Himself for us.

Rome's statement that a new sacrifice is not offered should not be misconstrued to mean that the Mass for the Catholic is symbolic of the sacrifice of Christ. The Council of Trent, along with other Church documents, makes it patently clear that in the Mass a true and proper propitiatory sacrifice for sin is made to God, valid for both the living and the dead. The sacrifice in the Mass is identical with the sacrifice of the cross inasmuch as Jesus Christ is both priest and victim. The difference lies in the manner and form of the offering, which was bloody upon the cross and bloodless on the altar. It has been estimated, according to the faith of the Vatican, that globally Christ is sacrificed afresh and offered to God on behalf of the supplicants as often as two hundred thousand times per day. For Catholics, the remembrance of the Lord's death becomes a new enactment of that sacrifice.

Let's take an excursion into Catholic dogma to reinforce what I have just said as to their understanding of the sacrificial efficacy of the Mass.

The theologians of Trent were not behind the door in expanding how they saw the nature of the sacrifice on the altar. In a decree dated 1562 and entitled *Doctrine Concerning the Sacrifice of the Mass*, the second chapter contains these words:

> And inasmuch as in this divine sacrifice which is celebrated in the mass is contained and immolated in an un-bloody manner the same Christ who once offered Himself in a bloody manner on the altar of the cross, the holy council teaches that this is truly propitiatory and has this effect, that if we, contrite and penitent, with sincere heart and upright faith, with fear and reverence, draw nigh to God, we obtain mercy and find grace in seasonable aid. For, appeased by this sacrifice, the Lord grants the grace and gift of penitence and pardons even the gravest crimes and sins. For the victim is one and the same, the same now offering by the ministry of priests who then offered Himself on the cross, the manner alone of offering being different. The fruits of that bloody sacrifice, it is well understood, are received most abundantly through this un-bloody one, so far is the latter from derogating in any way from the former. Wherefore, according to the tradition of the Apostles, it is rightly offered not only for the sins, punishments, satisfactions and other necessities of the faithful who are living, but also for those departed in Christ but not yet fully purified.

Dr. Ludwig Ott, a well-known Roman Catholic theologian, wrote the *Fundamentals of Catholic Dogma*, and although written prior to Vatican II, his perspectives continue to be shared by many Catholic apologists and theologians. Concerning the sacrifice of the Mass, Ott believes that Christ's sacrifice on the cross is made present, its memory celebrated, and its saving power applied. He articulates this position in the following extraction from *Fundamentals of Catholic Dogma*:

> While the Sacrifice on the Cross is an absolute sacrifice, as it is neither the commemoration of a past sacrifice nor the archetype of a future sacrifice, the Sacrifice of the Mass is a relative sacrifice, as it is essentially linked to the Sacrifice on the Cross. [Ott then cites from Trent] ... The sacrifice of the Mass is the presenting again of the Sacrifice of the Cross, in so far as the sacrificial Body and the sacrificial Blood of Christ are made present under separate species, thus symbolically representing the real separation of the body and blood of Christ on the Cross ... But it is not a mere commemorative celebration ... it is also a true and proper sacrifice. Finally, the sacrifice of the Mass is the means whereby the fruits of the Sacrifice of the Cross are applied to mankind in need of salvation.[23]

Note please that Ott's words are formally and firmly rooted in the soil of Trent. He frequently cites from the decrees of Trent and uses Trent as the foundation for many of his definitions and formulations.

Turning to *The New Catechism* we will observe that the theological furniture regarding the sacrifice of the Mass remains to this present hour untouched and unmoved. Listen to this extraction.

> The Eucharist is thus a sacrifice because it re-presents (makes present) the sacrifice of the cross, because it is its memorial and because it applies its fruit:
>
>> [Christ], our Lord and God, was once and for all to offer himself to God the Father by his death on the altar of the cross, to accomplish there an everlasting redemption. But because his priesthood was not to end with his death, at the Last Supper "on the night when he was betrayed," [he wanted] to leave to his beloved spouse the Church a visible sacrifice (as the nature of man demands) by which the bloody sacrifice which he was to accomplish once for all on the cross would be re-presented, its memory perpetuated until the end of the world, and its salutary power be applied to the forgiveness of the sins we daily commit.
>
> The sacrifice of Christ and the sacrifice of the Eucharist are one single sacrifice: "The victim is one and the same: the same now offers through the ministry of priests, who then offered himself on the cross; only the manner of offering is different." "In this divine sacrifice which is celebrated in the Mass, the same Christ who offered himself once in a bloody manner on the altar of the cross is contained and is offered in an un-bloody manner."[24]

In summation, we underline the fact that Rome teaches the continuation of the cross in the sacrifice of the Mass, since they are one and the same offering, for in each Christ is both the offerer and the offering. Each Mass presents again in an unbloody manner the sacrifice of Christ on the cross, and is coupled with the belief that the Mass appeases God and effects the expiation and release of the sinner from the punishment of sin. Furthermore, the benefits of this sacrifice can be applied to both the living and the dead.

What are we to say in the light of such darkness? There can be no doubt in our minds that this is a watershed issue between biblical Christianity and Roman Catholicism. Tolerance of the proposition that espouses the continual sacrificing of Christ will break the back of true theology and stop the heart of our living gospel.

Our protest must be vehement and made in the strongest possible terms in the face of such brazen heresy concerning the true message of Christ's death on the sinner's behalf.

Let Me Begin My Protest Against the Doctrine of the Mass as a Propitiatory Sacrifice with the Assertion That the Concept of an Ongoing Sacrifice for Sins is Foreign to the Word of God

Hebrews 10:18 tells us in no uncertain manner that "there is no longer any offering for sin." The assertion in verse 18 concerning the finality of Christ's sacrifice is unequivocal and once is enough when it comes to an understanding of the death of Christ in the New Testament.

In answering the claims of the Catholic Church regarding the Mass on this matter, Erwin Lutzer in his book *All One Body Why Don't We Agree?* strikes out at Rome with these comments:

The Roman Catholic Church bases its understanding of sacrifice on the Old Testament rituals, where sacrifices were continuously offered. This explains why Catholicism teaches that salvation is a process that is never finished. Even if the past is forgiven, tomorrow is another day. Mass, confessions, prayers to Mary—these never settle one's relationship with God forever. Consistency dictates that Christ's sacrifice on the cross is never finished either. He is offered up repeatedly.

However, the New Testament Book of Hebrews explicitly states that Christ's sacrifice was sufficient for God, thus it was offered **once for all.** Four contrasts are made between Christ's sacrifice and those of the Old Testament (Heb. 10:10-14):

- In the Old Testament many priests offered sacrifices; in fact, they worked in shift. But now there is only one High Priest who lives forever.

- Many sacrifices were offered, day after day, whenever sin was committed. But Christ offered "one sacrifice for sins for all time." His work ended the sacrificial system forever.

- The Old Testament sacrifices could only take care of past sins—which was the reason they had to be re-occurred. But of Christ we read, "For by one offering He has perfected for all time those who are sanctified" (v.14).

- The former priests were not allowed to sit down while working their shift. But Christ sat down on the right hand of God the Father because his work was finished.[25]

Christ's work is finished and the Father has accepted the sufficiency of that sacrifice granting our Lord a seat of honor.

The Testimony of Or Lord Jesus Christ Himself From the Cross demolishes and Levels any Notion That His Sacrifice Upon the Cross is to be Extended and Repeated

Just before He gave up His spirit upon the cross, our Lord and Savior cried victoriously, "It is finished!" (John 19:30). The Greek verb used in this verse is in the perfect tense, conveying a process, but viewing that process as having reached its consummation and existing in a finished state. In other words, the saving work of Christ was completed once and for all and continues in a state of completion. Fundamentally, this is directly contrary to Rome concerning the repeating and representing of Christ to the Father in the Mass.

To further enlighten you, let me share something of the etymology and usage of this Greek verb as highlighted for us by Warren Wiersbe in his book *The Seven Last Words*. In speaking of the word "tetelestai" Wiersbe states:

> *Servants*
> If you were to check the Greek lexicons, you would find that the servants and the slaves used this word. A master would tell his servant to go do something, and when the servant had completed the task, he would come back and say, "tetelestai—I have finished the work that you gave me to do."
>
> The Lord Jesus Christ was God's suffering servant. Philippians 2 informs us that Jesus Christ came as a servant. He did not come as a sovereign but as a servant, not as a ruler but as a slave. The Lord Jesus

Christ had a work to do. He said in John 17:4, "I have finished the work which thou gavest me to do."

Priests

You will discover that the priests also used this word. The Jewish people had to bring the sacrifices to the priest to be examined, because it was against the law to offer an imperfect sacrifice at the altar of God. After the priest had examined the sacrifice, he would say, "It is perfect." (Of course, he would use the Hebrew or the Aramaic word, but it would be the equivalent of tetelestai.)

Jesus Christ, dying on the cross, was God's perfect, faultless sacrifice—the Lamb of God who takes away the sin of the world. How do we know Christ is a faultless sacrifice? God the Father said that He is. When the Lord Jesus was baptized, God the Father spoke from heaven and said, "This is my beloved Son, in whom I am well pleased" (Matt. 3:17). God the Father put His seal of approval upon God the Son, and God the Holy Spirit came down as a dove and added His witness (see v.16). Even the demons admitted that Jesus was the Son of God (see 8:28, 29). His enemies had to admit that He was faultless, because they had to hire liars to bear false witness against Him. His followers found no fault in Him. None of the apostles ever said, "We heard Jesus tell a lie" or, "We saw Jesus do something wrong." He is the spotless, perfect sacrifice.

Pilate said, "I find no fault in this man" (Luke 23:4). Even Judas said, "I have betrayed innocent blood"

(Matt. 27:4). Tetelestai! The priests used this word; it means "a perfect, faultless sacrifice." You will not find any other sacrifice for your sins who is perfect, spotless and faultless. Jesus Christ is the only one.

Artists
The servants used this word, and the priests used it as well. The artists also used it. When a painter completed his work, he would step back and say, "Tetelestai—it is finished!" It means, "The picture is completed."

When you read the Old Testament, you have a rather difficult picture. In the Old Testament are ceremonies, types, prophecies and some mysterious symbols. Even those of us who have been studying the Word of God for many years often find serious difficulties as we study the Old Testament Scriptures. The Old Testament was God's picture gallery in the shadows. So many Old Testament passages seem incomplete and hard to understand. When Jesus Christ came, He completed the picture and turned on the light! He is God's wonderful completion to the Old Testament revelation.

I like that scene in Luke 24 where those two discouraged men were walking on the road to Emmaus. A stranger joined them, and they told him about the death of the Lord Jesus. (Can you imagine telling Jesus about His own death?) Jesus said to them, "O fools, and slow of heart to believe all that the prophets have spoken" (v. 25). Beginning at Moses and all the prophets, the Lord Jesus went through the Old Testament Scriptures and explained the total picture. Calvary completed the picture. Tetelestai—it is finished!

We today read the Old Testament, and even though there are some difficulties and some things that are hard to understand, because we know Christ, the light is shining. The portraits are no longer in the shadows; we can see the complete picture that God has painted.

Merchants
It was a familiar word. The slaves used it, the priests used it, and the artists used it. The merchants also used it. To them, it meant "the debt is fully paid." If you had purchased something, the merchant would take your money and then would give you a receipt. That receipt would say "Tetelestai—it is finished." The debt had been fully paid.

You and I as sinners are in debt before God, and we cannot pay this debt. We have broken God's law, and we are bankrupt. The wages of sin is death. But Jesus came and paid the debt for us. That is what tetelestai means. It was a familiar word. The servant had finished the work. The perfect sacrifice had been offered. The picture had been completed. The debt had been paid.[26]

Rome Has Turned the Table of remembrance Into an altar of Sacrifice, and in Doing So Has Flown in the Face of Christ's Command to do This Very Thing in Remembrance of Him

The word remembrance is a Greek word, which literally means a memorial. The Lord's Supper is a commemoration not a crucifixion. It is a memorial to our living Lord not an offering of our dying Savior.

In his book, *Rome at the Judgment Bar of History*, William Webster addresses the call to remembrance:

> This becomes yet clearer from the identification of the Lord's Supper with the Passover memorial of the Old Testament. The Lord's Supper was first celebrated at the time of the Jewish Passover and Jesus specifically identifies it as an equivalent when he says: "I have earnestly desired to eat this Passover with you before I suffer" (Luke 22:15). What exactly was the Passover? It was an annual feast established by God in which the Jews would remember the night in which the angel of death 'passed over' those families that had applied the blood of the lamb to their doorposts (Ex. 12:1-13). "Now this day will be a memorial to you, and you shall celebrate it as a feast to the Lord; throughout your generations you are to celebrate it as a permanent ordinance" (Ex. 12:14). This was a "memorial" to a specific act of God in redeeming his people from bondage and death. The "memorial" served to bring to remembrance an important event. It did not repeat the

event but kept it vivid in the memory through a physical representation.

Just as God instituted a memorial of remembrance of redemption in the Old Testament, he has done the same in the New Testament. 1 Cor. 5:7 states, "For Christ our Passover also has been sacrificed." His death is an accomplished fact. Now we are called, not to a sacrifice, but to a feast: "Let us therefore celebrate the feast . . . with the unleavened bread of sincerity and truth" (I Cor. 5:8). When Christ states that the bread is to be eaten and the wine drunk in remembrance of him, he is employing the same language as that of the Old Testament memorial in reference to the Passover. The Lord's Supper is not a sacrifice, it is the commemoration of a sacrifice.

Theologically and Logically it is a Nonsense to Talk of a Bloodless Sacrifice

On the theological side, Calvary was a very bloody scene as the Lamb of God carried away the sin of the world. The Bible distinctly states that "without the shedding of blood there can be no remission (of sins)" (Heb. 9:22). Yet the un-bloody emulation of Christ upon the Roman altar is deemed to have propitiatory benefits. On the logical side, they have not explained to us how there can be an un-bloody repetition of Calvary. Catholicism claims that the Mass is the "un-bloody" sacrifice of the body and blood of Jesus Christ. How wonderful? What kind of blood is "un-bloody" blood? What kind of a body is a "bodiless" body? One may as well speak of a lifeless life, a horseless horse or a manless man. Such must be the thought of thoughtless thinkers.

Collectively these scriptural rebuttals become the rock upon which the popish doctrine of the sacrifice of the Mass perishes. God the Father is satisfied with the once forever sacrifice of His Son and so should be every true child of the Father.

The Sacrilege of the Roman Mass

By now you will have seen that the Mass is not an alternative view of the Lord's Supper as Jack Hayford seems to understand it when he calls the Promise Keepers to be involved in redeeming worship, but is in fact a diabolical doctrine patented in Hell, intended to undermine the souls of men, and undervalue the sacrifice of Christ. It defaces the true gospel beyond recognition, and blinds the eyes of those who seek reconciliation with God. To be blunt, it dooms millions and denies the uniqueness and sufficiency of Christ's death upon Golgotha's Hill. It is not worship, it is sacrilege; it is not a true propitiatory sacrifice, but Satan's ploy to circumvent the cross. If he failed to get Jesus to come down from the cross, he will do the next best thing and take people to a false cross and a fake Christ.

This writer firmly and definitely declares the Romanist understanding of the Eucharist meal at best an unbiblical novelty and at worst a theological heresy; and as the whole system of Romanism rests upon it, that system is therefore founded not upon the Rock of Ages but the sand of human reason, and it will perish in the storms destined to overthrow every system of error (2 Thess. 1:7-9; 2:9-12).

Let me expand on what I have just said by offering the following.

The Roman Mass Blights the Souls of Men

The Word of God warns that the evil one, through doctrines of demons and damnable heresies, has a full time occupation of blinding the minds of men lest the light of the gospel should shine in. Satan seeks to trap the souls of men in error, in the belief that it is truth (II Cor. 4:4-5; 11:3, 13-15). To see this in operation, one need only look at the Roman Mass to view a masterpiece of deception.

In the Mass, the priest offers to the communicant a counterfeit Christ. Rome teaches that to receive the consecrated wafer is to receive Christ, and added to this is the belief that sin is being atoned and forgiveness secured in the sacrifice of the Mass. To top it all, the liturgy of the Mass requires Catholics to involve themselves in the practice of idolatry in affording the wafer the same worship attributed to God.

The sad result of this is that Catholics receive a crumb of bread in place of the Bread of Life Himself. As the worshiper approaches the altar, he is unconsciously deceiving himself, thinking that he is drawing nearer to God, when in reality he is moving further away. Sadly, the Mass actually erects a barricade on the road to Christ because it is just one more thing the Church gives the people to do in order that they might be saved; one more act that takes the place and displaces a personal relationship with Christ; one more ritual that makes the Church of Rome a surrogate Savior.

This is a damnable heresy that robs men and women of the peace to be found in the finished work of Christ, leaving them in the darkness of dread to doubt their relationship with God rather than bringing them into the light and liberty of the true gospel of Jesus' atoning death. Martin Luther once knew that dread, but later discovered the glorious light of our Protestant gospel.

Martin Luther was one who struggled with his sins. Before his break with the Catholic Church he went to confession every day and was so guilt-ridden by his sins he would almost have gone every hour.

On most nights Luther slept well, but he even felt guilty about that, thinking, 'Here am I, sinful as I am, having a good night's sleep.' So he would confess that. One day the older priest to whom Luther went for confession said to him, "Martin, either find a new sin and commit it, or quit coming to see me!"

Luther wrestled in search of peace with God, a peace, as Paul wrote, that could only be found through faith in our Lord Jesus Christ and what He has done on our behalf. When Luther discovered that "the just shall live by faith," he entered into the light of the gospel. The change was dramatic and has been illustrated in a commonly known story that comes from his life:

> It is said that the devil approached Luther one day and tried to use the fact that every person is fallible. He presented the Reformer with a long list of sins of which he was guilty. When he had finished reading, Luther said to Satan, "Think a little harder; you must have forgotten some." This the devil did and added other sins to the list. At the conclusion of this exchange, Martin Luther simply said, "That's fine. Now write across that list in red ink, 'The blood of Jesus Christ, His Son, cleanses us from all sin.'" There was nothing the devil could say to that.

It must be our sincere wish before God that many more Catholics like Luther will find the truth of the gospel and realize that their sins are forgiven fully and forever. That must be our prayer for those whose souls are enslaved by Roman theology.

The Roman Mass Slights the Sacrifice of Christ

The doctrine of the Roman Mass is abhorrent to every true Evangelical because it proclaims the insufficiency of Christ's death upon Calvary's tree (Hebrews 10:12, 14; John 19:30). To teach that the sacrifice of Calvary needs to be supplemented and augmented by the daily offerings upon Roman altars is to rubbish the united and vocal testimony of Scripture and join those around the cross who spat in the face of Christ along with the purpose of His mission.

To perpetuate the sacrifice of Christ for the payment of sin is to insult both God the Father and God the Son. Why? Because if a benefactor pays a creditor the debt someone owes, the debt is gone forever. It would be meaningless and insulting to speak of representing or reenacting or perpetuating the payment in the present. One could well remember with gratitude the payment that was made, but no re-enactment would be necessary or have any virtue since there no longer remains any debt to be paid. Therefore, to perpetuate the sacrifice of Christ and offer Him again and again to the Father is an insult to the Father and the Son of the highest order. The Mass in its re-enactment serves to question the Father's acceptance of the payment and to devalue the Son's payment.

In a relative sense, this very point and principle is illustrated in the following:

> A wealthy English merchant who lived on the European continent was satisfied with nothing but the best. This attitude extended even as far as the cars

he owned. His pride and joy was a Rolls-Royce coupe that he had owned for years and that had given great service all that time. One day, while driving down a bumpy road, his car hit a deep pothole, resulting in a broken rear axle.

The owner had the car shipped back to the Rolls plant in England and was surprised by the quick repair that was performed. He received no bill for the work and, knowing his warranty had run out, he had expected one. He waited for months and still no bill came. So he finally communicated with the company about the bill for his car repairs. Again the response from the factory was immediate. The reply said, "We have thoroughly searched our files and find no record of a Rolls-Royce axle ever breaking."

A search on our part of the biblical record will turn up an absence of complaint on God's part to the workmanship of Christ on behalf of the sinner towards God. To question the excellence and durability of that work is to risk the reputation of Jesus Christ Himself, but that is exactly what Roman Catholic Mass does. The Roman Mass slights the work of Christ, and therefore must be hated and regarded for its error and arrogance in risking the reputation of Christ's person and work.

By way of conclusion, let me address a question that is often asked. Should Protestants ever be found in attendance at a Mass?

Historically, Protestants would say No. At the time of the Reformation, Protestant leaders would not agree to Christians attending the Mass without making a protest against it. Calvin, who met and prayed with Thomas Cranmer during a crucial time for the Reformation in England, had very firm views about attendance at the Mass. In his day, Reformed Christians were in danger if they failed to attend, and many of them wanted to conceal the fact that they were Protestants. Although it made Calvin deeply unpopular in some quarters, he maintained "on the strongest grounds that Christian men ought not even to be present at the Mass."

J. C. Ryle chronicled in *The Five English Reformers* that most of the English martyrs were killed for their denial and non-attendance of the Mass, and Protestants would have refrained from attending the Mass.

Based on Biblical Theology, Protestants should be unanimous in their objection to attendance to the Mass. The Roman Mass as a service is idolatrous and doctrinally erroneous, therefore we must be separate from it (1 Cor. 10:14; 2 Cor. 6:6-17; Rev. 18:4).

Writing in the late 19th century, Bishop J. C. Ryle, first Bishop of Liverpool, argued:

> ". . . the Romish doctrine of the real presence, if pursued to its legitimate consequences, obscures every leading doctrine of the Gospel, and damages and interfered with the whole system of Christ's truth. It produces an idolatry to be abhorred of faithful Christians."[27]

Set against the background of this study and the words of Bishop Ryle, I cannot but conclude that attendance of the Mass is nothing short of complicity in error and idolatry, something forbidden to the believer in the New Testament.

In the Scriptures, we find clear teaching on this very subject from the pen of the Apostle Paul in his first letter to the Corinthians. In chapter ten, Paul deals with the question of attendance at sacrificial feasts in heathen temples (10:14-22).

Such attendance, Paul writes while under the authority of the Holy Spirit, is considered sinful and an act of idolatry. It is important to underline that Paul condemns the act of participation apart from the motive or intention behind it. Participation brought them into communion with demons and is forbidden (vv. 18:20).

Charles Hodge, in his exposition of 1 Corinthians, makes a pertinent application to the words of Paul under consideration when he wrote:

> The same principle also applies to the compliance of Protestants in the religious observances of Papists. Whatever their intention may be, they worship the host if they bow down to it with the crowd who intend to adore it. By the force of the act we become one with those in whose worship we join. We constitute with them and with the objects of their worship one communion.[28]

Therefore, theologically and historically, it seems a very bad idea to be found in the company of Catholics in worshiping the host and sacrificing Christ. Separation and not participation is the direction we should be heading in.

---

1. James Breig, *Why Go to Mass?*, (Missouri: Liguori Publications, 1978) 7.

2. Thomas Cranmer, *The True and Catholic Use of the Lord's Supper.*

3. Michael de Semlyen, *All Roads Lead to Rome?*, (England: Dorchester House Publications, 1991) 38.

4. *Catechism of the Catholic Church*, (Missouri: Ligouri Publications, 1994) Para. 1210- 1212.

5. *Mysterium Fidei,*No. 38.

6. *Catechism of the Catholic Church*, Para. 1364.

7. Ibid., Para. 1366.

8. Ibid., Para. 1367.

9. Ibid., Para. 1371.

10. Ibid., Para. 1407.

11. Ibid., Para. 1389.

12. Ibid., Para. 1389, 2042, 2181.

13. Ibid., Para. 1407, 2042.

14. Ibid., Para. 2181.

15. Semlyen, 11.

16. J.C. Ryle, *Five English Reformers*, (London: Banner of Truth Trust, 1960) 29.

17. David Gillies, *Unity in the Dark*, (London: Banner of Truth Trust, 1964) 45.

18. Mother Teresa, *In the Silence of the Heart*, (1983)

19. *Catechism of the Catholic Church*, Para. 1373-1374.

20. Ibid., Para. 1378.

21. Herbert Carson, *Faith of the Vatican*, (England: Evangelical Press, 1996) 156-7.

22. Dave Hunt, *A Woman Rides the Beast*, (Oregon: Harvest House, 1994) 386.

23. Dr. Ludwig Ott, *Fundamentals of Catholic Dogma*, (Illinois: Tan Books, 1960) 407.

24. *Catechism of the Catholic Church*, Para. 1366-1367.

25. Erwin Lutzer, *All One Body Why Don't We Agree?*, (Illinois: Tyndale, 1989), 109.

26. Warren Wiersbe, *Jesus' Seven Last Words*, (Lincoln: Back to the Bible Publication, 1981) 59.

27. Bishop J. C. Ryle, *Why Were Our Reformers Burned?*, (Belfast: Every Home Crusade)

28. Charles Hodge, *Exposition of the First Epistle to the Corinthians*, (London: 1994) 194.

CHAPTER 6

HEAVEN BY THE BACK DOOR

Hebrews 1:1-4

O_{nce} a woman was taking a confirmation examination. "What is matrimony?" the young priest asked her. She answered, "Matrimony is a state of terrible torment which those who enter into are compelled to undergo for a time to fit them for heaven." The priest responded in astonishment, "Oh, no, that's not the definition of matrimony. That's the definition of purgatory." The elderly bishop interrupted with; "Maybe she knows more about it than we do."

This woman's definition of the Roman Catholic doctrine of purgatory is indeed a correct one and taken outside the context of this story is a matter of lament rather than laughter. For as it stands today, the faith of the Vatican holds to the belief that before a soul who trusts Christ can be eternally wedded to Him and live happily ever after in the Father's house, it must first be purified and perfumed in the anteroom of purgatory. For Roman Catholics, heaven must wait, as death becomes a door into the posthumous penitentiary of purgatory. Over the centuries popes and bishops have taught heaven by the side entrance and back door of purgatory. For the Protestant to die is gain, for the Catholic to die is pain. In the case of the vast majority of Roman Catholics, death will bring neither heaven nor hell.

Listen to the words of Cardinal Gibbons in his work, *The Faith of our Fathers*, as he underlines my opening remarks:

> The Catholic Church teaches that, besides a place of eternal torments for the wicked and of everlasting rest for the righteous, there exists in the next life a middle state of temporary punishment, allotted for those who have died in venial sin, or who have not satisfied the justice of God for sins already forgiven. She also teaches us that, although the souls consigned to this intermediate state, commonly called purgatory, cannot help themselves, they may be aided by the suffrages of the faithful on earth.[1]

In Roman Catholic teaching, purgatory is a place where the souls of believers go to be further purified from sin until they are ready to be admitted into heaven. According to this view, the suffering of purgatory and the suffrages of the faithful on earth are given to God in place of the punishment for sins that believers should have received in time but did not. For Catholics, purgatory is the final aspect of their justification before catching a glimpse of the face of God.

The case in question is another classic example of why any marriage between Evangelicalism and Roman Catholicism would be a wedding arranged in hell and officiated by Satan himself. Yet again we see in the doctrine of purgatory, Rome's meddling with the simplicity of the Gospel (2 Corinthians 11:3-4). This system is forever guilty of adding and augmenting the faith once delivered to the saints. Rome's gospel is a gospel with harmful additives. To faith and justification they have added baptism and works. To Calvary they have added the sacrifice of the Mass. To God's Word they have added tradition. To the Son of God they have added the Mother of God in the act of prayer. To heaven and hell we now see that they have added purgatory. Theirs indeed is another gospel. What we have in purgatory is another false doctrine pulled from the hat of Roman Catholicism. A doctrine, as we shall see more clearly as we proceed, that tarnishes the work of Christ, takes the shine off heaven, and clouds the souls of men with fear and foreboding.

This plank in Catholic theology deserves to be ripped up and sawn in two. Bishop Ryle cuts to the quick when he stated:

> The notion of purgatory after death, which shall turn sinners into saints, is a lying invention of man, and is nowhere taught in the Bible. We must be saints before we die, if we are to be saints afterwards in glory.

The doctrine of purgatory is another one of those foreign growths that has fastened itself like a malignant tumor upon the theology of the Roman Catholic Church. Rome is a doctrinally deceased body and ought to remain where our forefathers placed her in an isolation ward not to be visited by healthy Protestants and Evangelicals who value their life (1 Timothy 6:3-5). The merits of this health warning against the doctrine of purgatory can be better understood by considering several aspects of this doctrine under the microscope of Holy Writ.

The Theology of Purgatory

No one need doubt that the doctrine of purgatory, first articulated at the Council of Florence in 1439, remains an essential part of Catholic dogma. Admittedly, Rome attempts today to paint a brighter more positive picture of purgatory, compared to the dark and frightening concepts of medieval Rome, but as we shall see the principal and offending parts abide intact. Whether viewed as an incubator or an incinerator to borrow the terminology of Catholic apologist Peter Kreeft, purgatory remains as it always has, the final act of justification and the full payment for the remittance of sin in the life of the faithful Catholic. The body of this theology is alive and well since its birth in 1439 no matter how modern theologians dress it up in new language and thought.

In getting our arms around this doctrine that we might possess a better understanding of it, we need to look at two things:

The Doctrine Defined.

Before we reduce this doctrine to a definition, let us scout out the theological geography of purgatorial dogma as mapped out by the Roman System in her councils and catechisms. The span of our reconnaissance will take us back to 1439 and bring us forward to 1994, proving the historical and theological correctness of this dogma within orthodox Catholicism.

The bedrock for recent and present statements on purgatory are the Councils of Florence (1439) and the Council of Trent (1563). These are cited for us in The Companion to the Catechism of the Catholic Church as follows:

> Council of Florence (1439): DS (1304) [De novissimis] It has likewise defined, that, if those truly penitent have departed in the love of God, before they have made satisfaction by worthy fruits of penance for sins of commission and omission, the souls of these are cleansed after death by purgatorial punishments; and so that they may be released from punishments of this kind, the suffrages of the living faithful are of advantage to them, namely, the sacrifices of Masses, prayers, and almsgiving, and other

works of piety, which are customarily performed by the faithful for other faithful according to the institutions of the Church.

Council of Trent (1563): DS (1820) Since the Catholic Church, instructed by the Holy Spirit, in conformity with the sacred writings and ancient tradition of the Fathers in sacred councils, and very recently in this ecumenical Synod, has taught that there is a purgatory, and that the souls detained there are assisted by the suffrages of the faithful, and especially by the acceptable sacrifice of the altar, the holy Synod commands the bishops that they insist that the sound doctrine of purgatory, which has been transmitted by the holy Fathers and holy Councils, be believed by the faithful of Christ, be maintained, taught, and everywhere preached.

Although separated by several centuries, the Second Vatican Council didn't move far from Florence and Trent in proclaiming and explaining purgatory—its existence, nature and purpose. In the section "Sacred Liturgy" of *Apostolic Constitution on the Revision of Indulgences*, No. 2, we read:

The truth has been divinely revealed that sins are followed by punishments. God's holiness and justice inflict them. Sins must be expiated. This may be done on this earth through the sorrows, miseries and trials of this life and, above all, through death. Otherwise the expiation must be made in the next life through fire and torments or purifying punishments.

Before drawing these strands of thought together into a definition, let us take a final look at the official propagation of this doctrine by Rome at her own hand and from her own mouth. The New Catechism of the Catholic Church was declared by Pope John II to be "a sure norm for teaching the Faith" and so our excursion would do well to end here. In the following paragraphs we read:

> All who die in God's grace and friendship, but still imperfectly purified, are indeed assured of their eternal salvation; but after death they undergo purification, so as to achieve the holiness necessary to enter the joy of heaven.

> The Church gives the name Purgatory to this final purification of the elect, which is entirely different from the punishment of the damned. The Church formulated her doctrine of faith on Purgatory especially at the Councils of Florence and Trent. The tradition of the Church, by reference to certain texts of Scripture, speaks of a cleansing fire: -

>> As for certain lesser faults, we must believe that, before the Final Judgment, there is a purifying fire. He who is truth says that whoever utters blasphemy against the Holy Spirit will be pardoned neither in this age nor in the age to come. From this sentence we understand that certain offenses can be forgiven in this age, but certain others in the age to come.

> This teaching is also based on the practice of prayer for the dead, already mentioned in Sacred Scripture: "Therefore [Judas Maccabeus] made atonement for the dead that they might be delivered from their sin.' From the beginning the Church has honored the

memory of the dead and offered prayers in suffrage for them, above all the Eucharistic sacrifice, so that, thus purified, they may attain the beatific vision of God. The Church also commends almsgiving, indulgences, and works of penance undertaken on behalf of the dead:

> Let us help and commemorate them. If Job's sons were purified by their father's sacrifice, why would we doubt that our offerings for the dead bring them some consolation? Let us not hesitate to help those who have died and to offer our prayers for them.[2]

Within the full circle of these quotations a definition and basic understanding of this centuries old doctrine is to be found. Catholicism, past and present, believes that those who die in God's grace and at peace with the Church, but who are not yet holy or perfect must undergo a state of suffering after death whereby sin is expiated by purifying punishments. For the Catholic, Calvary doesn't cover it all, for while Christ's atoning death makes it possible for sins to be forgiven, Rome teaches that the pardoned sinner must himself suffer an undetermined pain, of unknown intensity, for an unspecified time in order to be purged, cleansed and thereby made ready for heaven. While Rome opens the door to the possibility of being made fit for heaven, through the suffering of this life and one's death, the door seems to be mighty close to closed. So much so that the pope himself cannot be sure of squeezing through. Consequently, death for the Catholic is not a coronation as Paul viewed it in 2 Timothy 4, but an incarceration.

Purgatory, then, is a state of temporary punishment for those who, departing this life in the grace of God, are not entirely free from venial sins or have not yet fully paid the satisfaction due to their transgression. While hell is a jailhouse for the hardened sinner, purgatory by all accounts then is a reformatory school for the not so bad and the not so good.

While we have not yet begun to critique this doctrine, the latter thought is enough to frighten away any true biblical Christian. The category of not so bad and not so good is foreign to God's Word. The concept of being holy enough to miss hell, but not holy enough to enter heaven, is a million miles away from the truth of God's Word. This is man speaking, not God the Holy Spirit.

In his book, *Probing Heaven*, John Gilmore writes:

> The modern man does not believe he is wicked enough to deserve hell, but that he is sufficiently bad to require purgatory. Man is willing to spend some time in the neighborhood of hell, but unwilling to make hell his permanent residence. Purgatory gives man the option to suffer for his sins, but not eternally suffer for them. It appeals to his sense of modulation.

> Acceptance of purgatory outside the circle of the church reflects the fact that the average person no longer believes in the separating and absolute punishing power of divine holiness. Modern man has distaste for pain in any form, but he will accept a little if it leads to something better. But he holds both a definite dread and disdain for a brand of holiness, which will exact eternal retribution. He would prefer to empty and board up hell for good and he hopes that God's holiness would lack the severity and strictness that would keep hell going.[3]

By way of opening criticism of the doctrine as we find it defined by the Catholic Church, it has more to do with the rationale of men rather than the revelation of God. Rome would have us believe that this doctrine was borne out of a strong commitment to God's holiness, but in reality it pampers to people who look for and want a place to atone for their sins, and to have opportunity to un-live the lives they lived on earth.

The Doctrine Developed:

Working with this basic definition of purgatory, further clarification and further investigation is, I believe, required on a number of issues. Does God forgive the sinner and yet require satisfaction and reparations from the sinner? Is one sin greater than the other? Can others ease the pain of those detained in purgatory and effect their early release? Rome answers in the affirmative to all three questions and we need to know why and how.

In the first place, the concept of purgatory is supported by a unique and wrong understanding of sin's offense and forgiveness. A few definitions of uniquely Catholic terms will help. Rome teaches a distinction between "venial" and "mortal" sins. Basically, some sins are graver in the eyes of God than others. Venial sin also differs from mortal sin in the punishment assigned it. Venial sin merits a temporal rather than an eternal penalty. Catholicism, therefore, has a division of sin and a distinction of punishment. An outworking of this dichotomy is to be seen in that after the guilt of sin and its eternal punishment have been forgiven, temporal punishment remains. This temporal punishment can be atoned for by the sacrament of penance, which involves the priest declaring the penitent forgiven and prescribing deeds of penance for the person to perform.

Although written a number of years ago, some words from *The Secrets of Romanism* by Dr. Zacchello will help solidify and place these dichotomies within the context of purgatory.

> According to Roman teaching a person can commit two kinds of sin against God: mortal and venial. By mortal sin is meant a grave offense against the law of God or of the church. It is called 'mortal' because it kills the soul by depriving it entirely of sanctifying grace. Venial sin is a small and pardonable offense against God and the laws of the church. Then, this confusing and unscriptural doctrine continues: Two kinds of punishment are due to mortal sin, eternal (in hell forever), and temporal (in purgatory). Eternal punishment is canceled by the sacraments of baptism and penance, or by an act of perfect contrition with promise of confession. Temporal punishment is not canceled by these sacraments, but by works of penance, by almsgiving, by paying the priest to say mass, by indulgences, etc., which reduce the temporal punishment for mortal sins that would have to be suffered in purgatory. Thus even if all mortal sins of a Roman Catholic are forgiven in confession by a priest, and he does not perform enough of these 'good works,' he will go to purgatory and remain there in torture until his soul is completely purified.[4]

The doctrine of purgatory, therefore, is built upon the premise that while God forgives sins, His justice nevertheless cries out that the sinner must suffer the punishment due him for his sin, before he will ever be able to approach the gates of heaven with any hope of entrance. Such postulation, however, is threadbare of any biblical theology and lays an ax to the foot of the cross. Not only is this distinction absent of biblical justification, it lacks logic even according to human reasoning. For it manifestly would be unjust to forgive a criminal the guilt of his crime and still send him to prison to suffer for it.

Furthermore, the doctrine of purgatory is accompanied by the belief that others can cut the time served by the detainee through vicarious atonement by means of prayers, masses, alms giving, and the securing of indulgences upon the performance of specified deeds. This notion of vicarious atonement on the behalf of the dead is based upon a false understanding of the communion of saints, whereby one saint can traffic merit and reward in the direction of another saint. Basically, when one person has done more than enough to get to heaven he can transfer the surplus to a less fortunate brother. Such a possibility manifests itself in a number of ways with regards to purgatory.

The primary means of helping an inmate of purgatory, says the church, can be obtained by performing a Mass on their behalf. Parishioners can make a plea to a priest to say a Mass for the benefit of a person believed to be in purgatory and the request is normally accompanied by a small gift of money.

The New Catechism spells out this doctrine in the following excerpt:

> By virtue of the "communion of saints" the Church commends the dead to God's mercy and offers her prayers, especially the holy sacrifice of the Eucharist, on their behalf.[5]

Another way of helping prisoners of purgatory tunnel their way out is by the acquiring of special credits on their behalf called indulgences, which possess the ability to cancel out temporal punishment. Catholics can earn an indulgence from the church by accomplishing a defined deed of piety, such as praying the Rosary whereupon the church dispenses indulgences from a vast warehouse of merit called "the treasury of the church".

Again, *The New Catechism* advances the Church's position by way of expansion and explanation:

> In the communion of saints, "a perennial link of charity exists between the faithful who have already reached their heavenly home, those who are expiating their sins in purgatory and those who are still pilgrims on earth. Between them there is, too, an abundant exchange of all good things." In this wonderful exchange, the holiness of one profits others, well beyond the harm that the sin of one could cause others. Thus recourse to the communion of saints lets the contrite sinner be more promptly and efficaciously purified of the punishments for sin.[6]

> We also call these spiritual goods of the communion of saints the "Church's treasury", which is "not the sum total of the material goods which have accumulated during the course of the centuries. On the contrary the "treasury of the Church" is the infinite value, which can never be exhausted, which Christ's merits have before God. They were offered so that the whole of mankind could be set free from sin and attain communion with the Father. In Christ, the Redeemer himself, the satisfactions and merits of his Redemption exist and find their efficacy."[7]

> This treasury includes as well the prayers and good works of the Blessed Virgin Mary. They are truly immense, unfathomable, and even pristine in their

value before God. In the treasury, too, are the prayers and good works of all the saints, all those who have followed in the footsteps of Christ the Lord and by his grace have made their lives holy and carried their own salvation and at the same time cooperated in saving their brothers in the unity of the Mystical Body.[8]

What we have here is a treasury of meritorious works for the dead. According to the Catholic faith, in addition to the merit obtained and secured by Christ on the cross, there is a warehouse of merit deposited by the saints on which others can draw for help. In essence, those saints who have exceeded the quota of good deeds required for ultimate salvation, have put money into the bank of heaven, on which others still in debt to God can draw for their required deposit that will enable them to enter into heaven. These works are called works of supererogation, which occurs when works performed by an individual exceed the merit necessary for themselves. Indulgences then could be likened to a "withdrawal" of that portion of additional merit and then applied to the "account" of the person obtaining the indulgence or a prisoner of purgatory. Whichever way he chooses to apply is acceptable.

Surely no aspect of Vatican dogma more clearly illustrates the chasm between biblical Protestantism and the Roman teachings on salvation than the concept of a treasury of merit and the securing of indulgences. It mocks the cross and places salvation in the hands of man.

By way of final comment, prayers to and for the dead are integral to easing the pain and securing the release of those in purgatory. Catholic dogma is unequivocal in this position, as evidenced when Ludwig Ott wrote the following excerpt from *Fun-*

damentals of Catholic Dogma, "The living faithful on earth can come to the assistance of the souls in purgatory by their intercessions (suffrages)." The faithful are to be encouraged by the bishops to intercede on behalf of the dead, and to enlist the invocation of the saints in order to obtain favors from God through His Son for the poor and pained souls of those in purgatory.

A prime example of what we have just noted is related to us by John Phillips in his comments on Psalm 23:

> Some years ago Kenneth Opperman was granted an interview with Pope Paul VI. During the course of the interview, Opperman asked the pope if he was saved and the pontiff related some mystical experience he had received as a boy. It wasn't much to go on, but at least, it was a start. The visitor rephrased the question: "Sir, when you die, will you go to Heaven?" The pope's answer was most revealing. "Ah! Mr. Opperman, you have asked me a very hard question." It certainly was a hard question. If he had said, "Yes!" he would have demolished the Catholic Church then and there because the Catholic Church does not believe that people die and go to Heaven. According to Roman dogma they die and go to purgatory. Then the pontiff brightened. "Ah, but Mr. Opperman, when I die I shall have seven hundred million Roman Catholics praying for my soul." What darkness![9]

As evidenced, Catholic dogma propagates Purgatory as place or state of temporary punishment for those who departing this life in the grace of God but not yet entirely free from venial sins, or have not yet fully paid the satisfaction due to their transgressions. Release and relief for such sufferers is to be found in the merits and ministry of others in their behalf.

The Tyranny of Purgatory

While not wishing to spend too much time on this point, consideration must be given to the moneymaking, soul-imprisoning, and hell-originating nature of this doctrine. This doctrine, quite frankly, enriches Rome and enslaves Catholics. The true Gospel liberates men from the fear of death and can be possessed without money (Isaiah 55:1-2; 1 Peter 1:17-21; Hebrews 2:14-15), but not according to the gospel of Rome. By virtue of its Purgatory doctrine, the Church of Rome has placed in its possession the keys to the place of punishment in the afterlife. The Bible, however, says that Christ alone holds "the keys of death and Hades" (Revelation 1:18).

The practical and historical reality of this awful doctrine is that it shrouds the death and funeral of a Roman Catholic with darkness and dread. As stated earlier, for the Protestant to die is gain, but for the Catholic to die is pain. Instead of the expansion of the soul in heaven's glorious freedom, there is a shrinking of the soul into a place of unspeakable torment. How sad and scandalous that millions of Catholics should live and die chained to the fear of dying, and shackled to the miserable thought of spending an unknown time in the pain and anguish of a fictional place called purgatory. In general, the worst a Catholic can hope for is hell, and the best a Catholic can hope for is purgatory. Death brings detention and the grave brings suffering.

The net result of this doctrine is the enslavement of the Catholic soul to the priests and provisions of Rome. From the hand of the priest Masses are found, indulgences are bought, and penances are prescribed, all of which can alleviate the pains and sufferings of purgatory. For all practical purposes, the priest becomes a saviour and the church a redeemer to those who fear the woe and misery of this temporal hell. Faced with the foreboding threat of Purgatory, the sincere Catholic will easily and generously part with his money and make himself accountable to the church in the hope that the more satisfaction one makes while living, the less remains to be asked for in the life to come. This doctrine makes men slaves and popes millionaires.

It is a fraud and a financial scam that shames the Gospel and incarcerates men and women to a life sentence of bondage and fear of death. The writer of the book to the Hebrews tells us that Christ died to remove bondage and fear of death . It is a doctrine of exploitation while the Gospel is a doctrine of emancipation.

Read the following words of Dr. Robert Ketcham as he challenges Rome on this very ground,

> How do you know, Mr. Priest, when to stop praying and taking money from your parishioners for a given case? How do you know then that John Murphy is out of purgatory? His getting out is dependent upon the saying of masses paid for by his bereaved ones. If you stop one or two masses too soon, what then? If you keep on saying masses for the fellow after he is out, that is bad. It is bad either way you come at it. I ask seriously, Sir, Mr. Roman Catholic Priest, How do you know when to stop saying masses for a given individual? Do you have some kind of a connection with the unseen world?"[10]

The words of Father Chiniguy are no less poignant as he addressed himself to this issue out of the context of having been a priest for 50 years prior to his conversion to Protantism:

How long, O Lord, shall that insolent enemy of the gospel, the Church of Rome, be permitted to fatten herself upon the tears of the widow and of the orphan by means of that cruel and impious invention of paganism—purgatory?"[11]

We not only stand against this doctrine theologically, but also oppose it ethically. Jesus and His disciples warned about those who would play on people's emotions and peddle the Word of God for personal and financial gain (Matthew 23:14; 2 Corinthians 2:17; II Peter 2:1-3). The Church of Rome through its doctrine of purgatory is directly contrary to the teachings of Scripture.

The Travesty of Purgatory

In his book, *Catholicism and Fundamentalism*, Catholic apologist Karl Keating while speaking on the subject of purgatory, relates the following exchange between two great Englishmen, James Boswell and Samuel Johnson in 1769:

Boswell: "What do you think, Sir, of purgatory, as believed by the Roman Catholics?"

Johnson: "Why, Sir, it is a very harmless doctrine. They are of the opinion that the generality of mankind are neither so obstinately wicked as to deserve everlasting punishment, nor so good as to merit being admitted into the society of blessed spirits and therefore that God is graciously pleased to allow a middle state, where they may be purified by certain degrees of suffering. You see, Sir, there is nothing unreasonable in this."

Boswell: "But then, Sir, their Masses for the dead?"

Johnson: "Why, Sir, if it be at once established that there are souls in purgatory, it is as proper to pray for these, as for our brethren of mankind who are yet in this life."

After relating this story, Karl Keating goes on to say,

"Although Johnson was not a 'Catholic' he recognized that the doctrine of purgatory is not at odds with other tenets of Christianity. In fact, as he may know, there is considerable Scriptural warrant for it, even if the doctrine is not explicitly set out in the Bible."[12]

What ought to be our response? Is purgatory a harmless doctrine? Is it in agreement with the major tenets of Christianity? Does it have considerable Scriptural warrant? I believe our response ought to be one of obstinate rejection to any consideration that this doctrine be biblical and orthodox. To speak frankly, Karl Keating is talking theological blarney. As stated in the introduction to this section, this doctrine is a lying invention of men that tarnishes the work of Christ, removes the shine off heaven, and clouds the souls of men with fear and foreboding.

The rope with which we would like to hang this doctrine has three strands to it:

Purgatory Contradicts the Word of God:

Although Karl Keating suggests that the doctrine of purgatory has at its side considerable Scriptural warrant, I would argue to the contrary. It is my contention that this doctrine is built upon the sand of Church tradition rather than the rock of biblical revelation.

Upon investigation of the evidence presented by Catholic apologists and theologians in defense of purgatory, we will deduce that this doctrine does not even cast a shadow upon the wall of Scripture. The Bible does not give witness to this doctrine, but rather prosecutes a strong case against it.

It must be admitted that not all Catholic theologians echo the sentiments of Karl Keating. Some exegetes at this time would be inclined to say that although there is no clear textual warrant in Scripture for the later doctrine of purgatory, neither is there anything that is clearly contrary to that doctrine.

Two comments are in order here. First, finding nothing in the Bible against a view is not an adequate basis for making it an article of faith. A lack of evidence against someone in court may hinder prosecution, but it doesn't prove innocence. Second, I will presently take issue with the basic premise that Scripture does not contradict the doctrine of purgatory.

Let's wade directly into the controversy and consider the contradiction of purgatorial texts. Catholics rally a number of texts in support of purgatory: Matthew 12:32; 1 Corinthians 3:15; 2 Maccabees 12:42-46.

In Matthew 12:32, Jesus warns his detractors of the fact that anyone who commits blasphemy against the Holy Spirit "will not be forgiven, either in this age or in the age to come." From this verse Catholicism infers the possibility that sins are forgiven not only in this world, but also in the world to come. But Jesus does not say that some sins will be forgiven after death, as some have wrongly inferred from His words. Rather, He emphatically declares that he who commits this sin shall never be forgiven. The focus of Christ, as recorded by Mark, is the deadly nature and eternal consequences of this sin (Mark 3:29). It is simply flawed reasoning to say that something will happen in the age to come because it is stated that something won't happen in the age to come.

What is needed to prove the doctrine of purgatory is not a negative statement based upon inference, but a positive one that tells us that people suffer for the purpose of continuing purification after death. But the Bible is silent as to this point.

Also, purgatory involves only venial sins. However, this sin is not venial. It is mortal, being both eternal and unforgivable. How then can a statement about the unforgiveness of a mortal sin in the next life be the basis for an argument that non-mortal sins will be forgiven then?

Another text that Rome employs in the defense of purgatory is found in 1 Corinthians 3:15. Paul's words about being saved, yet as through fire, have been taken by Rome to speak of a transient purification punishment in the other world. This citation in defense of purgatory is, however, shot through with exegetical and contextual twists.

The passage in question is addressed to a company of believers who, according to Paul, had already been given a right standing before God through the death of his Son. Their sins had already been taken care of in the suffering of Christ (1 Cor. 1:2 and 6:11; 2 Cor. 5:21). An exegesis of the context also shows that the day in question was not referring to the time of death, but to the return of the Lord and the judgment seat of Christ. Paul is speaking of a day when believers will be given a reward for their service to Jesus Christ. The question here is not of sin and its punishment, but rather service and its reward. The fire consumes a man's work, not his sin, in essence revealing man's service and not expiating sin.

In his commentary on 1 Corinthians, John MacArthur sets the exegetical record straight concerning these verses and clarifies by implication the faulty and sloppy exegesis of Roman

Catholicism in their handling of this passage. Commenting on verse thirteen, MacArthur writes:

> A new building is usually checked out carefully before it is occupied or used. Cities, counties, and states have codes that require buildings to meet certain standards. God has strict standards for what we build for Him in and with our lives. When Christ returns, every believer's work will be tested as to quality. Fire is the symbol of testing. Just as it purifies metal, so will the fire of God's discernment burn up the dross and leave what is pure and valuable (cf. Job 23:10; Zech. 13:9; 1 Pet. 1:17; Rev. 3:18).
>
> As the following verses (14-15) make clear, that will not be a time of punishment but a time of reward. Even the one who has built with wood, hay, or straw will not be condemned; but his reward will correspond to the quality of his building materials. When wood, hay, or straw come in contact with fire they are burned up. Nothing is left but cinders. They cannot stand the test. Gold, silver, and precious stone, however, do not burn. They will stand the test, and they will bring a great reward.[13]

1 Corinthians 3:15 speaks then not of redemption in purgatory, but of reward in heaven. It speaks not of the destiny of our souls, but of the quality of our work for Jesus Christ. The works in question have nothing to do with my acceptance before God (Eph. 2:8-9; Titus 3:4-5; Rom. 4:4-5).

From the Apocrypha, 2 Maccabees 12:42-46, is also enlisted as proof for purgatory. In this text, it is to be observed that the Jews prayed for the fallen dead and sought to make atonement for the dead that they might be forgiven. What had happened was that the Jewish general, Judas Maccabeus, had lost some men in a battle with the Idomeans. When the time came to bury them with proper honor, they were found to be in the possession of tokens of idols, a sin in the Jewish religion. Judas took up a collection from his soldiers, which amounted to 2,000 drachmas and sent it to the priests in Jerusalem to provide sacrifices to expiate their sins.

Consequently, the practice of mass offered for the souls in purgatory is said to be similar to what Judas did and his deed is recorded in the canonical Catholic Scriptures.

By way of response, the following are offered. First, it is to be noted that 2 Maccabees is difficult to square even with Roman Catholic's teaching, because it advocates that soldiers who had died in the mortal sin of idolatry (which cannot be forgiven according to Catholic dogma) should have prayers and sacrifices offered for them with the possibility that they will be delivered from their suffering. Is there not an internal contradiction in Rome's citation of this passage? Second, it must be said that this literature is not equal to Scripture in authority, and should not be taken as a safe and authoritative source of doctrine.

In their book, *Roman Catholics and Evangelicals*, Norman Geisler and Ralph Mackenzie challenge this very issue and offer the following rebuttal:

> The Protestant response to the use of this text to prove purgatory is simple: II Maccabees is not part of the inspired cannon of Scripture, and therefore has no authority. It, along with the rest of the Apocrypha, was not accepted as inspired by the Jewish community that wrote them. They were not accepted by Jesus and the apostles, who never

quoted them in the New Testament. Many important early Fathers of the church, including Jerome, the great biblical scholar and translator of the Roman Catholic Latin Vulgate rejected them. Indeed, they were not infallibly added to the Roman Catholic Bible until after the Reformation (A.D. 1546), in a futile attempt to support purgatory and prayers for the dead which Luther attacked. Even then this polemical anti-Reformation council inconsistently rejected some apocryphal books, including one (2 [4] Esdras 7:105) which speaks against praying for the dead.[14]

In light of what we have just considered, Rome's textual arguments for purgatory are paper thin and easily shredded by careful and plain exegesis. Their arguments to defend purgatory are hardly worthy of "considerable Scriptural warrant!"

Having considered purgatorial texts and their contradiction with Scripture, let me further expose their contradictions.

In their Purgatory doctrine, Rome promotes prayers for the dead. Does such a notion have any Scriptural warrant or weight? Is Rome justified in encouraging "suffrages of the faithful on earth" for those in purgatory? In rebuttal to these questions, I will raise several objections to this practice that is foreign to biblical Christianity. First, it is foreign because it flies in the face of death and its separation. In biblical terms, death is the separation of the spirit and the body, and the separating of the living from the departed (Phil. 1:23; 2 Cor. 5:7). A great gulf exists between the living and the dead and it can't be bridged by prayer (Luke 16:26). From the Bible we are told that death is a veil that seals off the living from the dead (1 Thess. 4:13-18). The Scriptures voice a stern warning against any attempt to contact the dead. It is not only futile, but also forbidden (Deut. 18:11).

Added to these facts is the example of David, who while his baby was alive, but seriously ill, prayed for it fervently. However, when the baby died, he ceased praying for it immediately (2 Sam. 12:22-23). The notion that our prayers or works can do anything on behalf of the dead is a hammer blow to the all-sufficiency of the completed work of Christ on the Cross. His mediation and intercession is more than enough for the sinner who trusts in Him (2 John 2:1-2).

Second, Purgatory not only promotes prayers for the dead, but also invents a third place beyond the grave. There is not only a heaven to gain and a hell to shun, but also a purgatory to endure. Death for the Catholic will bring neither heaven nor hell. Can such a notion breathe within an atmosphere of biblical theology? Can the doctrine of purgatory make an entrance through the front door of Genesis or the back door of Revelation? To this the Scriptures shout a resounding NO!

A look at the Scriptures gives sufficient proof that purgatory is purely imaginary. Those passages that are clear about the world beyond present only two possibilities. The broad way that leads to destruction, and the narrow gate that leads to life (Matt. 7:13,14). The tares are cast into the fire; the wheat is gathered into barns (Matt. 13:30). The wicked are thrown into the furnace of fire; the righteous shine forth in the kingdom of their father (Matt. 13:41-43,49,50). The foolish virgins stay outside; the wise virgins enter into the marriage feast (Matt. 25:21,30). The cursed, on the left hand, go away into the fire of eternal punishment; the blessed, on the right hand, receive the kingdom and eternal life (Matt. 25:33-46). The wicked rich man is in torments; Lazarus is comforted in Abraham's bosom (Lk. 16:22,23). Some are raised for judgment, and others awaken to everlasting life (Dan. 12:2). The wicked are cast into the lake of fire and brimstone; the elect are brought into the heavenly Jerusalem (Rev. 21:1-4,8).

Nowhere is there a question of any place other than heaven and hell. The texts brought forth by Rome to uphold the doctrine of purgatory are irrelevant, and provide no support or warrant for this doctrine.

Joseph Parker said of Spurgeon:

"The only colors Mr. Spurgeon knew where black and white. In all things he was definite. You were either in or out, up or down, alive or dead."

Like Spurgeon, the biblical writers spoke in black and white terms concerning heaven and hell, and knew nothing of a gray purgatory. There may be two ways to get to Scotland, the high road and the low road, but there is only one way to heaven, and that is through the front door of God's saving grace, not through the back door of purgatory. There is a heaven to gain and a hell to shun, and nothing else.

Purgatory is indeed in contradiction to Scripture. It is a theological vagabond that can find no home within the walls of biblical revelation.

Purgatory Challenges the Work of Christ:

Not only does this doctrine twist the Word of God, it tarnishes the work of Christ. The greatest sin and shame of this concept is that it dynamites the hill called Calvary, because by implication Christ failed to fully satisfy the justice of God on behalf of the sinner. The Reformers correctly viewed purgatory as an insult to Christ's saving work. As I said earlier, purgatory mocks the cross and places salvation into the hands of man. Salvation becomes an attainment by the works and merits of men rather than an obtainment by the work and merit of Christ (Ps. 49:7-8).

The combined message of the New Testament is that all our sins were judged, exacted, and punished in Jesus Christ on the Cross (Rom 3:23-26: Titus 2:14; Heb. 9:26-28, 10:14; Rev. 1:5). He felt the banishment of God in bearing our sin, and His soul became a sheath for the sword of God's justice. (Isa. 53:10). There is therefore now no condemnation the them that are in Christ (John 5:24; Rom 8:1). The conclusion of Scripture is that while purgation was necessary for the sinner before he could enter into heaven, Jesus Christ did the purging and completely absorbed the pain caused by all our iniquities (Heb. 1:3). There is a purgatory, but it is not after death, it was in Christ's death. The biblical record declares the completed, sufficient nature of the work of Christ (Jo. 19:30). Christ left nothing for man to do, He had finished it on the cross. These and other passages deny legitimizing the view that we must do or can do something extra to please God and inch the doors of heaven open.

The doctrine of propitiation freely and fully through Christ, is sufficient alone to drive the last nail into the coffin of purgatorial dogma, and to render as baseless the concept of a treasury of merit (Rom. 3:25; 1 John 2:2). The Greek word employed by Paul is hilasterion. Propitiation carries the basic idea of appeasement or satisfaction. In ancient pagan religions as in many religions today, the idea of man's appeasing a deity by various gifts or sacrifices was common. In the New Testament, however, propitiation always refers to the work of God, not of man. Man is utterly incapable of satisfying God's justice except by spending eternity in hell. This is highlighted to us in the one other New Testament use of this noun. In Hebrews 9:5, this term refers to the mercy seat of the tabernacle's Ark of the Covenant. There a bull's blood was sprinkled on the Day of Atonement to cover (atone) Israel's sins (Lev. 16;14), and satisfy God for another year. Jesus' death on the cross was that final and perfect sacrifice which completely satisfied God's just demands against sinful people, thus averting His wrath from those who believe. What was once hidden from view in the tabernacle has now been set forth in the person and work of our lovely Lord Jesus. The doctrine of purgatory is redundant and offensive in the full glare of such glorious truths. What Catholic doctrine and its adherents have failed to grasp, is that sin, when propitiated in the New Testament sense, the wrath of God, including the punishment due to sin, is satisfied and wiped out. Jesus Christ alone is the sufficient satisfaction for sin and the sufficient Savior for sinners. To affirm that we must suffer for our own sins as Roman Catholicism teaches is the ultimate insult to Christ's atoning death. Purgatory cheapens the cross, devalues the blood, and implies a blemish upon the Lamb of God. Purgatory exalts men to the status of cooperative saviors with Jesus Christ. In Catholic theology, Calvary is a start; but for Protestant theology, Calvary is the end of the matter. Protestant doctrine teaches that Jesus paid it all and all to Him I owe. Catholic doctrine promulgates that Jesus paid a part and that part to Him I owe, but the rest is up to me. The latter is both ignorance and arrogance in the face of Gospel truth.

Is it any wonder that John Owen, the Welshman, wrote concerning purgatory, "It is a groundless fable; an invention set up in competition with the sanctification of the Spirit and the blood of Christ." The Great Reformer, Calvin, demonstrated his disgust for the notion of purgatory when he wrote:

[It] is a deadly fiction of Satan, which nullifies the cross of Christ. . . . If it is perfectly clear . . . that the blood of Christ is the sole satisfaction for the sins of believers, the sole expiation, the sole purgation, what remains but to say that purgatory is simply a dreadful blasphemy against Christ?[15]

The story of Hudson Taylor's conversion has often been told, but it is one that gets more wonderful with each telling. His mother had left him home alone for a while as she visited a friend's home nearly one hundred miles away. Impressed by the Spirit to pray for her son, she left the table, went to her room, locked the door, and prayed for hours until she sensed in her heart that young Hudson had trusted Christ. Back at home, Hudson had found a tract in his father's library and was reading it primarily for the interesting stories that it might contain. While he was reading it, he was struck by the phrase, "The finished work of Christ." Immediately the words of Scripture leaped into his mind: "It is finished!" Hudson Taylor said to himself, "If the whole work was finished and the whole debt was paid, what is there left for me to do?" He fell to his knees and yielded himself to Christ, and when his mother returned home two weeks later, she told him she already knew!

Oh that the advocates of purgatory and the fearful faithful within Catholicism would learn along with Hudson Taylor that "the whole work was finished and the whole debt was paid and there is nothing left for us to do!" There is no value in a supposed treasury of merit. There is no place for a place called purgatory. There is no prayer, but the sinner's prayer.

Listen to the words of a hymn whose author is unknown to me, but whose heart beats with the concern and point of this section of our argument:

Not what these hands have done
Can save this guilty soul;
Not what this toiling flesh has borne
Can make my spirit whole.

Not what I feel or do
Can give me peace with God;
Not all my prayers, and sighs and tears,
Can bear my awful load.

Thy work alone, O Christ,
Can ease this weight of sin;
The blood alone, O Lamb of God,
Can give me peace within.

I bless the Christ of God,
I rest on love divine;
And, with unfaltering lip and heart,
I call this Saviour mine.

Purgatory not only contradicts the Word of God, but also challenges the work of Christ. It attacks both the blood and the Book and ought therefore to find no friends within the family of God.

Purgatory Clouds the Welcome of Heaven:

According to the Bible, death is but a door into the presence of God for those who die in Christ. Death is but the black limousine that carries us to the very gates of glory. Death is but an usher that shows us to our seat in the heavens. Once a believer has died, though his or her physical body remains on the earth and is buried, the Bible shows that at the moment of death the soul (or spirit) of that believer goes immediately into the presence of God with rejoicing. Death does not rupture our fellowship with Christ, but rather opens us to a greater experience of God in His immediate presence. Paul, under the inspiration of the Holy Spirit, wrote to the Church at Philippi, to die is gain, not pain (Phil. 1:21). To leave this life behind is to look forward to the sunshine of His near presence, not the darkness of purgatory.

Ron Rhodes in his book, *The Undiscovered Country*, seeks to open the eyes of his readers to view the immediacy and the intimacy of Christ's presence for the believer following his departure from earth's scene:

> Christians are in continuous fellowship with Christ in the intermediate state. This is evident in numerous passages. Jesus told the thief on the cross, "I tell you the truth, today you will be with me in paradise" (Lk 23:43). While being stoned to death, Stephen prayed, "Lord Jesus, receive my spirit" (Acts 7:59). The apostle Paul said, "I desire to depart and be with Christ, which is better by far (Phil. 1:23).

> It is interesting to note that the word for "depart" in Philippians 1:23 was used in Bible times in reference to a ship being loosed from its moorings to sail away from the dock. The "mooring" that kept Paul from departing to heaven was his commitment to work among believers on earth until his task was complete. His ultimate desire, however, was to "sail" directly into God's presence.

> The word "depart" was also used in Bible time to speak of freeing someone from chains. Here on

earth, we are anchored to the hardships and heartaches of this life. In death, these chains are broken. We are set free for entry into heaven.

Along this same line, Paul said in 2 Corinthians 5:8 that he preferred "to be away from the body and to be at home with the Lord." The Greek word for "with" in the phrase "home with the Lord" suggests very close fellowship face to face. It is a word used of intimate relationships. Paul was saying, then, that the fellowship we would have with Christ immediately following our physical death would be greatly intimate.[16]

In the light of these words, how tragic and sad are the pronouncements of the Catholic Church to her people. The valley of the shadow of death holds no rays of sunshine for the Catholics as they move towards purgatory. Death brings misery, not release. Paul speaks of chains being broken; Rome speaks of imprisonment and detention in this non-eternal hell. Paul speaks of seeing Christ face to face, but the Catholic sees only the back of God in purgatory and wonders when he will see God face to face. Purgatory not only tarnishes the work of Christ, but also takes the shine off heaven. It padlocks the gates to heaven, placing the keys into the hands of the Church and her ministries.

Lorraine Boettner, when stating the following, encapsulates the argument against the doctrinal heresy of purgatory:

> Since none but actual saints escape the pains of purgatory, this doctrine gives to the death and funeral of the Roman Catholic a dreadful and repellent aspect. Under the shadow of such a doctrine death is not, as in Evangelical Protestantism, the coming of Christ for His loved one, but the ushering of the shrinking soul

into a place of unspeakable torture. It is no wonder that millions of people born in the Roman Catholic Church, knowing practically nothing about the Bible but believing implicitly in the doctrines of their church, should live and die in fear of death, in fear of spending an unknown number of years in the pain and anguish of that place called purgatory. How tragic that these people live in fear and servitude to the priests, who they are taught to believe hold in their hands the power of life and death, when all the time Christ has paid for their redemption in full. Even their own Roman Catholic Bible says: "Wherefore because children have blood and flesh in common, so he in like manner has shared in these; that through death he might destroy him who had the empire of death, that is, the devil; and might deliver thee, who throughout their life were kept in servitude by the fear of death" (Heb. 2:14,15, Confraternity Version). These words, "Kept in servitude by the fear of death," describe the spiritual state of even devout Roman Catholics. All their lives they are kept in bondage through fear of this imaginary purgatory.[17]

Oh that dear Roman Catholics would see the error of their ways and leave the servitude of Rome for the serenity of Christ. That they would see through the blood of Christ that death ushers us into a better state, not a bitter state (Rev. 14:13). There is rest beyond the grave and not pain.

The great preacher, Charles Spurgeon, told the following story that will help illustrate this point and touch upon the restful joys that await the child of God beyond the threshold of death:

I remember standing in the pulpit one sultry summer afternoon, preaching on the joys of heaven. And there was one woman's eye that especially caught my attention. I knew not why it was, but it seemed to fascinate me. And as I spoke of heaven, she seemed to drink in every word, and her eyes flashed back again the thoughts I had uttered.

She seemed to lead me on to speak more and more of the streets of gold and the gates of pearl, till suddenly her eyes appeared to me to be too fixed. At last it struck me that, while I had been talking of heaven, she had gone there!

I paused and asked if someone in the pew would kindly see whether the friend sitting there was not dead. And in a moment her husband said, "She is dead, sir."

I had known her long as a consistent Christian. And as I stood there, I half wished that I could have changed places with her. There was neither a sigh nor a tear. She seemed to drink in the thoughts of heaven, and then immediately go there and enjoy it.[18]

I trust by now that you agree with the comment to be found in the introduction to this topic. "The notion of purgatory after death which turns sinners into saints is (indeed) a lying invention of man, and is nowhere taught in the Bible. We must be saints before we die if we are to be saints afterward in glory." Purgatory is to be rejected because it robs God's Word of its plain sense, robs God's Son of His sufficiency and robs God's people of their hope.

As we draw this topic to a close, a danger presents itself. It would be easy but wrong of us to walk away from this subject feeling theologically smug: that Rome is wrong and we are right. But to act that way would be to turn eternal issues into a doctrinal football where the name of the game is to score points against our opponents. The consequence of this study ought to be a renewed effort to bring the hope and assurance of the Gospel to our Roman Catholic friends and family members who sit in the shadow of death without Christ. May our souls be troubled and our hearts anxious for them as they have become the victims of a deception that tells them they are not bad enough to merit hell, but not good enough to win heaven. Believing they are going to purgatory, they are in reality going to hell. Knowing therefore the terror of the Lord, ought not we to persuade them to be reconciled to God (2 Cor. 5:10-21)? Ought not we to seek to snatch them out of the fires of hell and pluck the brand from the burning (Zech. 3:2; Jude 23)?

On 12 December 1984 dense fog shrouded M25 near Godstone, in Surrey, a few miles south of London. The hazard warning lights were on, but were ignored by most drivers. At 6.15 a.m. a lorry carrying huge rolls of paper was involved in an accident, and within minutes the carriageway was engulfed in carnage. Dozens of cars were wrecked. Ten people were killed. A police patrol car was soon on the scene, and two policemen ran back up the motorway to stop oncoming traffic. They waved their arms and shouted as loud as they could, but most drivers took no notice and raced on towards the disaster that awaited them. The policemen then picked up traffic cones and flung them at the cars' windscreens in a desperate attempt to warn drivers of their danger; one told how tears streamed down his face as car after car went by and he waited for the sickening sound of impact as they hit the growing mass of wreckage further down the road.[19]

Many dear Roman Catholics are traveling in a doctrinal fog to eternal disaster, unaware of the danger. Many think that after death they will eventually get to heaven, blind to the biblical fact that without complete trust in the saving work of Christ they will immediately go to hell. Oh that we would weep and stand in the way of eternal wreckage for Catholics down the road.

1. Cardinal Gibbons, *Faith of our Fathers*

2. *Catechism of the Catholic Church*, (Missouri: Ligouri Publications, 1994) para. 1030- 1032.

3. John Gilmore, *Probing Heaven*, (Grand Rapids: Baker House, 1989) 139-140.

4. Lorraine Boettner, *Roman Catholicism*, (New Jersey: P & R Publications, 1962) 218- 219.

5. *Catechism of the Catholic Church*, para. 1055.

6. Ibid., para. 1475.

7. Ibid., para. 1476.

8. Ibid., para. 1477.

9. John Phillips, *Exploring the Psalms*, 2 vols. (New Jersey: Loizeaux Brothers, 1985) 1: 176.

10. Robert Ketcham, *Let Rome Speak for Herself,* 20.

11. Source unknown.

12. Karl Keating, *Catholicism and Fundamentalism*, (San Francisco: Ignatius Press, 1988) 190.

13. John MacArthur, *Commentary on I Corinthians*, (Chicago: Moody Press, 1984) 84.

14. Norman Geisler and Ralph Mackenzie, *Roman Catholics and Evangelicals— Agreements and Disagreements*, (Grand Rapids, Michigan: Baker House, 1995) 334- 335.

15. John Gilmore, *Probing Heaven*, (Grand Rapids, Michigan: Baker House, 1989) 142.

16. Ron Rhodes, *The Undiscovered Country*, (Oregon: Harvest House, 1996) 43-44.

17. Lorraine Boettner, *Roman Catholicism*, (P & R Publishing, 1962) 219-220.

18. Rhodes, 45.

19. John Blanchard, *Whatever Happened to Hell?*, (England: Evangelical Press, 1993) 297.

CHAPTER 7

MARY, MARY, QUITE THE CONTRARY

Luke 1:26-56

Today we are witnessing the defrosting and thawing of relations between Evangelicalism and Roman Catholicism on an unprecedented scale. Old enemies have become new friends in a world that has become increasingly hostile to any form of Christianity. Both sides have called for a moratorium on their polemics against each other so as to form an alliance to fight together to save Western civilization.

This new spirit of understanding and cooperation can be seen starkly in the endorsements by J. I. Packer and Charles Colson of Peter Kreeft's new book entitled *Ecumenical Jihad.* The book is a call to both Catholics and Protestants to become involved in the cultural war, by advocating broad and united fronts between the faiths in order to retard rampaging sin in our culture and redeem society from moral chaos. Kreeft's book, however, advocates not only a unity based on a common moral issue, but as a Roman Catholic apologist and author, he defends the central place of the Eucharist within the Christian community and declares the real presence of Christ within the Eucharist. The following excerpt clearly identifies his position:

> "He is really, truly, objectively and fully present there—the very same Christ, the whole Christ,

body and blood, soul and divinity—as He was present on Calvary. And the wine I drink is not wine but is as truly His blood as His blood is His blood."[1]

Kreeft then adds:

"The Eucharist is perfect for us, because it gives us, without pain, what the cross gave Christ with pain."[2]

In *Ecumenical Jihad*, Kreeft declares not only Eucharistic devotion but Marian consecration. Faced with cultural crisis, Kreeft urges Catholics to draw upon the advocacy of Mary for both strength and ultimate victory. In the following articulation, he proclaims Mary's greatness:

Concentrate your life to the Immaculate Heart of Mary. She is the one who will win this war. She is the one (as the Bible says) who triumphs over Satan. She is the one all the early church Fathers call the "new Eve". (See Genesis 3:15) She is the "woman clothed with the sun" who will destroy the "dragon" (the Devil). (See Revelation 12)[3]

Despite Kreeft's proclamations concerning both the Eucharist and Marian devotion, Charles Colson was neither dissuaded nor even slightly tempered in describing Peter Kreeft as one of the premier apologists in America today. An enthusiastic J. I. Packer could not refrain from employing such words as racy, entertaining, and insightful to describe Ecumenical Jihad.

Indeed, a new day has dawned as Evangelical leaders add their stamp of approval to a book that promotes Eucharistic adoration and Marian devotion. The aroma of change is in the air and it has a foul smell to it. The stench of compromise must be detected in these endorsements. In the conflict between

Protestantism and Catholicism, the difference between tradition and Scripture is never more evident than in the cult of Mary. The Marian tradition is at complete odds with God's word, and the more Scripture is studied, the more the foundations of the Marian cult will be shaken.

The purpose of this study, therefore, is to prove the shaky and flawed foundation of the Marian cult and consequently call a halt to the building endeavors of ecumenically minded Evangelicals. It is Christ who always causes us to triumph, not Mary. (2 Cor. 2:14) No man or movement is worthy of our trust or cooperation that ties our future and ultimate success to the creature rather than the creator. Marian theology should prove to be the thin ice upon which ecumenical dialogue flounders and sinks.

Mariology a Main Doctrine

Roman Catholicism, in the past and especially in the present, confesses readily to a never- dying, ever-increasing love for and devotion to Mary. The cult of Mary is alive and well within the faith of the Vatican; and to varying degrees it would be true to say that radicals, traditionalists, and charismatics alike all raise their hand in a vote of support for Marian theology and liturgy.

A survey of the last century finds evidence that far from curbing the Marian cult, modern popes have been the leading advocates. Roman Catholics have been living in a Marian era since the middle of the nineteenth century. Philip Edgcumbe Hughes traces the development of increasing admiration for Mary in a *Christianity Today* article entitled "The Council and Mary".

> The dogma of the Immaculate Conception of the Blessed Virgin was proclaimed in 1854 by Pope Pius XI, speaking infallibly ex cathedra; 1858 saw the

institution of the shrine of Mary at Lourdes in France and 1917 the shrine of Fatima in Portugal, not to mention many other less celebrated centers where the cult of Mary thrives; in 1891 Pope Leo XIII affirmed in his encyclical Octobri mense that, "as no one can come to the Most High Father except through the Son, so, generally, no one can come to Christ except through Mary"; in 1904 Pope Pius X in his encyclical Ad diem praised Mary as the restorer of a fallen world and the dispenser of all the gifts of grace won for us through the death of Christ, and in 1907 he sanctioned February 11 as the Feast of the Apparition of Our Lady of Lourdes; in 1918 Pope Benedict XV stated that Mary had redeemed the human race in cooperation with Christ, and his successor Pope Pius XI approved the practice of calling Mary Co-Redemptrix"; in 1942 Pope Pius XII dedicated the world to Mary's Immaculate Heart; in 1950 the same pope promulgated the dogma of the Bodily Assumption of Mary, speaking infallibly ex cathedra, and in 1954 he inaugurated May 31 as the Feast of Mary Queen of Heaven. But surely the ultimate was said in 1946, again by Pope Pius XII, at the time of the coronation of Mary's statue at Fatima: "Mary is indeed worthy to receive honor and might and glory. She is exalted to hypostatic union with the Blessed Trinity. . .Her kingdom is as great as her Son's and God's. . .Mary's kingdom is identical with the kingdom of God."[4]

Although Vatican II slew a few sacred cows and raised Roman Catholic eyebrows around the world with its ecumenical tones and liturgical reforms, it sacrificed nothing on the part of Marian dogma. A wind of change may have blown through the windows of the Vatican, but it didn't shake or dislodge Rome's love affair with her. The cult of Mary is as strong as ever and remains antithetical to Protestant doctrine.

The present pope, John Paul II, has actively campaigned to bolster the Marian movement, and has emerged as one of the most eager papal proponents for Mariology. His motto is "Totus Tuus sum Maria" (Latin for "Mary I am all yours"). Shortly after ascending to the papal throne in 1978, he launched a campaign to revive the cult of Mary in the church. Before a watching world he visited almost all of her noble shrines, weeping in prayer before her grotto at Lourdes, France. He has given Mary credit for his recovery from an assassination attempt and for an escape from a second one unharmed. He believes Mary is also responsible for the disintegration of communism in Eastern Europe.

In a pamphlet entitled *The Teaching of Pope John Paul II on Mary, the Mother of God*, Bishop Kevin McNamara, Bishop of Kerry in Ireland, writes:

> In the mind and heart of Pope John Paul II, Mary, the Mother of God, holds a unique place. She is never far from his thoughts. Her name recurs constantly in his teaching. His personality, his prayer, his spiritual experience, his whole life and work are deeply marked by her influence.

> Pope John Paul II sees Mary as inseparably linked to Christ and as intimately associated with the life and mission of the Church. This has been clear from the very beginning of his pontificate, when he placed his entire future ministry under Mary's maternal care.[5]

Pope John Paul II not only places his entire future ministry under Mary's maternal care, but at the close of a Sunday Mass in August 1993, in Denver, he consigned all youth and the entire world to Mary's protection and guidance, when he said:

> "Mary of the New Advent, we implore your protection on the preparations that will now begin for the meeting [World Youth Day]. Mary, full of grace, we entrust the next World Youth Day to you. Mary, assumed into heaven, we entrust the young people of the world...the whole world to you!"[6]

The aforementioned statements clearly illustrate Rome's veneration and promotion of Mary, demonstrating that it is more than tangential to the faith but that it is dear to its heart. Without a doubt, Mariology is a cornerstone of the present papacy and remains a keystone in Catholic dogma. New Rome is old Rome concerning the cult of Mary, and as such should be repugnant to any self-respecting believer because Mariology elevates tradition, sidelines the Holy Spirit, exalts the creature, and usurps the glory of Jesus Christ.

In further developing our understanding of this main doctrine I want to consider Mariology assimilated historically and accommodated theologically.

Mariology Assimilated Historically

Rome's devotion to Mary is one not of obedience to the Word but conformity to the world. Mariology has its roots in the paganizing of the churches following the fourth century rapprochement with the state during the reign of the Emperor Constantine.

The pagan world worshiped many female deities. For example, the citizens of Ephesus worshiped the goddess Diana

(Acts 19:29). In Corinth stood the pagan Temple of Aphrodite, the goddess of love. Religious prostitutes served its devotees. After Constantine, Christianity became the official religion of the state, and the worship of the female fertility goddesses was transferred to Mary, even to the point where the worship of Mary rose above the worship of the goddesses. In *The Virgin Mary*, author Giovanni Miegge details Mary's usurpation of the status acclaimed to pagan divinities.

> This substitution of Mary for the pagan divinities took place partly through a spontaneous transfer of the popular piety of the converted masses, and, after Constantine, imperfectly converted. In part it corresponded with a program of exorcising of the pagan cults by the Church which destroyed paganism when it could, and when it could not, or found it preferable, took its place by transforming it. The reconsecrations of temples, the location of new sanctuaries in the vicinity of pagan shrines are evidently intentional.[7]

The roots of Mariology go down deep into this historical soil. During Constantine's reign and those who followed, paganism was Christianized and Mary was paganized. There is not the slightest evidence that there was a cult of Mary or a worship of her person up until this point. Roman Catholic authors admit themselves that the Marian doctrine cannot be verified from the early tradition of the church as found in the writings of the Church Fathers.

The cult of Mary emerged from the wedding of paganism and Christianity under Constantine. The Church was unable, or perhaps even unwilling, to make a clean break from the 4th Century AD religious culture, that held dearly to the then popular notion of a mother goddess. Thus, Mary replaced the pagan deities of that time as noted by Herbert Carson in his book The Faith of the Vatican.

> As we noted . . . the very titles of the goddess used then, 'Our Lady' and 'Stella Maris', have been adopted. The picture of Isis and Horus, the Mother Goddess with the child on her knee, has been repeated innumerable times in the picture of the Madonna and the infant Jesus. It is noteworthy that the cult developed in its early days in those centers where the devotion to the Mother Goddess was established. Egypt was the center of the worship of Isis. Ephesus has long been associated with the worship of Artemis—witness the riot recorded by Luke (Acts 19:23-41) when the enraged devotees of the goddess erupted in fury against Paul's preaching, with its exclusive claims for Christ. Another important center was Phrygia, where the great mother Cybele was the focus of devotion.

> The cult had even earlier roots, as we discover in the denunciations of Jeremiah (Jer. 7:18-20; 44:17, 25). God's judgment was pronounced on the devotees of the 'queen of heaven'—another title which has come down through the centuries.

> This deity has older Canaanite roots in the cult of Ashtoreth, or Astarte (1 Kings 11:5). One can understand the popular appeal of these ancient cults with their emphasis on the motherly care of the goddess. This concept has percolated into popular Catholic piety and the kind of argument used by Catholic apologists. Who, they will ask, could be

more sympathetic than a mother, and who could have greater influence with her son?[8]

Historically, Mariology is nothing more than baptized paganism. The Roman Catholocism syncretism of such pagan beliefs as have been chronicled led her to unbiblical teaching about Mary.

Mariology Accomodated Theologically

Painting therefore from the wrong palette, Rome has proceeded to give us a portrait of the Virgin Mary distinctly different than that of the New Testament writers. Exalted in status and taking the place of former female deities, Mary had to be underwritten theologically. Rome made room for such a godlike figure by changing and adding to the biblical record of this lowly handmaiden through theological adaptation. Once Mary was accorded special honor, various traditions about her were accepted.

Let's note the major changes and developments in this theological redress of the Virgin Mary by the Church of Rome.

The change beyond recognition with regards to Mary first begins with the doctrine of her *Immaculate Conception*. This is the belief first popularized by a British monk named Eadmer in the 12th century, later to be declared a dogma by Pope Pius XI in 1854, which teaches that Mary herself was conceived without original sin. It is proposed that Mary was conceived as other human beings, but at the time of God's creation of her soul in its infusion with the bodily matter from her parents, she was preserved from the stain and guilt of original sin. Thus, she was spared from the defect and effect of original sin by the unmerited grace of God.

The papal Bull 'Ineffabilis,' which is written below, made the belief of this doctrine binding upon all Catholics.

We declare, announce, and define that the doctrine which holds that the most blessed Virgin Mary, in the first instance of her conception, by a singular grace and privilege granted by Almighty God, in view of the merits of Jesus Christ, the Savior of the human race, was preserved free from all stain of original sin, is a doctrine revealed by God and therefore to be believed firmly and constantly by all the faithful.

According to the gospel of Rome, God redeemed Mary from sin so that she might be a fit habitation for Christ. According to Catholic dogma, Mary was destined to play an unparalleled role in God's saving plan, thus it was necessary that she be redeemed in an altogether singular way and to a surpassing degree. Such a notion is propped up by the belief that the seed promised in Genesis 3:15 is ultimately Mary, and the grace spoken of in Luke 1:28 must be of unique perfection.

The change beyond biblical recognition with regard to Mary continues with the doctrine of *Mary's Sinlessness*. Born without the stain of original sin, Mary, according to the gospel of Rome, remained sinless and free from all motions of concupiscence. Although subject to general human limitations and defects just as Christ was, Mary nevertheless lived sinless. Catholic doctrine teaches that Mary had neither the tendency to sin nor did she ever actually sin during her entire lifetime.

The Council of Trent was unequivocal in its pronouncement of Mary's sinless nature as cited in Ludwig Ott's *Fundamentals of Catholic Dogma*:

No justified person can for his whole life avoid all sins, even venial sins, except on the ground of a special privilege from God such as the church holds was given to the blessed Virgin.[9]

The departure deepens and the change increases as Rome adds the doctrine of *Mary's Perpetual Virginity* to the two previous aspects. That Mary was a virgin when she conceived Christ, is of course taught in the Bible and agreed upon by every true believer (Is. 7:14; Matt. 4:18-22; Luke 4:26). But the Catholic Church doesn't stop here, but proceeds to teach that Mary remained a virgin to her dying day. Although she later married Joseph, the faith of the Vatican advocates that Joseph and Mary did not have sexual relations. In fact, Rome teaches that the birth of Christ was as supernatural as His conception in that Mary experienced no pain in the delivery of the child and that her virginal integrity was not disrupted.

The *New Catholic Catechism* addresses Mary's perpetual virginity:

> The deepening of faith in the virginal motherhood led the Church to confess Mary's real and perpetual virginity even in the act of giving birth to the Son of God made man. In fact, Christ's birth "did not diminish his mother's virginal integrity but sanctified it." And so the liturgy of the Church celebrates Mary as Aeiparthenos, the "Ever-virgin."[10]

The gospel of Rome professes that a virgin conceived, a virgin gave birth, and a virgin remained. The dogma itself was stressed by the Lateran Synod (649 A.D.) under Pope Martin I. Argument is made by Catholic scholars that by inference from the question put by Mary to the angel concerning the fact that she did not know a man, that she had taken a vow of virginity on the ground of divine enlightenment (Luke 1:34). It is also argued that Mary must have had no other children but Jesus, since the dying Redeemer placed her into the care of John (John 19:26). As to the references in Scripture to Jesus' "brothers" (Matt. 13:55; Mark 6:3; Gal. 1:19), Rome conveniently reassigned them to the status of cousins. As a matter of fact, this doctrine found allies that included Origen, Ambrole, Jerome, Augustine, and even Martin Luther himself.

The makeover becomes complete in the doctrine of *Mary's Bodily Assumption* to heaven. Given such an entrance into this world by means of immaculate conception, it should come as no surprise therefore that Mary's departure of this life would be nothing less than spectacular. Tradition became doctrine when on November 1, 1950, Pope Pius XII sanctioned as doctrine, Mary's assumption, which he claimed was revealed by God.

The Catechism of the Catholic Church catches the flavor of this doctrine:

> The Most Blessed Virgin Mary, when the course of her earthly life was completed, was taken up body and soul into the glory of heaven, where she already shares in the glory of her Son's Resurrection, anticipating the resurrection of all members of his Body.[11]

As the glorification of Mary developed, Rome revolted against the idea that a glorious Mary could have suffered the corruption of the grave. They claim that she, who was extraordinary in life, was extraordinary in death. Bodily assumption was the final attainment, and represents the highest crown of her privileges and paved the way for Mary being exalted by the Lord to become the Queen over all things.[12] Mary's assumption, therefore, not only made possible her escape from death, but also brought about her enthronement as the Queen of heaven and governess over all things through her Son.

To sum up what we have thus far observed and documented, we have, with the words and demonstrations of Catholic dogma, witnessed Mary's unique experience of grace which removed from her the stain of original sin (immaculate conception), and preserved her from sin during the course of her life. Her body was never impaired (perpetual virginity) nor did it decay at death (assumption).

Rome, however, was not satisfied to leave it there, but has cast her as a co-Redemptrix and Mediatrix with Christ for men. According to Rome, Mary has and continues to contribute significantly to the work of redemption, although in a subsidiary and secondary manner.

Mary's place and role as co-Redemptrix was secured according to Rome by virtue of her fiat and acceptance of God's invite to bear his Son (Luke 1:35-38). It is argued by some that if salvation is dependent on Mary's 'fiat' (her assent to give birth to the Savior) then salvation stems from two components—the act of God in Christ and the act of Mary. Mary uniquely was a collaborator and contributor to the history and accomplishment of redemption through Christ. Through her obedience she became the cause of salvation for herself and the whole human race. The knot of Eve's disobedience was untied by Mary's obedience. Death through Eve and life through Mary, is a frequent claim of the papacy.

According to the Roman Catholic Church, Mary's participation in the incarnation was only the beginning of her role in salvation. Mary not only gave life to Christ but was party to his death in a singular sense also. United to her son, Mary offered him on Calvary's hill to the eternal Father together with the holocaust of her maternal rights and motherly love. Not only did Mary offer her Son to God, but she remained at the Cross to suffer with Christ.

In their helpful book, *The Cult of the Virgin*, authors Elliot Miller and Kenneth Samples cite two quotations of modern popes that provide insight into grasping Catholic understanding on this matter.

Pius X in *Ad Diem Illum* contributed significantly to twentieth-century thought on Mary as co-Redemptrix:

> "The most holy Mother of God had not only the honor of 'having given the substance of her flesh to the only begotten Son of God, who was to be born of the human race', and by means of this flesh the victim for the salvation of man was to be prepared, but she was also entrusted with the task of tending and nursing this victim and even of offering it on the altar at the appointed time."

Benedict XV further elaborated the role Mary played:

> Thus, she (Mary) suffered and all but died along with her Son suffering and dying; thus, for the salvation of men she abdicated the rights of a mother toward her Son, and as was hers to do, she immolated the Son to placate God's justice, so that she herself may justly be said to have redeemed together with Christ the human race.[13]

From the above quote, Mary's redemptive role is to be seen in that she gave herself to God in the birth of the Savior and also that she gave her Son to God in the death of the Savior, thereby becoming an indispensable figure together with Christ in the redemption of the human race. Redemption, as we underlined earlier in the pronouncement of the Catholic Church, stems from two components—the act of God in Christ and the act of Mary.

In addition to her role in the history of redemption, Rome positions Mary as central to the ministry of intercession and mediation. Rome teaches that by virtue of her participation in redemption, Mary has earned the privilege of being the one through whom God dispenses His grace. According to the Church, Mary has been designated by God as a channel for grace whether in the person of Christ historically or the provision of God presently. It is proposed that while Christ is the mediator between God and man, Mary is the bridge between Christ and men.

By way of analogy, it is stated within some Catholic literature that Mary is the "neck" within the mystical body, through which everything that comes to us from the head (Christ) must pass, and through which also we must pass in order to reach the head.

Pope Leo XIII decreed that,

> Nothing according to the will of God comes to us except through Mary, so that, as nobody can approach the Supreme Father except through the Son, similarly nobody can approach Christ except through the Mother.[14]

In the *Catechism of the Catholic Church*, Rome avers to Catholics Mary's prominence in the order of grace and her role as dispenser of that grace.

> This motherhood of Mary in the order of grace continues uninterruptedly from the consent which she loyally gave at the Annunciation and which she sustained without wavering beneath the Cross, until the eternal fulfillment of all the elect. Taken up to heaven she did not lay aside this saving office but by her manifold intercession to bring us the gifts of

eternal salvation. . . . Therefore the Blessed Virgin is invoked in the Church under the titles of Advocate, Helper, Benefactress, and Mediatrix.[15]

Since Mary gave (through birth) the source of all grace (Christ) to men, it is to be expected, says Rome that she will also cooperate in the distribution of all grace. From this, the idea emerges that Christ is our Brother and Mary our Mother. In the following words, the current pope, John Paul II, affirms Mary's role as intercessor:

> The fundamental mission of the girl of Nazareth was, therefore, to be the link between the Savior and mankind.[16]

Intercession remains at the heart of Catholic thinking concerning the role of Mary. Rome advances her role as Mother, as one of linking Christ to man, and bringing his saving love as near to them as possible. Again, recent Catholic pronouncements affirm Mary as intercessor, with the following excerpt taken from the Second Vatican Council.

> Mary occupies a place in the Church, which is the highest after Christ and also closest to us.[17]

Therefore, the Blessed Virgin is invoked in the Church under the titles Advocate, Helper, Benefactress, and Mediatrix.

Aware of the negative reaction such position statements arouse, especially within Protestantism, Rome goes to great lengths in its official announcements to protect Christ's supreme Mediation. Mary's function is said to be subsidiary, and in no way diminishes the unique place of Christ but rather rests upon his mediation and draws all its power from it.[18]

Rome, however, commits contradiction in its depiction of Mary as Redemptrix and Christ's role as redeemer. From one side of its mouth it cannot say that everything we need we get from Christ, and from the other side of its mouth speak of Mary's unique role and ability to get from Christ what we need. The Church of Rome seems to have entangled itself upon the horns of a dilemma wherein either Mary's role is rendered superfluous, or the all-sufficiency of Christ's mediation is diminished.

Practically, it is a mute point because in Marian devotion little restraint and reserve is shown with regards to this theological balancing trick. Mary is nearest to Christ and closest to us; therefore, she, not Christ, is often the object of Catholic prayer. Among the all-too-accessible examples of this practice, consider the following excerpts from *Novena Prayers in Honor of Our Mother of Perpetual Help*, a booklet published by the Sisters of St. Basil with official church approval (Nihil Obstat and Imprimator):

> Have pity, compassionate mother, on us and our families; especially in this my necessity (here mention it). Help me, O my Mother, in my distress; deliver me from all my ills; or if it be the will of God that I should suffer still longer, grant that I may endure all with love and patience. This grace I expect of thee with confidence, because thou art our Perpetual Help.[19]

> *We have no greater help,*
> *no greater hope than you,*
> *O Most Pure Virgin; help us, then,*
> *for we hope in you, we glory in you,*
> *we are your servants.*
> *Do not disappoint us.*[20]

Come to my aid, dearest mother, for I recommend myself to thee. In thy hand I place my eternal salvation, and to thee I entrust my soul. Count me among thy most devoted servants; take me under thy protection, and it is enough for me. For, if thou protect me, dear Mother, I fear nothing; not from my sins, because thou wilt obtain for me the pardon of them; nor from the devils, because thou art more powerful than all hell together; not even from Jesus, my Judge, because by one prayer from thee, he will be appeased. But one thing I fear, that in the hour of temptation, I may through negligence fail to have recourse to thee and thus perish miserably. Obtain for me, therefore, the pardon of my sins, love for Jesus, final perseverance, and the grace to have recourse to thee, O Mother of Perpetual Help.[21]

To bring this point to a conclusion, let us take one last look at the colorful portrait of Mary painted for us within the framework of Catholic dogma. This main doctrine portrays Mary as having received a unique experience of grace, which preserved her from sin both in conception and conduct. Her body and its virginal integrity were never impaired, nor did it decay in death. When her sojourn was completed, she was assumed into heaven by God, and according to the Roman church, has been crowned the Queen of Heaven and given the title and office of Mediatrix. It is accordingly supposed that she cooperates with the Lord Jesus in mediating salvation to sinners.

Having traced the historical development and the theological departure of the Marian cult, I will now focus on the vanity of Catholic devotion to Mary.

Mariology a Vain Devotion

As Mary grew in spiritual stature within the Roman doctrine, the Church evolved into an adoring audience. Her dignity as the Mother of God coupled with her fulness of grace leat Rome to teach the faithful to greatly venerate Mary. The genesis for such devotion developed in the early centuries of church history when there was the growing veneration of martyrs, among whom Mary was singled out for special honor because of her unique relationship to the Lord. Since then, she became more and more prominent in the consciousness of the people.

This thought is crystallized in the Second Vatican Council pronouncement, *Dogmatic Constitution on the Church* which states:

> Mary has by grace been exalted above all angels and men to a place second only to her Son, as the most holy mother of God who was involved in the mysteries of Christ: She is rightly honored by a special cult in the Church.

Catholic scholars are quick to explain that this devotion and veneration of Mary is not to be understood as being on the same plane as that of worshiping God. Catholicism is eager to head off any charge that might be leveled at them concerning the issue of idolatry. This they attempt to do by pointing to three degrees of honor recognized by the Church.

The first degree of honor is "latria," which is the highest form of adoration and is to be given to God alone. The second is "dulia" or veneration, which may be directed to the saints and angels. The third is "hyperdulia," which is one step below worship and which among all created beings may be offered to Mary alone. In theory, these categories are intended to prevent idolatrous worship of created beings, but in practice however, they afford no more protection to the honor of Jesus Christ than a paper bag on a rainy and windy day. In practical terms, what we have here is little more than a public relations exercise on the part of Rome to silence its theological critics.

The reality that Mary is, and has been for centuries, worshiped in the place and alongside Jesus Christ by millions of Catholics all over the world is barely arguable. The Latin words of latria, dulia, and hyperdulia have a hollow ring to it in practical terms. By granting to Mary the attributes, honors, and functions of Jesus Christ, she is de facto elevated to a seat beside the throne of Jesus Christ. Mariology has become Mariolatry as the Holy Spirit is sidelined and Jesus Christ rivaled.

Should you consider that to be an overstatement, consider then the sharp critique of Vatican II Council's teaching on Mary by Philip Edgcumbe Hughes in *Christianity Today*.

> Despite all qualifying clauses, the effect, in both logic and practice, of the Mariology of the Roman church is to rob Christ of the uniqueness of his redemptive and mediatorial office. How can it be otherwise, when Christ declares that it is he who gives life to the world (John 6:33), whereas the council, without disputing this, affirms that Mary "gave life to the world" (DV II, 86); when the apostles consistently declare that the witness to which we are to be conformed is that of Christ (Rom. 8:29; 2 Cor. 3:18; Phil. 3:21; 1 John 3:2), whereas the council affirms that Mary is "the church's model" and that those who "strive to increase in holiness . . . raise their eyes to Mary who shines forth to the whole community of the elect as a model of the virtues"

(DV II, 86, 93); when the Scriptures consistently declare that Christ alone was without sin (2 Cor. 5:21; Heb. 4:15; 7:26; 1 Pet. 1:19; 2:22; 1 John 3:5), whereas the council affirms that Mary was "entirely holy and free from all stain of sin," was "adorned from the first instance of her conception with the splendors of an entirely unique holiness," and in what she subsequently did was "impeded by no sin" (DV II, 88); and when the New Testament consistently declares that Christ is the sole and unique mediator between God and man and the only Redeemer of our race (1 Tim. 2:5; Heb. 9:15; John 14:6; Acts 4:12; 1 John 2:1), whereas the council— though, as we have mentioned, it acknowledges this—applies the title "Mediatrix" to Mary and affirms that by her "cooperating in the work of human salvation" there was a "union of the Mother with the Son in the work of salvation" (DV II, 84). In other words, though the term itself is not used, Vatican II propounds the heresy that Mary is Co-Redemptrix with Christ."[22]

Mary's exaltation within the Roman Church is at the direct expense of our Lord Jesus Christ. Catholicism has helped Mary elbow her way almost into the Trinity itself. If that seems incredulous, then note the words of Bishop Alponsus de Liguori, canonized saint and renowned bishop in his celebrated work *The Glories of Mary*, when he wrote:

'At the command of Mary all obey—even God.' St. Bernardine fears not to utter this sentence; meaning, indeed, to say that God grants the prayers of Mary as if they were commands . . . the Mother, then, should have the same power as the Son, rightly has Jesus, who is omnipotent, made Mary also omnipotent; though, of course, it is always true that where the Son is omnipotent by nature, the Mother is only so by grace.[23]

What are we to say in the face of such vain devotion to the Virgin Mary? In Rome's veneration of Mary, are we witnesses to honor taken too far or idolatry brought too near? When one considers the promotion of the cult of Mary by Catholicism through her festivals, shrines, teaching, worship, and liturgy, one cannot help but come to the conclusion that what we encounter is a deep corruption of worship and a demotion of Jesus Christ. Mary is not the champion of the Christian cause as Peter Kreeft implied in our introduction, but Christ alone is the chief cornerstone in the household of faith. To them who believe He is precious (1 Peter 2:4-10).

Biblically, there is no support for the conclusions drawn by Catholics, namely, that Mary can and should be venerated above all creatures, a status second only to the Lord. Mary was a woman of singular virtue or she would never have been chosen to be the mother of the Lord Jesus Christ. For that role she deserves respect and honor (Luke 1:42). That recognition of her blessedness was clearly stated to be among women and not above women. It is indeed, strange logic to argue that being the most blessed among women makes Mary more worthy than all other women. For instance, Eve was the mother of all the living (Gen. 3:23), a distinctive honor held by no other person, including Mary. Yet Catholics have chosen not to venerate Eve in accord with her blessed status. The Scriptures teach that a man is blessed when sin is forgiven, but such blessing produces humility not honor. The apostle Paul labeled himself the chief of sinners greatly forgiven, and thus considered himself the least of all apostles (1 Tim. 1:15; 1 Cor. 15:9).

Furthermore, we note in two specific instances in the Gospel that Mary was afforded no special or privileged status by Christ himself. In Mark 3:31-32, Mary along with Jesus' brothers tried to assume some special privileges based upon their earthly relationship to him. But Jesus described his mother and brothers in terms of those who do the will of God, therefore implying that familial relationships to him gain Mary and his brothers no special spiritual recognition. That truth is specifically applied to Mary in the gospel of Luke. (Luke 11:27-28).

Is it not also striking that the last reference to Mary in Scripture is in the book of Acts and not the epistles? The silence of the epistles, which form the doctrinal core of the New Testament, is especially significant. That the New Testament is devoid of the worth and work of the Virgin Mary as told to us by the faith of the Vatican is a damning indictment on the cult of Mary within Catholicism.

In closing this point, the voice of protest is sounded loudest on the grounds that the cult of Mary sins grievously, in that it steals glory which belongs to God alone, and exalts the creature in vain devotion. Miller and Samples give expression to this protest when they wrote:

> In the Bible we find consistent emphasis on an all-encompassing distinction between God (Father, Son, and Holy Spirit) on the one hand and the entire spectrum of creation (including all angels and human beings) on the other hand. God commands he alone be worshipped (Luke 4:8; 1 Cor. 1:29). He makes it clear that no created being will glory before him; he will share his glory with no one (Isa. 42:8).

Even angels emphatically refuse worship, insisting that all angels and humans are on an equal footing of humanity before God (Rev. 22:8-9). In the New Testament we find that even the greatest of the apostles would not stand for being given any of the reverential treatment that is reserved for God alone (Acts 10:25-26; 14:11-15). We must conclude then that biblically all prayer, glory, and devotion belong to God and to his son, Jesus Christ."[24]

Jesus Christ must reign supreme upon the throne of our affection. In the context of our worship, it must be Jesus only (Matt. 17:4-8). The cry of our souls and the voice of our heart must forever communicate the recognition that He must increase and we (including Mary) must decrease (John 3:30). Christianity is nothing more and nothing less than Christ. The business of Christians is the exaltation and magnification of Christ (Phil. 1:19-21).

James Denny once said,

> You can never at the same time convince people that you are a great preacher and that Jesus Christ is a great Savior.

William Carey the father of modern missions said on his deathbed,

> When I am gone, say nothing about Dr. Carey; speak about Dr. Carey's Savior.

The message of Christianity is "O what a Savior." The message of Catholicism is "Hail Mary, full of grace, the Lord is with thee."

There is an episode in the life of John Knox, the great Scottish Reformer, that signposts the reaction of every true believer when confronted with the cult of Mary:

> In 1548, he was a prisoner on a French slave ship, chained to a rowing bench and lashed constantly by the guards. He was there because of his preaching of the word of God and his refusal to submit to Catholicism. One day the lieutenant brought aboard a wooden image of the Virgin Mary and demanded that the slaves kiss it. Knox refused, and they pushed it violently against his face. He grabbed it and threw it overboard, shouting, "Let our Lady now save herself: she is light enough; let her learn to swim."[25]

Mariology is not part of the cargo of Biblical Christianity and must be tossed overboard. Theologically speaking, it is a Jonah because of the words of Jesus, the silence of the epistles, and the centrality and exclusivity of Christ in Christian worship.

Mariology a Plain Departure

Bishop Gustaf Aulen, speaking of modern Roman theologians and the Marian dogmas of 1854 and 1950, complains:

> In neither case have they shown any concern to justify these dogmas on the basis of Scripture or even the tradition of the ancient Church. In reality these two documents are foreign to Scripture and contrary to the ancient tradition of the Church.[26]

Bishop Aulen's missive is a direct hit in underlining the fact that Catholic dogma concerning Mary is a stranger not a relative to Biblical theology. The foghorn of discernment ought to sound loudly in the mind of every believer in that Marian theology has plotted a doctrinal course outside of the Bible (1 Tim. 4:1-2; 2 Tim. 4:1-5). This dogma is a plain departure from God's Word.

As stated in the introduction, the conflict between Romanism and Biblical Christianity is intensified by Catholic's embrace of both tradition and Scripture, and the resulting schism is greatest in the cult of Mary. The gulf separating the doctrine of Rome from the Gospel becomes quite visible. Like two parallel lines, this dogma's historical development is mirrored by its theological departure. Let us therefore detail the departure beyond the borders of Biblical doctrine by advocates of the cult of Mary.

Mary's Immaculate Conception and Her Resultant Sinlessness

How do we answer Rome's assertion that Mary was redeemed super abundantly and protected against the effects of sin in her birth and life? Four things are offered by way of rebuttal.

First, the texts frequently used to support the above assertion are weak and improperly interpreted. The texts that Catholics identify as foundational to Marian doctrine are Genesis 3:15 and Luke 1:28. In the Genesis reference, Catholic scholars maintained that while the seed of the woman is indeed made in reference to Christ, by implication the mother of our Lord came to be seen in the woman. Mary is the new Eve of the new creation and therefore was to be found at birth and throughout life in a perfect state of sanctifying grace. The fact remains, however, that the literal, grammatical, and historical interpretation of this passage yields no other understanding of this verse other than Eve and her offspring. Ludwig Ott admits himself that the "literal sense" of the text does not refer to Mary but Eve and her posterity. Even if by extension or culmination we saw Mary through the telescoping of this text in some indirect fashion, it is still a gigantic leap from that to her immaculate conception and sinlessness, which is neither stated nor conferred in the text.

The second verse which is thought to support Marian dogma is Luke 1:28. The Angel Gabriel came to Mary and said, "Rejoice, highly favored one, the Lord is with you." The crucial word here is the one translated "favored." On this word, Catholics have built their view of Mary's unique experience of grace with all the implications that follow. According to Arnt and Gingrich, the word means "to bestow favor upon, favor highly." However, in Ephesians 1:6, which is the other use of this word in the New Testament, it is used of all Christians who have experienced the forgiving grace which God "freely bestowed on us in the beloved." If we can deduce from Luke 1:28 that Mary was conceived without sin, lived without sin, and was assumed into heaven, can we not too deduce from Ephesians 1:6 that all Christians have similarly been conceived without sin, live without sin, and will rise from the grave shortly after being buried? But of course, this is ridiculous and simply proves the Alice in Wonderland approach taken by Rome in advocating biblical credence for the cult of Mary. We would say to the cultists of Mary not to begin their defense of this doctrine in the Bible, because you cannot.

Another argument against this aspect of Marian theology is the biblical revelation of the universality of sin. According to the Bible, the stream of humankind has been polluted by the toxic of sin (Rom. 3:23, 5:12). Throughout the Scriptures the judge of all the earth has decreed that all men are under the condemnation and constraint of sin (1 Kings 8:46; Ecc. 7:20;

Gal. 3:22). Sin waits lurking to attack every baby born into this world (Psa. 51:5). Sin rules every heart as the monarch of man and the lord of the soul from whom no one ever escapes. Every person on the globe has been infected with the virus of sin and to deny this is to deceive one's self and call God a liar (I John 1:7-9). The Bible is quite clear that Jesus was the only person who ever entered this world and passed through it without the stain of sin (Heb.7:26; John 8:46).

In advocating the Immaculate Conception and Mary's sinlessness, Rome is guilty of two great sins, in that they make God a liar concerning the universality of sin, and they rob Christ of His glory in diminishing the significance of the incarnation. Mary was undoubtedly a sinner because all have sinned and Luke shows the reality of that in Mary's participation in a sin offering at the temple (Luke 2:22-24; Lev.12:2,8).

The rebuttal against this dogma builds when you consider a third aspect, namely Mary's own confession in her Magnificat. In an essay on Mary, S. Lewis Johnson Jr., picks up this line of reasoning when he writes:

> . . . it is Mary herself, the biblical picture of whom has been so distorted, who underlines this in her Magnificat when she explains, "My soul glorifies the Lord and my spirit rejoices in God my Savior, before he has been mindful of the humble state of his servant. From now on all generations will call me blessed, for the Mighty One has done great things for me—holy is his name" (Luke 1:46-49). The Lord, she says, is her "Savior." Her state is "humble," and she will be called "blessed," for great things have been done "for me." That she calls God her Savior is an acknowledgment of the fact that she has by birth the same fallen

status that all have. She claims no special prerogatives with respect to sin. She is "blessed," but by
virtue of what has been done for her. Berkouwer is
correct: "Mary herself is not in the least the prophet-
ess of the Mariology of after times."[27]

S. Lewis Johnson brings us to see in these words that
Mary herself is the chief witness in the prosecution case against
Rome under the charge of theological and historical vandalism
of Mary's character.

Last but not least in our denial of this doctrine, we
acknowledge the fact that virtually all of the leading Catholic
theological authorities of their day soundly rejected the notion
of Immaculate Conception and sinlessness. Thomas Aquinas,
Bonadventure, Peter Lombard, and Alexander of Hales are but
a few who denied Mary the status she has been assigned. This
presents a problem, does it not, because the consent of the
Fathers and the tradition of the church are afforded such a pivotal role in the deciding of the authenticity of truth within
Catholicism. Where is the consensus and unity?

Mary's Perpetual Virginity

What response do we offer to Rome's proposal that
Mary's virginal integrity was not violated in the conception and
birth of Christ and that sex was never entered upon within the
marriage resulting in no children to Joseph?

In considering the biblical data regarding the birth of
Christ and Mary's marriage to Joseph, the dogma of perpetual
virginity has few legs to stand on. For example, in his gospel,
Matthew makes it clear by the use of the preposition "until"
with reference to Joseph's abstinence of sexual relations with
Mary, that after the birth of Christ, Joseph and Mary entered

upon a normal marital relationship, sexually speaking (Matt. 1:24-25). The birth of Jesus ended and terminated that period of restraint on the part of Joseph towards Mary. Nuptial rights were restored between Joseph and Mary as shown by the many references to the brothers and sisters of Jesus within the gospel. The union of Joseph and Mary produced children other than Jesus (Mark 3:31-35; 6:3-4; 1 Cor. 9:5; Gal. 1:15).

In clashing swords with Rome over the proposed perpetual virginity of Mary, we would thrust further by citing Luke's reference to Jesus as "the first-born son of Mary" (Luke 2:7).

In his book, *Protestants, Catholics, and Mary*, Stephen Benko speaks admirably on this matter when he points out:

> Luke 2:7 states that Jesus was the first-born son of Mary. The word used here is prototokos, which several manuscripts include in Matthew 1:25. The word in itself does not necessarily mean that other children followed the "first-born." However, since the gospels do mention brothers and sisters of Jesus, it is logical to conclude that this word refers to the oldest of possibly many children. A further argument in support of this interpretation is the fact that in a case where it is important to know that only one child is meant, the Greek New Testament uses another word, namely, the word monogenes. This term is used, for example, in connection with the dead man of Nain who was the "only son of his mother" (Luke 7:12); with the "only daughter" of Jairus (Luke 8:42); and with the "only child" whom Jesus was asked to free from an unclean spirit (Luke 9:38). All of these references are from Luke, which shows that the Evangelist is quite familiar with the

word monogenes when an only child is meant. Why then does he not use this word in 2:7, instead of pro-totokos? The answer lies at hand: Because Luke knew that Jesus was not the "only son" but the "first-born son," and that other children followed.[28]

On the basis of what we have just noted, the Catholic Church remains deaf to the voice of the synoptic Gospels and their presentation of the marriage between Mary and Joseph following the virgin birth as normal and one that produced children. The Gospels give no sign of a vow of chastity on the part of Mary or a divinely prescribed state of perpetual virginity. In fact, for Joseph and Mary to have maintained abstinence throughout their marriage would be contrary to biblical revelation concerning marriage. In the Old Testament, we find the ideal woman of virtue set forth as a faithful wife and homemaker (Prov. 31). While childbearing (within marriage) is exalted (Psa. 127:3-5; 1 Sam. 1:11), celibacy is never advocated. The New Testament likewise honors the holy state of matrimony (Heb. 13:4), never promoting abstinence within marriage. In fact, the only time it is touched upon is by Paul in his letter to the Corinthians and it comes with clear qualification and great limitation (1 Cor. 7:4-5). The doctrine of Mary's perpetual virginity clearly militates against God's intention for marriage and the principle of "one flesh" which is foundational to any biblical marriage (Gen. 2:24).

John Calvin puts the matter into perspective in writing of Mary and her supposed state of perpetual virginity:

> She would, in that case, have committed treachery by allowing herself to be united to a husband, and would have poured contempt on the holy covenant of marriage . . . although the Papists have exercised

barbarous tyranny on this subject, yet they have never proceeded so far as to allow the wife to form a vow of continence at her own pleasure.[29]

Mary's Assumption to Heaven

In view of Mary's sinless perfection, Roman Catholicism teaches that Mary's body did not undergo decay at the end of her life. That God miraculously took her up to heaven. The Roman doctrine of assumption is in direct conflict with Biblical teaching. What are we to believe?

The verdict on the part of biblical Christianity is false for a number of sound reasons. First, the Bible has no mention of Mary's death or her assumption. Second, the Biblical revelation that all have sinned and must suffer death as the penalty for sin is applicable to all (Rom. 5:12). Furthermore, our bodies will decay in the grave under the curse of sin and Mary is no exception to that reality (Job 4:10; 19:26; 21:26). Finally, victory over the grave and its offense will only be known at the Second Coming of Christ and not before (1 Cor. 15:50-58; Phil.3:20-21).

In compliment to the aforementioned criticisms concerning Mary's assumption to heaven, we would also align the prophesied and witnessed resurrection of Jesus. The Old Testament and New Testament present a string of promises concerning Christ's resurrection along with a list of witnesses who personally encountered the risen Lord. That is why we are so persuaded that Jesus truly conquered death and rose again. But where are the prophecies about Mary's assumption? Where are the witnesses to this event? To both these charges Rome responds with a deafening silence. The doctrine of Mary's assumption in the light of these considerations is no more than a presumption on the part of popery.

Mary the Dispenser of Grace

Crowned Queen of heaven, Mary is presented by Rome as the neck in the body of Christ, dispensing grace from Christ to his body. Mary is said to be closest to us and occupy a position of Mediatrix in the scheme of redemption. What might be our response?

All things considered, this represents the darkest side to this doctrine. Rome has declared war on the gospel and has stretched the relationship between Protestantism and Catholicism beyond breaking point. In her supposed role of Mediatrix, the meaning of prayer is twisted, the word of God is vandalized, and the Son of God rivaled.

In assigning Mary as the Dispenser of grace, Roman doctrine both vandalizes and injures God's word disclosed in John 19:26. Rome suggests that in John we have a representation of the whole of redeemed humanity, which was given over to the maternal care of Mary our spiritual mother. God's children can rest secure in the knowledge that they are to be cradled in the arms of Mary's powerful intercession according to the gospel of Rome.

To advocate this interpretation concerning the message of this text is unworthy of anyone claiming the name of scholar. One of the rules of hermeneutics is that when the literal rendering of the text makes good sense, there is no need to seek any other sense. Protestants would contend that what we have here is predisposed ambition to produce a "spiritual mother" at whatever exegetical cost to the text. That Jesus had only John in view and not all men and women is made abundantly clear by John's own testimony that from that day on he took Mary into his care.

Not only is the word of God violated in the proposed role of Mary as Mediatrix, but also the true meaning of prayer is twisted. In assigning this role of mediation and distribution to

Mary, Rome argues that just as Christians pray to God on behalf of one another, and in this sense could be called mediators, so Mary acts as Mediatrix for Christians still on earth.

In his book, *Rome at the Bar of History*, William Webster takes issue with such reasoning when he insightfully writes:

> The argument sounds innocent enough. After all, Christians do pray to God for one another. But there is a fallacy in this proposed defense. In praying to God on behalf of other individuals, the Christian is not a mediator. Of course, we intercede for others with God—but when Scripture speaks of Jesus as mediator, it stresses that he alone is the mediator who can reconcile God and man. It is through Christ and him alone that God mediates his saving grace to mankind. It is through Christ alone that men and women are granted access into the presence of God. When Christians pray for other men and women, they go directly to God through Jesus Christ and offer their intercession. In no way are they acting as mediators who can mediate grace to other men. If someone asks me to pray for them they do not look to me as a channel of grace which they can depend upon to meet their spiritual need.
>
> To pray for someone is one thing, to be a mediator in the biblical sense is quite another. The one is sanctioned in Scripture, the other is strictly forbidden—for there is only one mediator, the Lord Jesus Christ.[30]

The key words in the rebuttal of Rome is that to pray for someone is one thing, to be a mediator in the biblical sense is quite another. The Bible is adamant that there is only one mediator between God and man, the man Christ Jesus (1 Tim. 2:5; John 10:1-11; 14:6; Heb. 1:2-3; 10:12). The context of 1 Timothy 2:5 shows that while there are other human intercessors (2:1-2), there is only one mediator. Just as there is (only) one God, there is (only) one mediator between God and man. Paul is no more a polytheist than one who would ever lend his support to the idea that Mary should fulfill the role of Mediatrix (1 Tim. 2:5; Acts 4:12; John 14:6).

Finally, and most gravely, Rome errs in making Mary a dispenser of grace by creating a rival to the glory and uniqueness of Christ Jesus; essentially Mary has been transformed into a duplicate redeemer. Mary, like Christ, was immaculately conceived, sinless in life, suffered at the Cross, and ascended to heaven. Just as Jesus is King, Mary is Queen. According to Rome, the Cross was as much Mary's as Christ's, and death did no more claim her than claim him. As the Queen of heaven she shares Christ's throne in the governance of redemptive history. The gospel of Rome denies the preeminence of Christ, which is in direct contrast to Pauline theology (Col. 1:18; Phil. 2:10-11).

Throughout the New Testament, the divinely inspired writers go to great lengths to show and underline the greatness and supremacy of Jesus Christ as God's son and man's Savior. The book of Hebrews is a megaphone of praise extolling and exalting the virtues and excellencies of Jesus' person and work. To quote Miller and Samples once again:

> Christ is seen in Hebrews as the sole and entirely sufficient agent in effecting our redemption from beginning to end. He alone was worthy to serve as a sacrifice for our sins (9:12-14; 10:1-10). As our great high priest, only he could offer this sacrifice of himself (9:14, 25-26; 10:11-12). Having perfectly satis-

fied men's debt of sin before God (10:10-18), he now sits as our high priest and advocate at the right hand of God (8:1; 9:24; 10:12). On the basis of his complete identification with man and full participation in the human experience, he perfectly sympathizes with our plight and continually makes intercession for us (2:16-18; 4:14-15; 7:25). Because of the superiority and permanence of his high priestly work, all other mediators have been set aside (7:23-28; 8:6, 13). We obtain confident access to the very throne of God through him, receiving all of the grace and mercy we need (2:18; 4:60; 10:19-22); thus there is no need for any other's mediation.[31]

Christ is not an angry son who needs to be wooed by his mother, but according to the book of Hebrews, perfectly sympathizes with our plight and alone is able to succor those that will come to God by him. The book of Hebrews is the rock upon which the cult of the Virgin perishes. Christ is supremely and singularly our high priest before God. We have an advocate, and his name is Jesus (1 John 2:1-2).

One of the greatest biographies of all times is Sandberg's biography of Abraham Lincoln. In one of those many volumes he tells the story of Lincoln's little boy, Tad. Tad had a speech impediment—a cleft pallet. Because of his weakness and his impediment, his father loved him all the more and would give him anything he wanted. One day a group of frontiersmen had come from Kentucky to see President Lincoln. They'd known him. He studiously avoided seeing them for a week for political reasons. He just didn't want to see them. As they were outside the grounds of the White House, they were half-cursing and saying to themselves, "Ole Abe won't see us."

Tad Lincoln heard them and said, "Would you like to see Ole Abe?" They said, "Yes." Tad said, "You can see him." He went in and said, "Papa, there are some friends of mine outside." Abraham Lincoln said, "Any friends of yours are friends of mine. Bring them in." Tad Lincoln brought in to him every one of those men that he hadn't wanted to see for a whole week. With dignity he introduced them, and Abraham again took his little boy in his lap, kissed him, and said, "If they are your friends, they are my friends and they are welcome anytime."

Although a lame, tame, and anemic illustration of a greater reality, this story reminds us of the fact that in Jesus Christ we have a friend who will plead our cause before an offended God. He alone is the way to the Father (John 14:6). Christ is worthy of all my trust for he alone is worthy (Rev.4:9-10). Mary joins us in that song (Luke 1:46-56).

When you reduce this doctrine to its fundamental core, it is nothing less than a slight upon the finished and satisfactory work of Christ on behalf of his people. It is a failure to glory in the Cross (Gal.5:14).

To close, I would like to leave this challenge with my fellow believers. In his book, *The Mother of Jesus, Her Problems and Her Glory*, A.T. Robertson, the great New Testament scholar, makes this observation:

> As Christianity has made its way over the earth, the fame of Mary has grown. This was inevitable. Her life was literally wrapped up in the work of her Son. She was the greatest of mothers. She was the mother of the greatest of men, one called the Son of Man, but she was more. In some way still incomprehensible to us, as to her, she was the mother of the Son of God. The double mystery still baffles us, though our

very reason compels acceptance and faith. Mary would not have us give her credit for aught save that she did her part well. The goodness and grace of God chose her as the channel for this mercy to the human race. So she occupies the highest pedestal among others, and mothers rank above all other persons. But this is not to place her above mortals because of the duty of her wondrous Son. She has her consolation in high duty nobly done and in the supreme character and service of her Son. That is her coronation. She needs no other . . . But, if Roman Catholics have deified Mary, Protestants, as a rule, have neglected her. This is largely due to a reaction against the adoration by the Catholics. Protestants have often been afraid to praise and esteem Mary for her full worth lest they be accused of leanings in sympathy with the Catholics. Hence it has come to pass that the noblest of mothers is still the most misunderstood of mothers and of women. Cold neglect on the one hand is hers while adoring worship greets her memory in countless statues on the other hand. The God whom multitudes worship today is Mary. Protestants fight Mariolatry in order to stand up for the worship of Mary's Son, our Savior."[32]

Indeed, if Mary has been met with adoring worship on the part of Catholics, has she not on the other extreme been treated with cold neglect on the part of Protestants? That ought not to be the case because in Mary we find a pattern for motherhood and a model for godliness. She was a woman who put God's glory before her reputation and comfort, and put obedience before answers. In Mary we see a life conformed to the Word of God. In using her, God wants to teach us that he can use us also. The blessed Mary is a blessed message.

1. Peter Kreeft, *Ecumenical Jihad*, (San Francisco: Ignatius, 1996) 152.

2. Kreeft 153.

3. Kreeft 169.

4. Philip Edgecumbe Hughes, "The Council and Mary," *Christianity Today*, 8 Dec. 1967: 7.

5. Kevin McNamara, *Mary the Mother of God*, (London: Catholic Truth Society) 1.

6. Dave Hunt, *A Woman Rides the Beast*, (Oregon: Harvest House, 1994) 439.

7. Giovanni Miegge, *The Virgin Mary*, 77.

8. Herbert Carson, *The Faithful of the Vatican*, (Evangelical Press, 1996) 121-122.

9. Dr. Ludwig Ott, *Fundamentals of Catholic Dogma*, (Illinois: Tan Books, 1960) 203.

10. *Catechism of The Catholic Church*, (Missouri: Ligouri Publications, 1994) para. 499.

11. *Catechism of The Catholic Church*, para. 974.

12. *Catechism of The Catholic Church*, para. 966.

13. Elliot Miller and Kenneth Samples, *The Cult of the Virgin*, (Grand Rapids, MI: Baker House, 1992), 49.

14. Dr. Ludwig Ott, 213-214.

15. *Catechism of The Catholic Church*, para. 969.

16. Pope John Paul II, *Homily at Ephesus*, 30 November 1979.

17. Lumen Gentium, n. 53.

18. *Catechism of The Catholic Church*, para. 970.

19. *Novena Prayers in Honor of our Mother of Perpetual Help*, (Uniontown, PA: Sisters of St. Basil, 1968) 5.

20. *Novena Prayers in Honor of our Mother of Perpetual Help*, 16.

21. *Novena Prayers in Honor of our Mother of Perpetual Help*, 19.

22. Hughes, 10.

23. *The Glories of Mary*, ed. Eugene Grimm, (Brooklyn: Redemptorist Fathers, 1931) 180-182.

24. Miller and Samples, 71.

25. Gary Inrig, *Hearts of Iron, Feet of Clay*, (Chicago: Moody Press, 1969) 103.

26. *Christianity Today*, Dec. 8, 1967: 7.

27. *Roman Catholicism*, ed. John Armstrong (Chicago: Moody Press, 1994) 120.

28. Stephen Benko, *Protestants, Catholics, and Mary*, (Valley Forge, PA: Judson Press, 1968) 18-19.

29. Miller and Samples, 25.

30. William Webster, *The Church of Rome at the Bar of History*, (Edinburgh: Banner of Truth Trust, 1995) 85.

31. Miller and Samples, 52.

32. A. T. Robertson, *The Mother of Jesus, Her Problems and Her Glory*, (Baker House) 66-69.

CHAPTER 8

OUT OF WORK

Hebrews 7:1-28

Recently I read a story from Irish history that set me to thinking. Times were hard and thousands of persons were unemployed. To counter the high unemployment, the Irish government embarked on an ambitious road-building project. Many new jobs were created. Workers enthusiastically joined the project. Happy to be engaged in a significant task that would both feed their families and benefit their society, the workers sang as they worked.

But after awhile, the workers' level of motivation underwent a dramatic downturn. The work slowed and the singing ceased. Why? The workers discovered the roads led nowhere. The road-building project had been concocted only to provide jobs.

Providing jobs with no real benefit is indeed a strange and bogus plan, and yet I believe the Roman Catholic priesthood commits such folly. This assumption is borne out in the fact that today Roman Catholicism employs over 400,000 men around the world in the role of mediating priest between God and man, a role which the Scripture declares to be uniquely and singularly Christ's (1 Tim. 2:5; Heb. 7:24-25).

Despite this redundancy, Roman Catholic dogma advocates a priesthood empowered with the power to forgive sins, and the power to consecrate the eucharistic elements, making present the body and blood of Christ with His entire manhood and Godhead in the form of bread and wine during the sacrifice of the Mass. For Roman Catholics, the power to forgive sins and to offer sacrifice for sins is vested in the priesthood.

The force and significance of this twofold ministry and what it really entails is shown in a pastoral letter written in 1905 by Johannes Katschtaler, Prince Bishop of Salzburg. Since Vatican II and the New Catechism (see para. 1461-62, 1566) have changed nothing of substance in this respect, the points made in this quotation are still valid:

> Honor the priest because of two inexpressibly high powers with which he is endowed.
>
> ... The Catholic priest has the power to forgive sins .. . God has, as it were, to this end surrendered his omnipotence for this moment to his representative on earth, the duly empowered priest. Of course, the priest does not possess this altogether wonderful power of himself, but because of his ordination and because he is so empowered through the holy Church ... Protestant pastors have not the priestly ordination.
>
> The priests have the power to consecrate ... to make present the Body of the Lord with the precious Blood, with his entire Manhood and his Godhead under the form of bread and wine ... There at Bethlehem Mary bore the divine Child and wrapped him in swaddling clothes; the priest does the same as he lays the Host on the Corporal. Once did Mary bring the divine Child into the world. But, lo! The priest does this not once, but hundreds and thousands of times as often as he celebrates ... But do they make the Body and Blood of the Lord merely present? No,

they sacrifice; they offer the sacrifice to the heavenly Father. It is the same sacrifice that Christ made by shedding his Blood on Calvary...[1]

Under the auspices of the Roman priesthood, forgiveness is offered to men, and Christ is offered to God. In the eyes of Rome, the priest is gainfully employed in the construction and maintenance of a sacramental road to God. Thus, through a properly ordained priest, saving and sanctifying grace travels to the sinner via the sacraments of penance and the Eucharist. Rome's doctrine is unambiguous in that the priesthood is indispensable in the mediation of salvation and the distribution of grace.

Father John O'Brien in his popular work, *The Faith of Millions*, captures the past and present position of the faith of the Vatican with reference to the centrality and vital nature of the Roman priesthood, when he writes:

> The Catholic Church differs from Protestant denominations in that it alone possesses an altar and a priesthood ... Without a priesthood, however, there can be no altar and no sacrifice (and, according to the Vatican Council II, no salvation). There can be preaching and prayer. But the essential element of worship, that is, sacrifice ... is lost without a priesthood.[2]

Like the workers in our opening story, the dutifully charged Catholic priest sees himself happily engaged in the significant task of building a path to God that will benefit a society of lost people.

That mood and mission must, however, undergo a dramatic downturn. Like the workers in our story, the Roman priesthood must be informed biblically that they are employed in a dead-end job. A job with no real work. In a day of ecumenical inflation and theological recession, few if any are prepared to face the facts or tell the truth. However, the true message of Calvary spells the loss of hundreds of thousands of jobs at the Vatican. The finished work of Christ puts pay to the Roman priesthood as it did to the Levitical priesthood (John 19:30; Matt. 27:50-51). Through his death on the cross, Jesus opened up a new and living way in man's approach to God making redundant and superfluous any need for a human go-between (Hebrews 10:19-22). The New Testament makes no mention of a special group of men set apart to minister as priests. The New Testament, and specifically the book of Hebrews, teaches that Christ has become the fulfillment of the Old Testament priesthood and now serves as the only mediator between God and man (1 Tim. 2:5; 1 John 2:1-2). New Testament doctrine is unequivocally opposed to an established priesthood between God and man to rule the Church and to control the means of grace as currently manifested in the Roman priesthood.

One grows indignant at Roman pretensions that the priesthood has the means to confer grace, to work regeneration, to forgive sin, and so forth. Such delusions make priestcraft no better than witchcraft in that it limits God to the actions of men, exalts itself, dishonors Christ, and deprives men of the dearly bought privilege of the gospel. Charles Spurgeon wrote of this indignation in the following:

> I reckon it of all crimes the greatest for a man to assume to mediate between men and God. Little as I respect the devil I prefer him to a priest who pretends to forgive sins; for even the devil has to much honesty about him to pretend to give absolution in God's name. There is but one pardoning priest, and he is the Son of the Highest. His one sacrifice has

ended all other sacrifices; His one atonement has rendered all future oblations an imposture. Today as Elias stood on Carmel and cried out against the priests of Baal, so would I. I count no words too severe. If my every speech should be a thunderbolt and every word a lightning flash, it would not be too strong to protest against the accursed system which once degraded the whole earth to kiss the pope's foot, and is degrading our nation still, and through a so-called Protestant church. O, God Almighty, thou God of Latimer and Ridley, God of the martyrs, whose ashes are still among us, wilt thou suffer this people to go back again to false gods and saints and saintesses, and virgins, and crucifixes, relics and cast clouts and rotten rags; for to this also will they come if thy grace prevent not. Oh, my hearers, Jesus is the only Savior of the sons of men. Believe in Him and live. This is the only gospel: at your peril reject it. I pray you receive it for Christ's sake.[3]

In defense of the Gospel that claims Christ as the only pardoning priest, and Calvary as the one sufficient sacrifice, I would like to consider two things that will unmask the priestly imposters of Rome.

The Absence of a Clerical Priesthood.

The Presence of a Corporate Priesthood.

The Absence of a Clerical Priesthood

In beginning this point, we must begin to understand the authority and ministry structure of the Catholic Church. The entire Roman structure is hierarchical in nature, which in its root meaning connotes the idea of "rule by priest." This hierarchy or priesthood is foundational to the Church's authority. The structure of the priesthood itself, and indeed the Roman Catholic Church as a whole, is similar to an army—a graduated system of power headed by a supreme and absolute commander (the pope) and operating downward through successive ranks of officers (the priesthood) until it finally reaches the privates (the laity), who have zero authority and but one responsibility which is obedience. It is therefore no coincidence that the technical term for conversion in Catholic parlance is "submission" to Rome.

To borrow again the language of the military, the arrangement of ranks considered simply would view the pope as the supreme commander, the bishops as the lieutenants, and the priest as the drill sergeants. In this we note for the purpose of our study that the priest is below the pope and bishop in the Roman hierarchy. In the line of duty, under his commanding officers, the priest serves in parish churches, where he is responsible for pastoring and administering the sacraments.[4] His chief duties are to offer the Sacrifice of the Mass and to forgive sins through the sacrament of penance.[5] Therefore, Rome not only has a priesthood of the people but a priesthood for the people.[6] It has both clergy and laity. It has a special corps of men who rule the church and control the means of grace.

Does the biblical record of the New Testament church offer support for such a clerical priesthood? To stroll through the landscape of the New Testament Scriptures is to fail to pick up the trail of a clerical priesthood. The New Testament unequivocally insists that there is no longer a priesthood in contrast to an unpriestly laity, but that the whole new people of God has become a priesthood, in one eternal Priest, our Lord Jesus Christ. (Rev. 1:16; 1 Peter 2:5,9) Every Christian is a priest, with the inestimable privilege of direct access into the presence of God and the sacred responsibility of interceding for others. Ritualistic Christendom has moved away from this apostolic position.

In borrowing a quote from the other side of the fence, let me cite Hans Kung as he correctly notes the absence of a clerical priesthood in the New Testament:

> The New Testament insists quite unequivocally that there is no longer a priesthood in contrast to an unpriestly laity, but that the whole new people of God has become a priesthood ... Although Christ's sacrificial death on the Cross is represented in the Lord's Supper, the Lord's Supper itself is not regarded as a sacrifice on its own, nor even a repetition of the unique sacrificial death of Christ. Thus the Lord's Supper is never referred to as a sacrifice in the New Testament ... It is only in writing outside of the New Testament ... And as time went on (that) the ideas and images associated with the priesthood of the Old Testament (and pagan religions) were increasingly transferred to these New Testament "priests" ... Two observations may be made which sum up the whole issue: The fact that the leaders of the community are called "priests" is unexceptional precisely because of the priesthood of all believers; but the fact that the leaders of the community exclusively are seen as "priests," and become a separate caste, after pagan and Judaic patterns, standing between God and men and barring the direct access to God which the whole priestly people should enjoy—this as we have seen is contrary to the New Testament message: both the message of

255

the one Mediator and high priest Jesus Christ and that of the priesthood of all Christians.[7]

Building upon these criticisms of the Roman Catholic priesthood and its pretension to offer forgiveness to men and to offer Christ to God in exercise of its rule and role, let me ask two questions in light of the New Testament data.

What about the Rule of a Clerical Priesthood?

What about the Role of a Clerical Priesthood?

Is the Rule of a Clerical Priesthood Biblical?

Is there common ground between the Bible and the proposition held officially by Catholicism that our Lord instituted a special caste of men in the episcopal order known as priests, who would be given an exclusive authority over the church, and ministry within the church, to reconcile men with God through the Mass and by means of confession and penance? It is my belief that the Bible does not affirm Roman Catholic assertions concerning an episcopal priesthood, because of the terminology of ministry and the superiority of Jesus Christ, our Great High Priest.

A sacerdotal class that, in contrast to the rest of believers, exercises priestly functions which others are not allowed to exercise, is not only unknown to the New Testament but is completely contrary to its whole spirit. The priestly theory of Christian ministry is without biblical authority. In several places, Paul lists the different types of ministries and men who where set apart by God and operative in the New Testament church, such as apostles, prophets, evangelists, pastors, and teachers (Eph. 4:11; 1 Cor. 12:28). In the expanse of Paul's New Testament writings, there is nary any mention of priests. The New Testament writers, as guided by the Holy Spirit, never assign the title of priest to the Christian minister. He is called bishop, pastor or elder but not priest (Phil. 1:1; 1 Tim. 3:1-13; Acts 20: 17,28; Titus 1:6-9; 1 Peter 5:1-5).

In Scripture, there are three categories that bear the title priest. First, the priests of the Old Testament order, which was still in existence in the days of Christ and continued to function, although rejected of God, until Jerusalem fell. Second, our Lord Jesus Christ Himself, who in His exaltation at God's right hand is "a priest forever after the order of Melchisedek." Third, all believers who are designated " a kingdom of priests," and "a royal priesthood," whose function now and hereafter is "to offer up spiritual sacrifices, acceptable to God by Jesus Christ" (1 Peter 2:5). A priestly class within the ranks of the redeemed is not to be found in the New Testament.

Standing in opposition to this special corps of men for the special mission of priesthood, the New Testament advocates that all believers in Christ, not Christian ministers alone, are called priests and called to be priests, *hiereis*. The minister, the pastor, the bishop, and the deacon are priests in no other sense than is true of every believer in Christ.

Bishop Hanley Moule of England, a Bible expositor of deep spirituality and ripe scholarship says:

"Never do the great founders of the Church, and never does He who is its Foundation, use the term hiereus, sacrificing, mediating, priest, as a term to designate the Christian minister in any of his orders."

Furthermore, the rule of a clerical priesthood is made obsolete by the sufficiency and superiority of Jesus Christ our great High Priest. The New Testament is at pains to point out that the person and work of Lord Jesus has become the fulfillment of the Old Testament priesthood and that He now serves as the only Mediator between God and man (1 Tim. 2:5; Heb. 7:24-25). It is highly significant that in the New Testament the word priest when used in the singular speaks only of Jesus. His unique sacerdotal priesthood effected at Calvary rendered all other priestly mediators eternally obsolete. Therefore any attempt on the part of man to act as such can only be understood as a blasphemous denial of Christ's once-for-all offering, and is a direct challenge to its efficacy.

Protestantism regards the high priestly work of Christ for man's redemption as finished on the cross, where He made by Himself, one perfect sacrifice, satisfaction, and oblation for the sins of the whole world (Heb. 1:3, 7:27, 10:13-14). Moreover, we regard the priesthood of Christ as unique and inalienable, that is, it cannot be transmitted to any other. The word used in Hebrews 7:24 is "aparabatos" which is defined "without successor." In this way it differed from Aaron's priesthood which was passed on to others. Christ's priesthood is perfect, complete, and peculiar to Himself (Heb. 7:28). Because He made a perfect offering for sin "once for all", He requires neither successor nor further sacrifice. The idea that Christian ministry should share in or perpetuate the sacrifice of Christ is alien to the teaching of the New Testament.

In his earlier work *Roman Catholicism Today*, Herbert Carson gets to the kernel of this matter in highlighting the superiority of Jesus Christ in comparison to the Old Covenant and the Levitical priesthood when he noted:

> The Epistle, which deals at length with this subject, is that to the Hebrews. Here the great contrast is drawn between the old covenant and the new, and thus between the Levitical priesthood of the Old Testament and the priesthood of Christ. The Leviti-

cal priests were many in number and, as each generation passed, so a new group emerged to take their place. But by contrast, under the new covenant, there is but one great High Priest, the Lord Jesus Christ Himself, who having offered the one final sacrifice for sins is seated at the right hand of God. They were sinful, facing not only the sins of the people but their own. He is the spotless and sinless Son of God. Theirs was a glory that was passing, while His is the glory, which surpasses and abides. He has offered once and for all the perfect sacrifice, which has been accepted, and so through Him we may draw near to the throne of God.[8]

Is the rule of a clerical priesthood biblical? In conclusion of this point, I would have to say a definite no. Though the apostles under the guidance of the Holy Spirit did bring organization to the organism with officers in each church, they never assigned to the new church any fragments of a sacrificial system that had been done away in Christ. As we noted, in the New Testament one never reads of priests and people, clergy and laity, but rather of bishops (elders), deacons, and saints (Phil. 1:1). Anything in addition to this is not only superfluous, but is a contradiction of biblical dogma and robs the humble believer in Christ of his blood-bought privilege. Having Christ and His complete sacrifice offered once for all we have no need for priest, altar, sacrifice, or holy water. With His finished work we rest satisfied, and in His all sufficiency we rejoice.

Is the Role of a Cletical Priesthood Biblical?

As noted earlier, Roman Catholic theology attributes two prerogatives to the priest that affords him the crucial and domineering place he holds in the lives of his parishioners. Theologically, the Roman priest has been invested with jurisdiction both over the natural and over the mystical Body of Christ. Jurisdiction over the natural body of Christ means the consecration of the sacrament of the altar when at the word of the priest, the bread becomes the very flesh and substance of our Lord.

With jurisdiction over the mystical Body of Christ, the priest is ordained with the power to forgive sins upon due penance. The power to bring Christ down upon the altar is said to have been bestowed by our Savior when in the upper room stated, "This do in remembrance of me," and the prerogative of absolution was declared in the upper room after the resurrection, when the Lord, breathing upon them, said: "Receive the Holy Spirit: If you forgive the sins of any, they are forgiven them; if you retain the sins of any, they are retained" (John 20:22-23). In addition, a similar intent is purposed in the words of Christ to Simon Peter at Caesera Philippi, "And I will give you the keys of the kingdom of heaven and whatever you bind on earth will be bound in heaven and whatever you loose on earth will be loosed in heaven" (Matt. 16:19). But is such a role concerning the mediation of the atonement and absolution of sin biblically sanctioned?

Furthermore, can it be said that there is any biblical legitimacy to the Catholic claim that through confession of sin to a priest when accompanied by a contrite heart, and by his absolution and the performance of the appropriate penance (making satisfaction for sin), that an individual can receive forgiveness of sins? The faith of the Vatican would vote yes.[9] The court of Scripture, however, fails to give such jurisdiction to the Roman priest.

First, there is no longer a need for a distinct priestly class or caste to mediate between God and man. In the distinctively sacerdotal epistle, Hebrews, the word for priest "hiereus" comes into the foreground, but there it is absorbed by the Lord Jesus. It is appropriated altogether to Him in His sacrificial work once done, and in His heavenly work now always doing, the work of mediating the salvific blessing which His great offering won (Heb. 2:14-18, 4:14-16). The Roman priest is clearly out of his jurisdiction when set against the enduring and exalted priesthood of Christ.

Second, when the historical facts are critically examined, Rome finds few allies for priestly absolution. William Webster surveyed the historical landscape and revealed the following facts that tear at the fabric of the Roman doctrine of priestly absolution.

+ The early church knew nothing of the doctrine of auricular confession, penance, purgatory, or indulgences.

+ Confession in the early Church was a public matter that related to grave sin and could be done only once. There was no judicial absolution by a priest.

+ At the end of the second and beginning of the third century, penances were introduced as a means of gaining forgiveness of sins and the distinction between mortal and venial sins became prominent.

+ The seed of purgatory came into Christianity through paganizing and philosophical influences introduced by Origen, and it was later given dogmatic authority by Gregory the Great.

+ Private confession to a priest did not come into prominence until the seventh or eighth centuries and it completely displaced public confession.

- The first recorded use of indulgences dated from the ninth century.

- There were conflicting opinions among theologians as late as the thirteenth century on the exact nature of confession and penance, and whether or not confession to a priest was necessary to receive forgiveness of sins.[10]

Third, the practice of confessing one's offenses to a priest in the sacrament of penance is met with biblical bemusement. There is not the slightest trace in Scripture concerning the compulsory confession to a priest. The Bible constructs no impediment or barrier on the road to repentance. That the soul of man might freely and directly seek the Savior, is the combined testimony of the Old and New Testaments. David, the sweet psalmist, didn't need a priest to play second fiddle when he owned up to his sin in the 32nd chapter of Psalms and confessed his sin directly to God (Ps. 32:5). And Ezra, though a Levitical priest himself, taught God's people to "make confession to the Lord God of your fathers" (Ezra 10:11).

Free and direct access to seeking the Lord is reinforced in New Testament doctrine. An open door of access was the privilege of every wounded and wandering child of God (1 John 1:9, 2:12; Heb. 4:16). No human mediary was needed to broker a settlement with God that could be sought and possessed face to face with God through Christ the only way to the Father (John 14:6, Acts 4:12).

These remarks are not ignorant to the New Testament provision for confession to a fellow saint when we have sinned against them (Matt. 5:23-24; James 5:16). There is room also for confession before the church when our sin has been an affront and offense to the assembly of believers (Matt. 18:15-18; 1 Tim.

5:19-20). However, the silence of the New Testament is deafening in regard to a Christian's confession to a priest.

Fourth, surely the human priest is ill equipped to exercise the office of a confessor. No priest knows based upon a few minutes of discussion with a faceless individual the breadth of their sin, the height of their guilt, and the depth of their contrition. The priest is blind-sighted to the spiritual condition of the sinner, so he cannot be sure whether the person's repentance is genuine or not. Only God knows the secrets of the heart (Ps. 44:21). The priest knows even less of the thoughts of God. He can in no way ascertain directly whether God has in fact pardoned the supposed penitent. Added to that it is presumption in the extreme that proceeds to assign what is to be considered as appropriate satisfaction for that sin. How can a finite creature decide the appropriate damages to an infinitely holy God? "Who can forgive sins but God alone?" (Mark 2:7)

Fifth, Christ's words in John 20:23 must not be interpreted to mean that Jesus gave to a select body of people the right to absolve sins and reserve a spot in heaven for certain ecclesiastical clientele. Jesus had spoken similar words before (Matthew 16:19), but He was not endowing the apostles (and their successors) as a "spiritual A team" to deal with the sins of the world. It must be remembered that the apostles were not alone in receiving this commission, for others were with them. We know from Luke's account that the group commissioned contained at least Cleopas and the other disciple who had been with him on the road to Emmaus (Luke 24:18,33; John 19:25), and probably others who were not apostles (Acts 1:14).

Further wreckage of the Roman doctrine of a spiritual elite possessing the power to forgive sins, is the fact that no New Testament book yields one instance of an apostle taking for himself the authority to absolve sin or pardon anyone. This is crucial because it points to an important rule of biblical inter-pretation, namely, that every text must be interpreted within its historical and biblical world and not in isolation. The conse-quence of this point is that the apostles by their behavior lend no support to the Catholic dogmatists interpretation of John 20:22-23. The apostolic pattern was to point the sinner to Christ as the one and only remitter of sin (Acts 10:43, 13:38). The apostles clearly understood that the authority of a preacher had been given to them, but not the authority of a priest.

Finally, the outworking of this text is to be seen not in the apostolic band exercising a priestly ministry of absolution in the confessional, but by the preaching of the gospel. Luke's account of the same event places this injunction not in the context of a sacrament of the church, but in the context of the spread of the gospel through the proclamation of the Gospel (Luke 24:46-48). Having received their orders, the early church marched for-ward with their feet shod with the preparation of the Gospel of peace, trumpeting the good news of forgiveness (Eph. 6:5; Matt. 28:18-20). If sinners would repent and believe on the Lord Jesus, it was announced that their sins would be forgiven them (Acts10:43). If sinners showed hardness of heart and refused to repent, it was proclaimed that they were still in their sin and under condemnation (Acts 8:21-22). All that the heralder could do was announce the message of forgiveness; God performs the miracle (Mark 2:7). We announce it. We do not create it. All who proclaim the Gospel are in effect forgiving or not forgiving sins, depending on whether the hearer accepts or rejects the Lord Jesus Christ as the sin-bearer (2 Cor. 2:12-17).

Support for this interpretation is to be found in the fact that Jesus, when quoted in John 20:23, was speaking in the Greek perfect tense. This indicates an action already performed. Jesus is speaking therefore of forgiving and retaining sins that have already been forgiven or retained. In fact, this means that the disciples had the authority to declare forgiveness to those whom God had already forgiven. As stated earlier, we announce forgiveness through the Gospel; we do not create it.

Linking all these parts together, we forge a solid chain of argument with which to arrest the Roman priest and charge him in his rule and role to being an imposter. Calvary alone is our altar, Christ alone the sacrifice, and the throne of grace alone the true confessional.

I like the reply of the old woman to the priest who made a last ditch effort to bring her back into the "church" as she lay dying. "I have come to forgive your sins," he said to her. "Show me your hands," the aged saint answered; then, when the astonished priest showed his hands, she said; "You cannot forgive my sins. The Man who forgives my sins has the marks of nails in His hands."

As Spurgeon stated, it is indeed a great crime for a man to assume to mediate between God and man. Even the devil has too much honesty about him to pretend to give absolution in God's name. The Christian minister is a witness to the message of forgiveness, not as Rome suggests a partner in the business of forgiveness.

A biblical perspective on the work of salvation and our relationship to it is perhaps offered to us in the following words of Robert Murray McCheyne.

> Early in his ministry, in 1834, when he heard that a sinner had turned to Christ through hearing him preach, McCheyne wrote in his journal: "The precious tidings that a soul has been melted down by the grace of the Savior . . . Lord, I thank Thee that Thou hast shown me this marvelous working, though I was but an adoring spectator rather than an instrument.[11]

The Presence of a Corporate Priesthood

Under the old covenant, God's people had a priesthood, but in the new covenant, God's people are a priesthood. When God places the robe of Christ's righteousness upon the naked and dirty soul of a man, He places with it the mitre of priestly status and function. Just as we are sons in the eternal and well-beloved Son, so we are priests in the one and only sacrificing and mediating Priest. Priesthood is not an exclusive club reserved for a few, but the inestimable privilege of all believers in all ages.

The apostle Peter assured his readers that they were priests (1 Peter 2:5,9). In describing an aspect of Christ's work on our behalf, the apostle John reveals that one of the intended ends of our redemption was to make us priests unto God (Rev. 1:16). Later in Revelation, a note of praise is sounded that amplifies the reality of a believer's status as priest unto God (Rev. 5:10). Every saint is a priest, who enjoys the wonder and privilege of direct access into the presence of God, and the sacred responsibility of servicing God and others. The only priesthood the Bible teaches is the priesthood of all believers.

The affirmation of the priesthood of all believers, however, is neither a repudiation of the church and its ministry, nor a declaration that Christianity is a religion of individuals only. It is an assertion of the individual believer's right and ability to approach God, his responsibility to do so, and also his right and duty to aid his brothers in their spiritual quest.

Historically, the doctrine concerning the priesthood of all believers served as a foundation for criticism of the Roman priesthood. There was to be no fundamental difference in status, between the minister of the Gospel, by whatever name they might choose to be called, and the ordinary believer.

But in drawing this study to a close, I would plead that this doctrine not only forms a foundation for criticism of Catholicism but serves also as a foundation for activism among Protestants. This is a doctrine that deserves more than lip service, it deserves elbow grease. It must be used as a tool to build the church not just as a weapon in the apologetic war. What do I mean? Under the old covenant the Old Testament priest offered animal sacrifices, but under the new covenant believers offer up spiritual sacrifices, acceptable to God by Jesus Christ (1 Peter 2:5). Ours is not an honorary priesthood but an active one. Roman priests may be out of work but biblical priests have plenty to do.

The following quotation by Warren Wiersbe accentuates this biblical role of Christians as priests.

> As God's priests, we bring "spiritual sacrifices:" to him through Jesus Christ who is our "altar" (Heb. 13:10). The word spiritual does not suggest "immaterial," because some of the sacrifices we give are definitely material. Rather, spiritual means "of a spiritual quality." If unsaved people offered them, these sacrifices would not be spiritual, nor would they be accepted by God.

> We have already noted that prayer is a sacrifice we offer to the Lord (Ps. 141:1-3), and so is our praise of God (Heb. 13:15). God sees our good works as spiritual sacrifices (Heb. 13:16), as well as the money we give for his service (Phil. 4:14-18; Rom. 15:27). God certainly wants our bodies yielded to him as a living sacrifice, not a dead one (Rom. 12:1-2); and he also wants us to give him our hearts (Ps. 51:17).

The winning of others to Christ is also an act of spiritual worship (Rom. 15:16). The words minister and ministering come from a Greek word that means "priestly service" and gives us our English word liturgy. Paul looked upon the Gentile converts as a sacrifice "offered up" to the Lord (Eph. 5:2; Heb. 10:5,8). This lifts evangelism to the highest plane possible, for when we witness to others and win them to Christ, we are performing acts of worship to the Lord. Witnessing is not "Christian salesmanship." It is a holy act of worship to the glory of God.[12]

Such is the ministry allotted to every true child of God. We don't pay men to do the ministry; we have been bought by Christ to serve Him and others (Titus 2:14).

A village preacher rushed down to the railway station every day to watch the train go by. Members of his congregation thought the pastime juvenile and asked him to give it up. "No gentlemen" the minister replied firmly, "I preach your sermons, teach your children, bury your dead, marry your sons and daughters and chair your meetings. But I won't give up seeing that train. It is the only thing that passes through this town that I don't have to push."

Churches would not lag behind and pastors would not have to push so hard if this generation would climb on board the biblical concept of the priesthood of believers. Against the notion of a clerical priesthood we must fight, but before the truth of a corporate priesthood we must fall in surrender. Every priest is not a Christian but every Christian is a priest.

1. David Samuel, *Pope of Gospel?* (Marshalls, 1982) 72.

2. John O'Brien, *The Faith of Millions*, (Huntington, Indiana: 1938) 262.

3. Ian Paisley, *Blue-print Union with Rome*, (1989) 35.

4. *Catechism of The Catholic Church*, (Missouri: Ligouri Publications, 1994) para. 1591- 1592.

5. Ibid., para. 1411, 1461, 1566.

6. Ibid., para. 1591-1592.

7. Hans Kung, *The Church*, (New York: Sheed and Ward, 1968) 328.

8. Herbert Carson, *Roman Catholicism Today*, (London: 1969) 61.

9. (NCC para. 1441-1445

10. William Webster, Church of Rome at the Bar of History, (Scotland: Banner of Truth) 99-100.

11. Warren Wiersbe, *Christians You Should Know*, (Grand Rapids, Baker, 1984) 18.

12. Warren Wiersbe, *Be What You Are*, (Illinois: Tyndale, 1988) 70.

CHAPTER 9

PUTTING THE POPE IN HIS PLACE

Matthew 16:13-20

Few people have the opportunity of a private audience with Pope John Paul II. One who did was journalist Tim Russert, *NBC News* Washington bureau chief, Meet the Press moderator, and former altar boy. In the *St. Anthony Messenger*, James W. Arnold relates Russert's story.

> I'll never forget it. I was there to convince His Holiness it was in his interest to appear on the Today Show. But my thoughts soon turned away from NBC's ratings toward the idea of salvation. As I stood there with the Vicar of Christ, I simply blurted, "Bless me, Father!" He put his arm around my shoulders and whispered, "You are the one called Timothy, the man from NBC?" I said, "Yes, yes, that's me." "They tell me you're a very important man," Taken aback, I said, "Your Holiness, there are only two of us in this room, and I am certainly a distant second." He looked at me and said, "Right."[1]

It's always wise to know your place and for NBC's Tim Russert this entailed the acknowledgment of John Paul's papal authority and role as Christ's Vicar on earth. Awe struck,

Russert took the allotted place of every good Catholic in giving submission and deference to Peter's alleged successor, as pastor of the entire Church. It seems that during the course of this private audience with the pope, Russert must of realized that standing before him was the bridge builder to God (the Pontiff), the one standing in the place of Jesus Christ (the Vicar of Christ). Russert's thoughts turned naturally towards the idea of salvation and appealed to the pope for a blessing.

Enclosed in the details of this story is yet another constituent part of the Roman Catholic controversy, the papacy. The term *papacy* refers to the office of the pope as head of the Church or as civil ruler in the Vatican State. The office is a matter of central importance in the Catholic tradition. In fact, belief in the *Petrine* ministry as exercised by the Bishop of Rome distinguishes Roman Catholicism from all of the other "Christian" traditions. There are two principal doctrines pertaining to the Petrine office that distinguish Catholicism: the primacy of the pope over the whole Church and the gift of infallibility which he enjoys when he solemnly speaks as earthly head of the Church on matters of faith and morals. Adherence to these tenets of Roman theology is expected of every true Catholic and has historically constituted a matter of life and death.

Recognizing the centrality and parallel controversy of this doctrine, let me first of all place it into a historical and creedal framework for the purpose of accurately and clearly introducing the subject.

Since the Middle Ages, Roman Catholicism has taught that submission to the bishop of Rome is necessary for one's salvation. This teaching was given dogmatic expression by Pope Boniface VIII in an ex cathedra statement in his bull *Unam*

Sanctum (A.D. 1302) and was later reaffirmed by subsequent Popes and councils such as Vatican I. His decree states:

> "Furthermore we declare, state, define, and pronounce that it is altogether necessary to salvation for every human creature to be subject to the Roman pontiff."[2]

The primacy and power of the papacy was further defended and declared by the Council of Trent when it frequently convened between 1537 and 1563. The Council asserted with regard to the supreme authority of the Roman pontiff:

> He sits in that chair of Peter ... and hence it is that in him the church recognizes the highest degree of dignity, and a universality of jurisdiction derived, not from decrees of men or councils, but from God himself. Wherefore he is the Father and guide of all the faithful, of all the Bishops, and of all the prelates, no matter how high their power and office; and as the successor of St Peter, as true and lawful Vicar of Christ our Lord, he governs the universal church.[3]

We should also add to these statements the present Catechism of the Catholic Church, that despite the march of time, is to be found in step with Catholicism of old regarding the matter of papal primacy. In a section apropos to the episcopal college and its head, the pope, we find these words:

> When Christ instituted the twelve, "he constituted [them] in the form of a college or permanent assembly, at the head of which he placed Peter, chosen from among them." Just as "by the Lord's institution, St. Peter and the rest of the apostles constitute a single apostolic college, so in like fashion the Roman

Pontiff, Peter's successor, and the bishops, the successors of the apostles are related with and united to one another."

The Lord made Simon alone, whom he named Peter, the "rock" of his Church. He gave Him the keys of his Church and instituted him shepherd of the whole flock. "the office of binding and loosing which was given to Peter was also assigned to the college of apostles united to its head." This pastoral office of Peter and the other apostles belongs to the Church's very foundation and is continued by the bishops under the primacy of the pope.

The pope, bishop of Rome and Peter's successor, "is the perpetual and visible source and foundation of the unity both of the bishops and of the whole company of the faithful." "For the Roman Pontiff, by reason of his office as Vicar of Christ, and as pastor of the entire Church has full, supreme, and universal power over the whole Church, a power which he can always exercise unhindered."[4]

It stands, therefore, on the basis of these declarations that the faith of the Vatican, both past and present, teaches that the pope as Peter's successor, is Christ's appointed king over His ecclesiastical castle and all who enter the kingdom of God must bow in subjection to him. According to Rome, the Apostle Peter, following Pentecost, transferred his seat of apostolic rulership and jurisdiction from Antioch to Rome, and there he served as the first Bishop of Rome until martyred during the reign of the Emperor Nero. From Rome he ruled the universal church as head of the world's bishops. Thus, whoever succeeds

Peter as the bishop of Rome also succeeds him as pope. As Bishop of Rome and heir to Peter's seat, the pope is thus recognized as the vicar or representative of Christ on earth, invested with universal power in the care of souls.[5]

In the light of these facts, Tim Russert certainly knew his status in the presence of John Paul II. Many Catholics recognize that it is best to have the Church as your spiritual mother and the pope as your spiritual father. The necessity of this is bound up in the teaching that you cannot have the Church without the pope, and you cannot find salvation outside the sacrament and sacraments of the Church.[6]

At this point some might think that to raise this controversy is to flog a theological dead horse. Surveys taken during the 1980s reflect serious questioning by rank and file Catholics concerning papal authority. A 1985 *New York Times* and *CBS* poll may give some support to this in that the poll found that 83 percent of the Catholic population between the ages of 18 and 39 favor the use of artificial birth control. In the same age category, 68 percent favor women priests; 69 percent favor letting priests marry; 80 percent favor permitting Catholics to divorce and remarry; and 86 percent think it is possible to disagree with the pope on birth control, abortion, or divorce and still be a good Catholic.[7]

Although there is dissension within the ranks of the Roman Catholic Church, the official position regarding the authority of the Church and the papacy remain as firm as ever. The pope is still the pope and retains the full vestment of papal privilege and power. Neither critics nor polls will change this reality.

Bearing these facts in mind, we now begin a deeper exposé of papal ministrations. Theologically "prodigal protestantism" challenges the claim that Christians need the Church of Rome as our mother and the pope of Rome as our father. In general, Protestants do not view the papacy as a catalyst for true Christianity but rather as an unholy stampede for power and wealth, that over the centuries has trampled the true gospel and Church of Jesus Christ. Evangelicals also maintain that the Word of God spills no ink in defending the notion of apostolic succession and Petrine primacy. Further protest is made over the hijacking of the biblical pattern of local Church leadership by the universal and unbiblical dictatorship of the papacy. Some have even gone so far as to see in the office and history of the papacy the viceroy of Satan not the Vicar of Christ.

Martin Luther was among the some when he wrote, "We are of the conviction that the papacy is the seat of the true and real Antichrist . . . Personally I declare I owe the pope no other obedience than that to the Antichrist." John Wesley, founder of Methodism, viewed the papacy in a similar light when he wrote, "He (the pope) is in an emphatical sense the Man of Sin, as he increases all manner of sin above measure. And he is, too, properly styled the Son of Perdition, as he has caused the death of numberless multitudes, both of his opposers and followers . . . He it is that exalteth himself above all that is called God, or that is worshipped . . . claiming the highest honour . . . claiming the perogatives which belong to God alone." While not all within Protestantism were so bold as to identify the pope as the Man of Sin, there was nevertheless a uniformed suspicion of the papacy as perhaps captured in the words of the Puritan Richard Baxter, "If the pope be not the Antichrist he hath the ill- luck to be so like him."

Historically, Evangelical believers have stood opposed to the fallacious claims and authority of the Holy See. Evangelicals are entrenched in their opposition to Rome's claim that

Christ gave Peter and his successors the primary jurisdiction over both the Church universal and the entire world. In the following pages, I will detail the historical and biblical contradictions to papal affirmation.

The Procession of Papal History

In seeking to deny the authority and infallibility of the pope, history's record of papal indiscretion will illuminate their darkness. The activity, morality and theology of a procession of Popes will act as a useful corrective to the inflated claims of the papacy. The story of the Holy See is anything but heroic. The record shows an unbelievable soap opera of lust, madness and murder. Throughout the centuries, papal behavior consistently abused its power, seeking to destroy those who threatened their political and religious hegemony. Among Peter's supposed successors are included mass murderers and master criminals. Are these to be considered in the line of the apostles as heads over the church of Jesus Christ?

The checkered history of the papacy is indeed one of the best arguments against the legitimacy of the papal office. Sir Winston Churchill, British prime minister and writer, in arguing against the policy of another member of the House of Commons said, "History will say that the right honourable gentleman was wrong in this matter. I know it will, because I shall write the history."[8] Rome, having written its own history in the lives of its Popes, has shown itself to be wrong in the matter of papal authority and infallibility. A careful exposé of papal history will yield a number of self incriminating pieces of evidence that will act as a saw laid to the legs of Peter's chair.

The Historical Fallacy of the Papacy

History does not support the Romanist claim that an unbroken papal line of succession extends from Peter to the present incumbent. A major breach for papal advocates is found in the lack of evidence that the Bishop of Rome held universal jurisdiction over the Church during the first five centuries. For six centuries following the time of Christ, none of the regional churches attempted to exercise authority over any of the other regional churches. The early ecumenical councils were composed of delegates from various churches who met on the level ground of equality.

Also deserving scrutiny it the roll call of Popes produced by the Roman Catholic Church. On several occasions it has had to be edited, with a considerable number of those formerly listed as Popes now listed as anti-Popes. Is it not stretching the bounds of truthfulness for Catholicism to claim and name with supposed certainty a list of Popes from Peter to the present one?

Norman Geisler and Ralph MacKenzie make telling comments on this very point when they write concerning the historical contradiction of a pope and an anti-pope existing at the same time:

> "Another riddle of Roman Catholicism is the scandalous specter of having more than one infallible pope at the same time—a pope and a anti-pope. The Oxford Dictionary of the Christian Church says 'there have been about thirty-five anti-popes in the history of the Church.' How can there be two infallible and opposing popes at the same time? Which is the true pope? Since there is no infallible list of popes or even an infallible way to determine who is the infallible pope, the system has a serious logical problem."[9]

Alongside this historical fallacy of an unbroken line of Popes, there is historically a significant problem of disagreement among the Church Fathers concerning the primacy of Peter and the office of pope. It is a simple fact that history is in disharmony with an interpretation of Matthew 16:18 that decrees the establishment of the papacy upon the rock Peter. Herbert Carson underscores this when he states:

> "Launoy, a seventeenth-century French Roman Catholic scholar, did a useful statistical survey of the varying views. Seventeen of the Fathers believed that the rock was Peter. Forty-four of them considered that it was Peter's faith, which had been expressed in his confession that Jesus was the Christ, the Son of the living God. Sixteen of them said that the rock was Christ and eight claimed that it referred to all the apostles. If the unanimity of the fathers is the prerequisite to understanding the word 'rock' then we are at an impasse!"[10]

Again we observe the illegitimacy of the Roman Catholic Church's historical argument of an unbroken line of Popes. Is it not strange that Rome, the champion of Church tradition, finds little comfort in the writings of the Church Fathers for such a crucial doctrine as the papacy?

In closing this point I would be remiss to overlook the question of Peter's bishopric at Rome. Did Peter ever serve as the Bishop of Rome? One can search the Scripture in vain to find any reference of Peter's leadership over the Church at Rome. If Peter were indeed the Bishop of Rome, is it not striking in his correspondence to the Church at Rome that Paul omitted Peter? His omission may have stemmed from the fact that he had yet to emerge, hence the absence of his name. But much later, when Paul actually stepped foot in Rome, there was a welcome from the saints but still no sign of Peter. When Paul, much later still, wrote his prison letters from Rome to believers in Ephesus, Philippi and Colosse, he sent greetings from the Christians in Rome. In his letter to the Colossians there is quite a register of names but no reference to Peter. Finally, when Paul wrote to Timothy in the anticipation of near death only Luke was with him, all others had abandoned ship. Where was Bishop Peter?

The Moral Iniquity of the Papacy

It is difficult to embrace the high sounding claims of the papacy given the historical account of vile papal behavior. As noted earlier, the story of the papacy is a horror show of madness, mayhem and murder, and is a damning contradiction to the biblical account of true Church leadership. Throughout the New Testament, Peter and Paul characterize the God appointed leaders of the Church as men of ethical integrity, moral fiber, sexual purity, doctrinal orthodoxy and financial balance (cf. 1 Peter 5:1-5, 1 Tim. 3:1-7). Christian leaders, serving as shepherds of Christ's flock, are admonished to love that which is good (Titus 1:8). Looking objectively at the line and lives of the Popes, history's account of their behavior belies any claim to papal purity. The legitimacy of the papacy has been damaged by the illegitimacy of the Popes themselves. How can a man stand in the line of Peter when he lives outside the circle of biblical Christ-like leadership? How is it that a man who lives like the devil can continue to claim to be the supposed Vicar of Christ (Isaiah 52:11)?

"Pornocracy" is the name given to the 10th-century papacy by the chronicler Liudprand, a bishop of Cremona. During that era, two powerful and cunning women—Theodora Theophylact and her daughter, Marozia—succeeded in having six Popes appointed over their lifetimes. Through those titular men, the two women ruled the Church and Rome itself.

Theodora, the wife of a powerful Roman judge, initially garnered influence because her daughter was the mistress of Pope Sergius III (904-11), who fathered Marozia's first child while she was still in her early teens. Following Sergius' death, Theodora exercised great influence in the election of three Popes, including the Archbishop of Ravenna, a family ally who may also have been Theodora's lover.

After her mother's death Marozia rose to power and masterminded the overthrow of John X. She allowed two inconsequential Popes to rule for a short time until her son, Pope Sergius' bastard child, was old enough to assume the papacy. Marozia's scorned second son by her first marriage, Alberic, eventually foiled his mother's grandiose aspirations; he led a revolt against her and became Prince of Rome. A few years later, Alberic's son became pope at the age of 18. Uninterested in religion, John XII was ill-mannered, and rumors circulated that he turned the papal residence into a whorehouse.

Another example of the moral iniquity that has marked the history of the papacy is found in a story related to Pope Stephen VI. In 897, Pope Stephen VI dug up the corpse of his predecessor, Pope Formosus, and put the dead pontiff on trial. During Formosus' life, Stephen had harbored fierce personal and political hatred for him. He charged him with perjury, violating the canons and aspiring to the papacy. Dressed in full papal garb, the rotting corpse was propped up on a throne and a deacon was appointed to answer for him. Not surprisingly, Formosus was found guilty. All of his acts and ordinations were then considered void, and the three fingers on his right hand that he used for blessings were chopped off before his body was thrown into the Tiber.

Just as remarkable as the previous accounts, are the numerous deaths that many of the Popes have suffered. It is believed that Pope John VIII was the first pope to be assassinated. According to the *Annals of Fulda,* a history produced by a monastery in the German city by which it was given its name, the ill-fated pope was poisoned and then clubbed to death by his entourage. During the so-called "Iron Age of the Papacy" (867-964), powerful Roman families had popes elected and then killed according to political expediency. Seven of 26 pontiffs succumbed to vicious deaths in that era. Throughout history it is thought possible that 15 Popes died at the hands of murderers.

One might assume that the Roman Catholic Church would wish to conceal the accounts of evil Popes and hide them from public view. Yet, despite such infamy and iniquity, the above Popes and many more godless Vicars of Rome remain claimants to Peter's chair and are to be found on the Vatican's official list of Popes today. Not only does history decry every pope as a pretender, the biblical standards for Christian leadership disqualify such men.

The Theological Heresy of the Papacy

Continuing the critique against the historical claims of the papacy, I wish to highlight a glaring incompatibility between the assertions and the reality of papal authority . Considering the fact that the Church is the ground and pillar of truth (1 Tim. 3:15) is it not strange that the supposed Head of that Church (the pope) can historically be shown as theologically errant in so many areas with regard to biblical doctrine and revelation? In his letter to Titus, Paul writes that the Christian leader will be a minister dedicated to theological accuracy coupled with courage and a ability to refute those that contra-dict the Bible (Titus 1:9). If the occupants of the Petrine office were God's true representatives on earth, how could they endorse the following doctrines:

+ the equal authority of tradition
+ prayers for the dead
+ indulgences
+ transubstantiation (the mass)
+ the worship of saints
+ the elevation of Mary
+ the idolatrous veneration of objects
+ the existence of purgatory
+ the salvific value of meritorious works

How can these advocates of aberrant dogmas be said to carry the mantle of Apostolic authority and ministry? Quite plainly they cannot. The Popes have proven themselves to be false teachers who Peter warned would slip into the Church bringing with them destructive heresies, even denying the Lord that bought them (2 Peter 2:1-3).

Another example of papal arrogance is found in the titles bestowed upon them. These grandiose titles reinforce the per-ception that the papacy stands at variance with Scripture and therefore with Christ Himself.

The first of these titles is that of "the Holy Father." This title of the pope is the commonly shortened translation of the Latin title *Beatissimus Pater* (The Most Holy Father), and it refers to his position as the spiritual father of all the Christian faithful. While the title is used in Scripture none other than the Lord Jesus employs it. When these words escape from the lips of our Savior they do so in the context of a intimate prayer to His own Father on the eve of His death (John 17:11).

What should be evidently clear to all those who study Scripture, is that this title belongs uniquely to the Lord God Almighty. This is a title that the Scripture hangs around no ones neck but God's. Jesus warned us Himself about calling any man our father for we have one Father who is in heaven (Matt. 23:9). Is it not the height of arrogance on the part of Rome to take to its leader a designation reserved for God Himself?

The second of these titles is "Supreme Pontiff." Derived from the Latin *pontem facere*, "to build a bridge," the title of Supreme Pontiff was reserved in ancient Rome for the emperor, who as head of the principal college of priests in Rome was seen as the bridge or bridge-builder between men and the gods. The title was given to the pope by Gratian in A.D. 375 to distinguish the Supreme Pastor of the sheepfold of the Church, as bridge-builder between God and man.

This title, as usurped by the papacy, stands in contrast to Hebrews, which proclaims and protects the singularity, sufficiency and supremacy of Christ's high priestly rule over the Church. Peter tells us that Christ alone has both the ability as God and the acceptance before the Father to bring us to God, having been put to death in the flesh but made alive by the Spirit (1 Pet. 3:18). Christ alone is the Shepherd and Overseer of our soul's salvation (1 Pet. 2:25).

The third of these titles is "the Vicar of Christ." This is a title meaning "one who takes the place of Christ," and is often used of the Bishop of Rome in particular. It was first used by the Roman Synod of A.D. 495 to refer to Pope Gelasius. It was introduced into Roman Curial usage, to refer to the Bishop of Rome, during the reign of Eugene III (1145-1153).

Once again we find the Church of Rome moving against Scripture in the assignation of this title to the pope. The only vicar of Christ on earth is the blessed Holy Spirit (John 14:16, 26). Jesus said this of the Holy Spirit, not of Peter, not of anyone (John 16:13-14). Of note alongside this is the truth that Peter referred to himself in much more humble terms as "an apostle" (1 Pet. 1:1) and "fellow-elder" (1 Pet. 5:1), not the supreme bishop, not the pope, or the Holy Father.

To those who may be thinking that the argument over titles is a straining at gnats, the words of Herbert Carson are once again rather pertinent:

> "So the papal titles are not simply somewhat grandiose designations which have evolved in the course of Christian history. They are rather a very grave usurpation of the titles of the Godhead. We bow and worship the Holy Father, our Creator, Lord and Judge. We come through the sole mediatorship of our Lord Jesus Christ, the Supreme Pontiff, the great High Priest (Heb. 4:15). We rejoice in the indwelling presence of the Holy Spirit, the Vicar of Christ, who makes the presence of the heavenly Christ a deep reality in our own experience. To take on our lips these great titles is to tread on holy ground as we are in the presence not of man, but of the triune God."[11]

Therefore, it must be said that to study the line of the Popes does not place one on a track back to the Bible but rather reveals a twisted tale of historical dishonesty, moral degradation and theological heterodoxy. The Popes have not been good shepherds of Christ's little flock but wolves in shepherds clothing (Acts 20:28-30). Hirelings who have sold the truth and their own souls for power, prestige and possessions (John 10:12-13; 2 Pet. 2:1-3).

It is reported that while Raphael was painting his famous Vatican frescoes a couple of cardinals happened to stop by to watch and criticize. "The face of the apostle Paul is too red," said one. Raphael replied, "He blushes to see into whose hands the church has fallen."

The procession of Popes and the history of the papacy are an embarrassment to all that is called biblical Christianity. It is a blight on Christ's name, an injustice to Peter and a corruption of the gospel. If you think that is too strong then listen to the words of John Calvin as he rejects the idea of the papacy in the strongest and yet soundest possible terms:

> "I deny that See to be Apostolical, wherein nought is seen but a shocking apostasy—I deny him to be the vicar of Christ, who, in furiously persecuting the gospel, demonstrates by his conduct that he is Antichrist—I deny him to be the successor of Peter, who is doing his utmost to demolish every edifice that Peter built—and I deny him to be the head of the Church, who by his tyranny lacerates and dis-members the Church, after dissevering her from Christ, her true and only head."[12]

In another context Calvin again sharply criticizes the preten-sions of the pope to be the leader of the Church when he wrote:

> "Will our mediators then have the audacity to give the name of Christ's Vicar to one who, after routing the truth of Christ, extinguishing the light of the gospel, overthrowing the salvation of men, corrupt-ing and profaning the worship of God, and tram-

pling down and tearing to pieces all his sacred traditions, domineers like a barbarian?"[13]

In seeking to contradict the claims of the See of Rome we have indeed been served well by history. The history of the papacy undermines the legitimacy of the papacy. Rome may wish to draw a straight line back to Peter and paint a rather flattering picture of papal life, but the facts betray that and show the history of the Popes to be a crooked path of behavior and belief written in the black ink of sin.

The Pretension of Papal Authority

The Roman Catholic writer James Cardinal Gibbons, once archbishop of Baltimore wrote in his book entitled *Faith of our Fathers* regarding the papacy:

> "The Catholic Church teaches that our Lord conferred on St. Peter the first place honor and jurisdiction in the government of his whole church, and that same spiritual authority has always resided in the popes, or bishops of Rome, as being the successors of St Peter. Consequently, to be true followers of Christ all Christians, both among the clergy and laity, must be in communion with the See of Rome, where Peter rules in person of his successor."[14]

Cardinal Gibbons continued this theme as he wrote:

> "The word Peter, in the Syro Chaldaic tongue, which our Saviour spoke means a rock. The sentence in Matthew 16 runs thus in that language: 'Thou art a rock, and on this rock I will build my church.' Indeed all respectable Protestant commentators have now abandoned, and even ridicule the absurdity of apply-

ing the word rock to anyone but Peter; as the sentence can bear no other construction, unless our good Lord's grammar and common sense are called into question. Jesus our Lord, founded one Church, which He was pleased to build on Peter. Therefore, any church that does not recognize Peter as the foundation Rock is not the church of Christ, and therefore cannot stand, for it is not the work of God. This is plain. Would to God that all would see it aright and with eyes free from prejudice"[15]

Is Cardinal Gibbons right? Is it the mark of a spiritual man to open his eyes to the truth that the See of Rome is where Peter rules in the person of his successor? Is it the measure of a biblical Church to recognize a Christ ordained foundation in Peter the rock? Have Protestant exegetes abandoned any other interpretation of Matthew 16:18 other than Peter as the rock? Can it be said to be a plain fact that the Popes, as Peter's successors, are the kings of Christ's ecclesiastical castle and the guardians of the gate to God's kingdom?

Also of note is Cardinal Gibbons' honesty in outlining the high stakes involved in these questions from a Roman Catholic position that declares authentic followers of Christ to be those in obeisance to papal authority.

In seeking to answer these vital questions, I wish to target the concept of succession and Gibbons' citation of Matthew 16:18. If the Bible does not teach apostolic succession, or Peter as the rock, then two keystones of Catholic theology are loose and threaten to bring the whole structure of this teaching crashing down.

The Succession Argument

As underscored by James Gibbons, the Roman Catholic Church posits the doctrine of apostolic succession, whereby the church's duly consecrated bishops, supremely the bishop of Rome, are the legitimate heirs of Peter and apostles. *The Pocket Catholic Dictionary* defines Apostolic Succession this way:

> "The method by which the episcopacy has been derived from the Apostles to the present day. Succession means successive consecration by the laying on of hands, performing the functions of the Apostles, receiving their commission in a lineal sequence from the Apostles, succession in episcopal sees traced back to the Apostles, and successive communion with the Apostolic See, i.e., the Bishop of Rome."[16]

This hypothesis of an unbroken line of apostolic successors to Peter is both historically and biblically unsound. The following will catalog the most salient arguments that stand in contradiction to this assertion of owning Peter's mantle:

As written earlier history, provides no record that Peter was ever Bishop of Rome therefore breaking the loop of succession before it begins. If Peter was not Bishop of Rome how then could he have had successors? Irenaeus, Bishop of Lyons (178-200), provided a list of the first 12 Bishops of Rome, identifying Linus as the first. Peter's name was conspicuously absent. In addition, Eusebius of Caesaria, the Father of church history, never mentioned Peter as Bishop of Rome. He simply pointed out that Peter made a trip to Rome about "the end of his days" and was crucified there. Papal succession has no historical merit when it identifies Peter as the first pope.

Scripture provides no indication that there is a difference in authority between bishops and elders. For example, while Acts 6:6 speaks of the apostles laying their hands on the seven at Jerusalem, Timothy received his gift when the elders laid hands upon him (1 Tim. 4:14). The New Testament reveals that with the passing of the Apostles (Eph. 2:20) elders took leadership of the church (Acts 14:23; Titus 1:5) and that title is used interchangeably with bishop in the New Testament (Acts 20:17, 28; 1 Pet. 5:1-3). Biblically speaking, the church leader is simultaneously a shepherd (pastor), overseer (bishop), and elder over the congregation. The New Testament is silent concerning a hierarchy of bishops in apostolic succession, standing over the local church leaders.

Papal advocates also give insufficient attention to Christ's direct exercise of lordship over the church. When He installed Paul without any intermediary, there were no other apostles involved, and Paul argued this point when he justified his apostleship (Gal. 1:15-17). Now if Paul received his office directly from God, might not others as well? In this one case apostolic authority does not rest upon a previous apostolic authority.

The New Testament distinguishes the apostles from other Christians as those who had been with the Lord from the beginning and had seen his resurrected body (Acts 1:21-22; 1 Cor. 9:1). There have been no successors with the same qualifications, position, or authority. The apostolic eyewitnesses to the Messiah's incarnation had a unique foundational ministry. But after the first century there were no eyewitnesses of the incarnate, crucified, and risen Messiah.

To expand on this point, the qualifications for a man to be an apostle of Jesus Christ were only true if the following happened in his life:

- He must, as we have already noted, have been an eyewitness of the resurrection of Jesus Christ. He personally saw the risen Lord.

- Jesus Christ must have personally taught him the divine truth, the Gospel (Gal. 1:11- 12; 1 Cor. 15:3).

- He received the gift of divine inspiration, or that the influence of the Holy Spirit made him errorless in the communication of the Word (John 14:26, 16:13; 1 Cor. 2:10-13, 14:37; 1 Thess. 2:13; 1 John 4:6).

- He was bestowed with the power of working various types of miracles, thus confirming his mission (2 Cor. 12:12; Rom. 15:18-19; Heb. 2:3; Acts 5:12, 14:3).

- He had the ability to confer miraculous gifts on others (Acts 8:18, 19:6).

- He could speak words of judgment in the name of the Lord and have them miraculously executed (John 20:23; Acts 5:3-11,13:10; 1 Cor 5:3-5; 1 Tim. 1:20).

- He exercised a position of authority over local churches and pastors, demanding obedience and compliance (1 Cor. 5:3-5; 2 Cor.10:6-8; 2 Thess. 3:14; Phil. 3:17-18).

- He taught nothing that was contradictory to the Word of God (Gal. 1:8-9)

- He preached the Word with great power and fruitfulness (John 15:16, 1 Cor. 9:2; 2 Cor 3:2; 1 Thess. 1:5).

- His life was one of holiness, humility, self-discipline and selfless dedication (1 Cor. 9:16-22; 2 Cor. 6:1-10; 11:22-33; 1 Pet. 5:1-4; 1 John 1:1-7).[17]

Which pope claims to possess all the above credentials? If they do only then are they worthy claimants to the mantle of

Peter and the Apostles of Christ. Which pope, past or present, has physically seen the Lord and been commissioned to be His witness? The office of apostle by its very nature defies permanence within the church. Those who claim to possess it or inherit its mantle without exhibiting its characteristics are deceived, and those who follow them do so to their own destruction.

The great American theologian, Charles Hodge, puts the importance of rightly answering this issue, when he stated:

> "The signs of an apostle were the insignia of the apostleship; those things which by divine appointment were made the evidence of a mission from God. When these were present an obligation rested on all who witnessed them to acknowledge the authority of those who bore those insignia. When they were absent, it was, on the one hand, an act of sacrilege to claim the apostleship; and, on the other, an act of apostasy from God to admit its possession. To acknowledge the claims of those who said they were apostles and were not, was (and is) to turn from God to the creature, to receive as divine what was in fact human or Satanic."[18]

Knitted together, these arguments against apostolic succession form a fourfold cord that is not easily broken. There is no pope because apostolic succession does not exist. The acknowledgement of the papacy is turning from God and His Word to the creature and his tradition.

The Scripture Argument

The Roman Catholic Church, using the teaching found in Matthew 16:18, insists that Peter is the rock and first pope upon which Christ promised to build His church. In James

Gibbons' mind any other interpretation is at variance with our Lord and the good sense of His plain speech. But is that really the case?

While not seeking to rob the Apostle Peter of any honor due him, it is my contention that the best interpretation of Matthew 16:18 lies in seeing Christ as the rock and not Peter. It is my hope to prove through sound hermeneutic principles that this verse is textual quicksand for the papist and his papal dream. When passed through the hermeneutic grid this text is christological in nature and focus, not papal.

Consider the following principles and the christological interpretation they yield.

• The Principal of Historical Appropriateness

One key rule in accurately interpreting the content and meaning of a passage is an understanding of how the intended recipients would have understood that passage. It is not hard to imagine that those who heard Jesus, namely the apostles to whom the question of Jesus' identity was addressed (Matthew 16:15), would have understood the imagery of the rock (Gk. petra) as pointing to God (Deut. 32:4; 1 Sam. 2:2; Ps. 18:31). In this case God made manifest in flesh the person of His Son, Jesus Christ. The cultural and historical environment would seem to support the proposed view of Christ as the rock. Matthew wrote his Gospel for a Jewish audience and he expected his readers to be familiar with the Old Testament imagery. As William Barclay notes, "One thing is clear. To call anyone a rock was the greatest of compliments; and no Jew who knew his Old Testament could ever use the phrase without his thoughts turning to God, who alone was the true rock of his defense and salvation."[19]

◆ The Principle of Historical Background

In examining Matthew's gospel and its purpose, more evidence is uncovered to support Jesus as *this rock* upon which the church will be built. There can be little doubt that the primary purpose of the book is the presentation of Christ as Israel's Messiah. As S. Lewis Johnson stated, "this atmosphere surrounds the book from the early question of the wise men, 'Where is he that is born King of the Jews?' to the final answer upon the superscription of the cross, 'This is the King of the Jews' (2:2, 27:37)."[20] The rejection of Israel's Messiah is another constant theme in this gospel. In no other gospel are the attacks against Jesus portrayed as strongly. In Matthew's account of Calvary, for example, no thief repents, and no loved ones or friends are seen at the foot of the cross. In His death, even God (27:46) forsook him. The shadow of rejection is never lifted from the story. The reality of that and its relevance to our issue is clearly seen in Jesus' application of the parable of the landowner (Matt. 21:42). Christ presents Himself as the stone which the builders, namely Israel, rejected but whom God has intended to become the chief cornerstone (Ps. 118:22-23). Therefore, to combine Matthew 16:18 and 21:42 within the flow and direction of this gospel brings one to see that the foundation stone of the church was a stumbling stone to Israel. A theme and contrast picked up elsewhere in the New Testament (1 Cor. 1:23, 3:11), even by Peter himself (Acts 4:8-12, 1 Pet. 2:4-8). Historically then, one of the purposes of the writer of this gospel is to present God's cornerstone and the nation's subsequent rejection of it, and that points again to the christilogical nature of this text. The rock revealed is the stone rejected.

• The Principle of Context

As someone has said, a text without a context becomes a pretext. Therefore, we must examine this biblical jewel in its original setting. Without a doubt, the context of verse eighteen is the true identity of Jesus as revealed to Peter and through Peter in his confession of Christ as the Son of the living God (Matt. 16:13-20). As James White says, "Any interpretation that takes the focus off of Jesus as Messiah is missing the point"[21] The context is not about Peter, it is about Jesus. It starts with a question that Jesus raises about his identity: "Who do men say that the Son of man is?" (16:13). It reaches a climax with Peter's declaration: "You are the Christ, the Son of the living God" (16:16). It concludes with the Lord warning his disciples "that they should tell no one that He was the Christ" (16:20). Therefore, when the Lord says, "And I also say to you that you are Peter and on this rock I will build my church and the gates of Hades shall not prevail against it," the focus has not changed. The subject of the passage *remains* the identity of Christ, found in the confession of Peter. In other words, the Lord Jesus as "the Christ, the Son of the living God," would be the solid rock upon which the Christian faith would rest. Jesus is not speaking of the identity of Peter; He is still speaking about himself and His church. Romanism misses the fact that the focus remains on Christ the whole way through.

In seeing Christ as the rock revealed in Peter's confession, support is found in the context again, in that, while the Lord is addressing Peter directly, He changes from direct address to the third person, "this rock," when speaking of Peter's confession. In making this very point, Stanley Toussaint says, "In the first place, The Lord could have easily said 'on you' to remove the ambiguity. Why should the Lord use the pronoun this if He were speaking directly to Peter as He is in the immediately pre-ceding and following contexts?"[22]

Not to be overlooked in this context either is the fact that Peter was the spokesman for the Twelve when he answered a question addressed to them all (Matt. 16:15-16, 16:20). Also Christ does not grant to Peter anything He is not willing to give to the other disciples (Matt. 16:19, 18:18), which again mitigates against any singular focus on Peter in this context. From a practical standpoint, it is impractical that Peter could be such a rock, for in the immediate context Peter is anything but sure and solid. He who was touched by heaven was also used by hell (Matt. 16:23).

- The Principle of Word Study

A word study of the terms found in Matthew 16:18, Peter (Gk. Petros) and rock (Gk. petra) will help shed light upon the meaning of the text. "Peter" in Greek is *Petros*. The word is masculine in gender and means stone, or a piece of rock. In Christ's statement that He would build His church upon the rock, He used *Petra*, which differs from *Petros*. Found sixteen times in the New Testament, it is used eleven times as designation for a big boulder-type rock. The other five times it is used metaphorically of Christ. *Petros* and *petra* always seem to be used in a different sense, which certainly appears to be the case in this passage.[23] On the basis of this distinction Robert Lightner comments, "Very likely as Christ spoke, he pointed first to Peter when he said, 'You are Peter.' Then he pointed to himself as he said, 'And upon this rock I will build my church.'"[24] It seems a play on words was used here keeping the focus on our Lord as the previous point concerning con-text underscored.

+ The Principle of the Priority of the Original Languages

In an attempt to scuttle the distinction brought out in the Greek, papal protagonists point to the lack of distinction in Aramaic between Peter and the rock (Aram. *kepa*) and the language's possible underlying use in this context. This, however, is a red herring in light of the principle of the priority of the original languages. Research does not rule out the possibility that Jesus spoke Greek, which was not unexpected of a Galilean who dealt frequently with Gentiles to converse in their language (Matt. 4:15; 21:11). Added to that is the reality that the inspired New Testament Scriptures were written in Greek, not Aramaic. What Jesus might have said in Aramaic is conjecture and in light of the previous point may even be redundant. Furthermore, if the Aramaic is clear but the Greek inadequate or confusing, why did not the Holy Spirit simply import the Aramaic words? There are many such examples in the New Testament. Examples of Aramaic words in the New Testament include *raca* (Matt. 5:22), Eloi (Mark 15:34), and *Rabboni* (John 20:16). Or why did not the Holy Spirit just repeat the word *petros*?

As Robert Gromacki points out, "Since there is only one word in the Aramaic for rock many have argued that Jesus must have regarded Peter as the foundation. If that is so, then why did Matthew, directed by the Holy Spirit, use two Greek words instead of one? Christ evidently made a play on words. Peter was a small rock hewn out of the large rock mountain. Peter recognized this difference (1 Pet. 2:4-8)."[25]

+ The Principle of Cross-Reference

One of the strongest arguments for Christ's primacy in Matthew 16:18 rests in the principle that Scripture interprets Scripture. As G. Campbell Morgan underlines, "If we trace the figurative use of the word rock through the Hebrew Scriptures, we find that it is never used symbolically of man but always of God."[26] In the Old Testament the word rock (Heb. sur) is applied repeatedly to God himself (Deut. 32:4, 32:31; 1 Sam. 2:2; 2 Sam. 22:32; Ps. 18:31; Isa. 44:8; Dan. 2:31-44).

The wider context of the New Testament also confirms that Jesus, not Peter, is the rock. Peter himself refers to Christ as the rock more than once (Acts 4:10-11; 1 Pet. 2:6-8). Paul also refers to Christ by the Greek word *petra* (Rom. 9:33; 1 Cor. 10:4). In 1 Cor. 3:11, Paul emphasizes that Christ is the *foundation* upon which the church is built. In Ephesians, Paul speaks of the church "having been built upon foundation of the apostles and the prophets, Christ Himself being the cornerstone" (Ephesians 2:20). Paul pictures Christ as the principal stone and the apostles and prophets as secondary stones. William Webster puts it well when he says, "To whom then do the Scriptures, Both Old Testament and New Testament, consistently point as the rock, the stone, the cornerstone and the foundation upon which the Church would be built? Jesus Christ the Lord, the Son of the living God, he alone is the rock of our salvation."[27]

Historically, contextually, grammatically and scripturally, the christological view has got strong legs to stand on.

• The Principle of the Clarity of Scripture

As one investigates the pertinent issues involved with Matthew 16:18, the clearest and most logical conclusion is to interpret the text as referring to Christ as revealed in Peter's confession. Although it is correct to see Peter as a pivotal character in the founding of the church, he along with the other apostles are but secondary stones compared to Christ the chief cornerstone. Other considerations regarding Peter's subsequent behavior most also be borne in mind. Peter never claimed any authority over the other apostles, but rather denied it (1 Pet. 1:1, 5:1-3; Acts 10:25-26). His actions, especially in relation to Christ, did not conform to his being the one on whom the church was to be built. Immediately following Christ's promise to build the church Peter denied that Christ should even die (Matt. 16:22). Furthermore, Peter slept in the garden while Christ prayed, and later denied him openly. If Peter was the foundation of the church, why was he not more active in the choice to replace Judas among the apostles (Acts 1:15-26)? Why was James the leader of the great Jerusalem council and not Peter (Acts 15)?

J.C. Ryle calls time on this debate when he comments insightfully, "To speak of an erring, fallible child of Adam as the foundation of the spiritual temple, is very unlike the ordinary language of Scripture."[28]

Unlike the papal rendering of this text, the christological interpretation clearly gives place to our Lord Jesus, which is in agreement with the whole Canon of Scripture.

> A businessman who was accustomed to presiding at business functions was called upon suddenly to offi-ciate at a church affair. He was used to the normal procedures of a business gathering when the minutes were read and he would move their adoption and approval. Somebody read the Scriptures, and this man absent-mindedly got up and said, "If there are no corrections, the Scriptures will stand as read."[29]

In light of the pretension of papal authority the Scriptures will stand as read. There is no ground for believing that the Popes are the apostolic successors to Peter. Neither is their reason to accept Cardinal Gibbons bravado in declaring that every respectable Protestant commentator has now abandoned and even ridiculed the absurdity of applying the word rock to anyone but Peter. Peter was indeed a pillar in the church (Gal. 2:9) but Christ alone is the chief cornerstone and head (Eph. 1:22-23, 2:20-22).

The Presumption of Papal Infallibility

In taking a last bite on this bone of contention between Evangelicalism and Romanism, it is necessary to engage the question of papal infallibility. According to the Faith of the Vatican the teaching magisterium of bishops is infallible when officially outlining and defining faith and morals for believers. One manifestation of this doctrine is popularly known as the "infallibility of the pope," which was declared a dogma in 1870 at *Vatican I*. The New Catechism states:

> "The Roman Pontiff, head of the college of bishops, enjoys this infallibility (professing the true faith without error) in virtue of his office, when, as supreme pastor and teacher of all the faithful—who confirms his brethren in the faith—he proclaims by a definitive act a doctrine pertaining to faith and morals ... The infallibility promised to the church is also present in the body of bishops when, together with Peter's successor, they exercise the supreme Magisterium, above all in an Ecumenical Council."[30]

Thus, when the pope speaks *ex cathedra* (from the throne) as the official interpreter of faith and morals, by virtue of his supreme apostolic authority and divine assistance, he is possessed of a freedom from error in teaching the universal church on matters of faith and morals. For the Catholic, this applies to revealed and may also include unrevealed teaching that is in any way connected with revelation.

The condition of the infallibility is that the pope speaks *ex cathedra*. When he speaks *ex cathedra* it is required that: a) he have the intention of declaring something unchangeably true; and b) he speaks as shepherd and teacher of all the faithful with the full weight of his apostolic authority, and not merely as a private theologian or even merely for the people of Rome or some particular segment of the Church of God. A papal pronouncement in this context with these conditions met is irreformable in itself and not in virtue of the consent of the church.

Based on papal infallibility, Catholicism loves to boast that they and they alone have a heavenly spokesman on earth who guides them in matters of the kingdom. She pities the poor blind Protestant who is left to grope in the shadow of uncertainty. An open heart and an open Bible before the Holy Spirit is insufficient in the mind of Rome.

The reality of this was illustrated to me some time ago when along with a friend, I attended a debate in Fullerton, California between Tim Staples and James White over the issue of *Sola Scriptura*. The Catholic apologist Tim Staples could not keep himself from taunting James White about the assumed fragmentary nature of Protestantism supposedly brought about by the din of competing theological views. Which from his viewpoint showed the weakness of the *Sola Scriptura* position. Mr. Staples' intended point by implication was that Protestants were losing out by turning a deaf ear to the unifying and certain voice of the papacy. Tim Staples appealed to the orphan Protestants in the audience to realize that in the pope one finds the oracle of God on matters of faith and morals. Is Tim Staples right? Is the pope God's press secretary? Do his pronouncements lay a straight path to the truth?

In answering the boast of Mr. Staples and confronting the dogma of *Vatican I*, let us mark the truth that papal infallibility is a doctrine that finds itself on the wrong side of both history and theology.

On the Wrong Side of History

In charting history it is interesting to observe that although the Roman Church was of great importance in the third century, the Council of Nicea (325 A.D.) knew nothing of the Roman Bishop's authority over the whole church. It was the controversies that began in the fourth century that led to the increased importance of the Bishop of Rome in matters of doctrine. The Synod of Sardica (343) permitted a bishop who had been disposed the right to appeal to the Roman Bishop. Innocent I (404) claimed supreme right to judge in all "the more grave and momentous cases."[31] In 451, at the Council of Chalcedon, Pope Leo I formulated the famous statement on the hypostatic union. This definitive statement of this doctrine increased the respect and authority of the bishop. However, despite the bishop's increased prestige, the writings of early church leaders give neither indication nor suggestion that he was the infallible head of the church. Early church statesmen such as Ireneus (c.200) who wrote against many heresies, Tertullian (c.220), or Gregory the great (c.600) who was a powerful pope and ardent defender of Catholic traditions, never wrote nor taught that the pope had infallible authority. Supporting this point, Dr. Geddes MacGregor states that:

> "in spite of the early recognition of the importance of the See of Rome . . . there is not even a hint of an ex cathedra notion before the eleventh century. Even in the fourteenth, in the lively debates on the nature of papal pronouncements, no such common notion was being either combated or upheld."[32]

This is interesting to note in light of the fact that papal power had reached its pinnacle in the eleventh, twelfth and thirteenth centuries under Hildebrand (1073-85) and Innocent III (1198-1216).

Again we find that historical fact and Vatican assertions are anything but partners. Papal infallibility is another feather-weight doctrine from the See of Rome when weighed in the scales of history.

On the Wrong Side of Theology

In addition to the lack of historical framework, the Bible itself provides no ground for believing in a papacy as we noted. Furthermore, the issue of infallibility is severely challenged by examples of heretical teaching by Popes throughout the centuries. An example of this is held up to ridicule in the words of Geisler and MacKenzie:

> Pope Honorius I (AD. 525-638) was condemned by the Sixth General Council for teaching the monothelite heresy (that there was only one will in Christ). Even Catholic expert Ludwig Ott admits that Pope Leo II (682-683) confirmed his anthema-tization. This being the case, we are left with the incredible situation of an infallible pope teaching fallible, yea, heretical, doctrine. If the papal teaching office is infallible, that is, if it cannot mislead on doctrine and ethics, then how could a papal teaching be heretical? What is more, this was a serious heresy—one relating to the nature of Christ. To claim that the pope was not infallible in this occasion is only to further undermine the doctrine of infallibility. How can one know when his doctrinal pronouncements

are infallible and when they are not? There is no infallible test. And without such a test, how can a Roman Catholic Church provide infallible guidance on doctrine and morals? If the pope can be fallible on one doctrine, then why not others?"[33]

Examples abound of biblical irregularity such as in 1633 when Urban VIII condemned the astronomer Galileo for saying that the earth moves round the sun, and warned him that he would be tortured if he did not conform to the papal pronounce-ment on this matter. But wait a minute you say, this was not a matter of Scripture but of science, and therefore not an issue of infallibility. That would be true if it were not for the fact that the pope declared the Copernican theory to be false and contrary to the Word of God. The passing of the years has shown that papal condemnation to be completely out of step with the cosmological facts. It must be underlined, therefore, that the Bible itself on this matter was not wrong but rather the erroneous interpretation the Roman Catholic Church had adapted.

In both citations the question regarding the possibility or impossibility of the Roman Church erring in her interpretation and teaching of essential Christian truth is answered. The Church of Rome and her Popes can err and have erred. History records more than one infallible pope living at the same time and more than one pope who taught heretical doctrines.

Papal Infallibility is really the capstone on the entire denial of *Sola Scriptura*. James White hits the nail on the head when he writes:

> We are told we can find an infallible guide in the per-son of the pope, one who can speak for the Church without question on matters of faith and morals. It is impossible not to point out the simple fact that in this

doctrine one finds the final step in a process that began with the first addition of human tradition to the Scriptures: the process of replacing the Holy Spirit of God with a structure of man's making. Before one reacts too strongly to that statement, consider well to what I refer. Who is to take Christ's place when He ascends to heaven? The Holy Spirit. Who is to teach Christians and lead them into truth? The Holy Spirit. Who is to guide Christians and enlighten their minds to the truths of God? The Holy Spirit. It is not enough to say, Well, the Church does all these things with the help of the Spirit." The truth of the matter is that the Holy Spirit's role has been taken over by the hierarchy of the Church, and the individual Christian is subject to that authority as a matter of his eternal salvation."[34]

The purpose of this chapter has been to scuttle such pretensions and intentions. Both on historical and biblical grounds we utterly reject the arrogance of a man who purports to be in the place of Christ and able to duplicate the ministry of the Holy Spirit.

What conclusions can we draw from the facts presented in this chapter? a) The apostles, including Peter, did not recognize Peter as pope. b) Matthew 16:18 is christological in nature not papal. c) Apostolic succession is a hoax played on men by those hungry for power. d) The emergence of the papacy did not occur until long after the church had been established. e) "Infallible" statements have been known to contradict Scripture. f) It is highly unlikely that Peter was ever bishop in Rome.

When Alexander the Great visited Diogenes the cynic, he asked what he could do for Diogenes. The cynic answered that there was only one thing which

Alexander could do for Diogenes, and that was to abstain from standing between him and the sun.

There have been many great and mighty men who like to stand between God and man, but they only obscure man's vision of God. The Popes of Rome have sadly been among that number. Jesus Christ however is the only one who can build a bridge to God and introduce sinful men to his Holy Father. Christ has designated the Holy Spirit alone to be his vicar on earth and anyone pretending otherwise is not of the Spirit of Christ.

That is why this book sounds an alarm over the Evangelical meltdown with regard to Rome and specifically to this issue. One must be concerned in light of the information shared to find men like Dr. Billy Graham singing the praises of the pope. When the pope visited the United States in 1979, Dr. Graham in a newspaper article described John Paul II "as the greatest religious leader of the modern world, and one of the greatest moral and spiritual leaders of this century." Dr. Graham continued in this fashion for pages, and then concluded:

> "During his visit to America Pope John Paul II was indeed a bridge builder, and that is something that this world desperately needs. In a world which often seems to have lost its way, his voice will continue to remind us of our responsibilities to each other— and to God."[35]

While we surely would not disagree with Dr. Graham that the world is in a spiritual fog and in need of a guiding light, we do know based on the study material of this chapter that the Popes, including John Paul II, have failed to truly light the path to God. How can an office that has been party to the extinguishing of the light of the gospel, the eclipsing of Christ and the Holy Spirit prove to be a lighthouse for lost men?

1. Craig Brian Larson, *Contemporary Illustrations for Preachers, Teachers and Writers*, (Grand Rapids: Baker Books, 1996) 113.

2. Henry Betteson, ed., *Documents of the Christian Church*, (London: Oxford Univ., 1963) 116. Vatican I after affirming that the bishops of Rome are the rightful rulers over the Church to whom all Christians must submit in matters of faith and morals and discipline states, "This is the teaching of Catholic truth, from which no one can deviate without loss of faith and salvation", cited by Philip Schaff, The Creeds of Christendom (New York: Harper, 1877) II:263.

3. John A McHugh and Charles J Callan, Trans., *Catechism of the Council of Trent for Parish Priests*, (New York: Joseph F. Wagner, Inc., 1937) 333.

4. *Catechsim of the Catholic Church*, (Missouri: Ligouri Publications, 1994) para. 880- 882.

5. Ibid., para. 936-937.

6. Ibid., para. 552-553, 1129.

7. *New York Times*, November 25, 1985.

8. Lance Davidson, *The Wits Thesaurus*, (New York: Avon Books, 1994) 186.

9. Geisler and MacKenzie, *Roman Catholics and Evangelicals*, (Grand Rapids: Baker, 1995) 217.

10. Herbert Carson, *The Faith of the Vatican*, (England: Evangelical Press, 1996) 53.

11. Ibid., 50.

12. John Calvin, "The Neccessity of Reforming the Church," in *Selected Works of John Calvin, Tracts and Letters*, ed. H. Beveridge and J. Bonnet (Grand Rapids: Baker, 1983) 1:219f.

13. John Calvin, "The True Method of Giving Peace to Cristendom and Reforming the Church," in *Selected Works of John Calvin, Tracts and Letters*, 3:274.

14. John Cardinal Gibbons, *The Faith of our Fathers*, (Rockford, Ill.: Tan Books, 1980) 78.

15. Ibid., 81-82.

16. John A. Hardon, S.J. *Pocket Catholic Dictionary*, (New York: Image Books, 1985) 27.

17. Edward N. Gross, *Miracles, Demons and Spiritual Warfare*, (Grand Rapids: Baker, 1990) 53-54.

18. Charles Hodge, *An Exposition of the First Epistle to the Corinthians,* (Grand Rapids: Eerdmans) 290-291.

19. William Barclay, *The Gospel of Matthew,* Vol. 2, 140.

20. S.Lewis Johnson Jr, *The Argument of Matthew,* Bibliotheca Sacra, Oct, 1955, 143.

21. James White, *Roman Catholic Controversy,* (Minnesota: Bethany House Publishers, 1996) 117.

22. Stanley Toussaint, *Behold the King,* 202.

23. Abbott and Smith, *Manual Greek Lexicon of the New Testament,* 359; Colin Brown, *The New International Dictionary of the New Testament Theology,* Vol. 3, 381-388.

24. Robert Lightner, *Evangelical Theology,* (Grand Rapids: Baker, 1986) 230.

25. Robert Gromacki, *New Testament Survey,* (Grand Rapids: Baker, 1974) 84.

26. G.Campbell Morgan, *The Gospel According to Matthew,* 211.

27. William Webster, *The Church of Rome at the Bar of History,* (Edinburgh: Banner of Truth, 1995) 39.

28. J.C.Ryle, *Expository Thoughts on the Gospels,* Vol. 1, Matthew, 119.

29. Vance Havner, *On this Rock I Stand,* (Grand Rapids: Baker, 1987) 75.

30. *Catechism of the Catholic Church,* para. 891.

31. E.Sehling,"Pope. Papacy, Papal System," in the *New Schaff-Herzog Encyclopedia of Religious Knowledge,* 126.

32. Geddes MacGregor, *The Vatican Revolution* (Boston: Beacon Press, 1957) 137.

33. Geisler and MacKenzie, 213.

34. James White, 124.

35. *The Saturday Evening Post,* February 1980, vol. 252, number 1, Billy Graham, "The Pilgrim Pope: A Builder of Bridges," 72-75, 89.

CHAPTER 10

The Outstanding Difference

Romans 3:21-26.

The story is told of the immigrant who enlisted in the US army during World War II. Being a foreigner he had great difficulty with the English language. One day as the troop prepared for inspection the men realized that unless they gave this soldier some help, he would fail due to his speech problem. So one of the men said to him, "Now look, in a few days the general is going to come around and unless you are extremely careful you will fail inspection simply due to your difficulty with English. Let me tell the questions he will probably ask and the answers you will need to give. The first question he will undoubtedly ask is, 'How long have you been in the army?' When he asks that, simply answer 'two years.' The second question he will undoubtedly ask is, 'How old are you?' When he asks that question answer, 'twenty-two.' The third question he will undoubtedly ask is, 'Have you been receiving good food and good treatment?' When he asks that tell him, 'Both.' Remember two, twenty-two and both. Whatever you do don't forget two, twenty-two and both."

The day of inspection came and sure enough the General asked three questions. The only problem was that he did not ask them in the order in which the soldier was prepared to answer them. Instead the general said, "I would like to ask you a few questions. First, how old are you? The soldier answered, 'Two.' The General looked at him and said, 'Well, how long have you been in the army?' The soldier answered, 'Twenty-two years.' The General looked at him and said, What do you take me for, an idiot or a fool.' The soldier then answered, 'Both.'"

I am sure that all of us are glad that we were not standing in the boots of that poor soldier during inspection. Yet we should all be keenly aware that one day we are going to participate in an even greater inspection when we will find ourselves summoned to stand before the God of heaven and Lord of earth (Ecc. 12:14). The God to whom we must give an account (Rom. 14:12; Heb. 4:13). On that great and terrible day our lives shall appear before Him as an open book and we shall give an account for every word recorded, every line written and every chapter closed (Rev. 20:11-15). With a pure eye and holy mind God shall read the record of our lives and see for Himself the transgressions we have committed, written in black and bold letters and hidden between every line (1 Kings 8:46; Rom.3:23; 1 John 1:8). In light of the infinite scrutiny of this all Holy God, none shall pass that inspection; therefore, none shall join the ranks of Heaven's hosts (Ps. 130:3). The Bible teaches that righteousness is the price of a ticket to heaven and yet there is none righteous, no, not one (Rom. 3:10-18).

Confronted with such calamity, Job's and Bildad's question seems rather pressing and pertinent: "How then can a man be right with God (Job 9:2, 25:4)?" How can a man ever expect to enter heaven by passing under the judgement of a Holy God whose eyes cannot put up with iniquity, knowing full well that he himself has sinned and fallen short of God's holiness? Job's question of rightness with God may be an old one but it is certainly timeless. It is a question that has and continues to stoke the fire of religious fervor and the flames of doctrinal controversy, as unjust sinners seek to become just in the sight of God and yet differ over how this is to be obtained.

This difference of opinion concerning rightness with God comes sharply into focus in the clash between the Roman Catholic and Protestant theories of justification and rightness with God. These theories, advanced in history by Catholics and Protestants, are the principal views that have violently collided. The dispute over the doctrine of justification in the 16th century was surely the most volatile and divisive in church history. The volatility of that debate lay in its subject matter, for the Reformation was not a squabble over ecclesiastical etiquette, but rather a furious argument over the means and meaning of eternal life (Acts16:30). It was a debate that left no margin for compromise since the eternal destiny of men lay at its core. The struggle between the Romanist and the Reformer was a matter of life and death, both temporal and eternal. The epicenter of the 16th century theological earthquake is traced to the issue of man's eternal salvation in its theological conception and experiential reception. Catholic and Protestant doctrine has considered it the fundamental heresy to be wrong about being right with God. It was a controversy that allowed no compromise.

The doctrinal controversy hinged upon the question as to the means and conditions by which the eminent blessings of the gospel, namely peace with God through the death of Christ (Luke 2:10-14, Col. 1:20), come to be appropriated by sinful man. Roman Catholics have believed that one's acceptance before God was achieved by one's cooperation with regard to the gracious work of God in a sinner. William Webster in his book, *The Gospel of the Reformation*, explains:

> When Rome states that an individual is justified by grace, she means that grace has been infused into the

soul of man. This makes him righteous before God and enables him to perform acts of righteousness. These then become the basis of justification and the means whereby he merits heaven. Justification is a process then by which the individual is made righteous in a moral sense. The Roman Catholic Church interprets the phrase the righteousness of God to mean righteousness which finds its source in the grace of God, channeled through sacraments. But the righteousness itself is the work of man cooperating with that grace. The righteousness of God then is not the righteousness of Christ, but rather the righteousness of man which results from the gift of grace, the source of which is God.[1]

Roman Catholic doctrine promotes the contradictory concept that justification is a gift for which man must work to achieve. According to the gospel of Rome, justification is a work in man by God, and a work of man to God, whereby the soul of man is progressively made righteous and acceptable to God. Thus, eternal life is the fruit of an amalgam of God's grace and man's endeavor. Justification is seen not to be an objective status but a subjective experience, and as such it is open to loss and regression. Because justification is therefore partially dependent on the work of human beings, it is imperfect and flawed.

Protestants have believed that one's acceptance before God was to be received by the hand of faith alone with regard to the gracious work of God for sinners through the Cross. For Protestants, justification was not a work done within the sinner but a work done on behalf of the sinner. A right relationship with God was viewed through the understanding that justification was an instantaneous gift received by faith alone, based solely upon

God's grace toward sinners, purchased by the atoning blood of Christ, and devoid of human work and religious endeavor. It was a judgment passed on man, not a work wrought within man. William Webster again proves helpful as he explains the Protestant viewpoint as it stands in opposition to Rome:

> Justification is an eternal declaration of God which happens the moment an individual is united to Christ. It is not a process dependent upon the works of an individual but an instantaneous act of God. The sinner is translated out of a state of sin and enmity with God into a state of forgiveness and acceptance with Him. He is reconciled to and has peace with God (Rom. 5:1). He is set free from all judgment and condemnation (Rom. 8:1). The believer is brought into a filial relationship with God through the New Covenant. He is adopted—made a child of God (Rom..8:15-17; Eph.1:5; 1 John 3:1-2).[2]

Again it is important to underline the concept that justification is a gift that man need not and cannot work for. Evangelical Protestantism purports that justification is a work of God apart from man, done outside and on the behalf of man, whereby man is instantaneously reckoned righteous before God. Eternal life is the fruit then of God's grace and Christ's work done on the behalf of sinners. Justification is viewed not as a subjective experience but an objective status granted by God, and as such is closed to loss and regression. Justification is completely dependent on the work of Christ and is perfect and abiding in nature. Christ imparts *eternal* life (John 3:16), and his work accomplishes an eternal redemption (Heb. 9:12) and provides an eternal inheritance (Heb. 9:15; 1 Peter 1:4).

Emerging from the vortex of this historical debate and disagreement, it is plainly evident that the Reformation was a critical fight over the Gospel and the means of our standing justified in the presence of a Holy God. The Roman Catholic says that man has an active part to play as God works with him to make him righteous. The Protestant, however, says that man has no part to play as God works for him in declaring him righteous. Peeling off all the contentious layers, the question that remains is whether God has partial or complete efficiency in the matter of justification. Does he reward the godly with justification or redeem the ungodly through justification? B.B. Warfield touched upon this when he wrote:

> "The battle of the Reformation was fought out under a banner on which the sole authority of the Scripture was inscribed. But the principle of the sole authority of Scripture was not to the Reformation an abstract principle. What it was interested in was what is taught in Scripture; and the sole authority of Scripture meant to it the sole authority of what is taught in Scripture. This, of course, is dogma; and the dogma which the men of the Reformation found taught in Scripture above every other dogma, so much above every other dogma that it summed up all the teaching of Scripture, is the sole efficiency of God in salvation. That is what we call the material principle of the Reformation. It was not at first known by the name justification by faith alone, but it was from the first passionately embraced as renunciation of all human works, and dependence on the Grace of God alone for salvation. In it the Reforma-

tion lived and moved and had its being; in a high sense of the words, it is the Reformation."[3]

With this discovery of the sole sufficiency of God in the free and full justification of the sinner, the Reformation began and centuries of darkness began to roll away. This Evangelical doctrine swept through nation after nation. In a short space of time, much of Europe had been won to the Reformation and the greatest revival since Pentecost, both in scope and importance, had taken place.

Within the context of this book and its concern over the race to reunion with Rome, we note with shock and sadness that even this great doctrine, the very touchstone of the Evangelical faith itself, is being auctioned for the cause of ecumenism. Once the dividing line between Romanism and Protestantism, the great doctrine of justification by faith alone has been relegated to a position of minimal importance by the very heirs of the Reformation itself and all for the purpose of maximizing fellowship, cooperation, and co-belligerence with Roman Catholics.

An example of this was underscored in the opening chapter of this book in showing that the ECT document dismisses the controversy of justification by faith alone by its unwillingness to mention it in the list of points of disagreements. A further example of this auction of truth for the purchase of peace surfaced in an article in the 7/20/97 issue of *Our Sunday Visitor*, an American Roman Catholic newspaper. The article concerned itself with the Evangelical Promise Keepers movement and their desire for greater Roman Catholic participation. An inclusion, it seems, that is desired on the part of Promise Keeper's leaders, even at the cost of the precious doctrine of justification by faith alone. The Sunday Visitor explains:

At its March meeting Promise Keepers board of directors welcomed Mike Timmis as a new member. A Detroit-area lawyer and businessman, Timmis is a longtime leader of the Catholic Charismatic renewal. At several rallies this year P.K's has spotlighted Catholic Evangelist Jim Berlucchi as a speaker ... and earlier this year P.K's amended its statement of faith revising the lines that Catholics had found offensive. P.K's founder Bill McCartney told *Our Sunday Visitor* that full Catholic participation was his intention from the start ... Last year, P.K's published a "Statement of faith" with lines that seemed to be crafted to exclude Catholics. Section five of the P.K's credo read, "We believe that man was created in the image of God but because of sin was alienated from God. That alienation can be removed only by accepting through Faith Alone God's gift of salvation which was made possible by Christ's death." "Faith alone" is a key doctrine of the Protestant Reformation ... Early this year P.K's revised the statement in a way that passed theological muster with those Catholics "Only through faith, trusting in Christ alone for salvation, which was made possible by his death and resurrection, can that alienation be removed."

What this amended wording represents on the part of Promise Keepers is their desire to maximize the common ground that exists between Protestants and Catholics concerning the sole agency of Christ in salvation, while sadly tip-toeing passt the battlefield of *sola fide*. Catholics can sign up to the truth that Christ alone saves, but they continue to reject that salvation comes by faith alone. What this revision constitutes is an agreement among Evangelicals to disagree with Roman Catholic's over the doctrine of justification by faith alone and yet pursue union. But is that legitimate? I think not! How is it possible to call ourselves brothers and sisters in Christ when we share neither a common heritage nor theology on how God becomes our Father? Protestants and Catholics agree, as they also did in the sixteenth century, that Christ alone saves us, but the key question is how does our Lord save? By faith plus works as advocated in Catholicism, or is it by faith alone as is proclaimed by Protestants?

Therefore, it is my aim in the rest of this chapter to highlight the deep and abiding differences that still exist between the faith of the Vatican and the gospel of Evangelicalism concerning the means and meaning of justification. As a result, we will conclude once again that any invitation to this supposed family reunion between long separated brothers and sisters in Christ is rather premature. It is undoubtedly a sad case of mistaken identity. Fellowship, according to the Apostle Paul, takes place within the context of a proper understanding and cherishing of the gospel (Phil. 1:5-7, 27). In Acts, Luke places doctrine and fellowship side by side (Acts 2:42). Fellowship, therefore, cannot be fostered without agreement over the content of the gospel. Fellowship must have a doctrinal foundation to it. In fact, the church exists because of the gospel being preached and received by faith, and where the gospel is absent the church ceases to exist (Matt. 28:18-20; 1 Cor. 4:15; Col. 1:3-8; 2 Thess. 2:14). J.C.Ryle has some rather telling words on this matter when he writes:

> Take away the Gospel from a Church and that Church is not worth preserving. A well without

water, a scabbard without a sword, a steam-engine without a fire, a ship without a compass and rudder, a watch without a mainspring, a stuffed carcass without life,—all these are useless things. But there is nothing so useless as a Church without the Gospel.[4]

To slightly modify these insightful words of J.C. Ryle, we add that the Evangelical fervor for reconciliation with Rome will condemn the Church, for such reconciliation is worth neither pursuing nor preserving. On the issue of justification, reconciliation with Rome will result in a failure to preach and cherish the gospel of justification by grace alone in Christ alone by faith alone. Therefore the goal of reunion with Rome is a pursuit that will ultimately lead us away from the gospel and towards the condemnation of God (Gal. 1:6-9).

Consider the doctrine of justification, which is of primary importance and the chief point of difference separating Protestantism and Roman Catholicism. In the following, we will seek to establish a biblical base for the Protestant view of seeing justification as a right standing before God and also show how this kingly doctrine has been betrayed by the hand of Roman Catholicism.

The Basis of Declared Righteousness

The importance of establishing a true and biblical basis to justification cannot be exaggerated. This is a debate that allows for no margin of error. At stake is the right answer to the most important of all human questions: How can a man or woman become right with God? John Calvin, for instance, in his *Institutes of the Christian Religion*, devotes more space to justification than to almost any other doctrine. As he introduces the subject he reminds his readers that "this is the main hinge on which religion turns" and therefore "we devote the greater attention and care to it. For unless you first of all grasp what your relationship to God is, and the nature of this judgment concerning you, you have neither a foundation on which to establish your salvation nor one on which to build piety toward God."[5] Thomas Watson, one of the finest of the Puritans, said, "Justification is the very hinge and pillar of Christianity. An error about justification is dangerous, like a defect in a foundation. Justification by Christ is a spring of the water of life. To have the poison of corrupt doctrine cast into this spring is damnable."[6] These statements are by no means overstatements. Justification is vital for we must become right with God or perish eternally.

It is disconcerting that we can be so wrong about being right with God, which is outlined in the context of Romans 10:2 and Acts 17:22. The Jews lacked knowledge of true righteousness and Greeks lacked knowledge of the true God. In the parable told by Christ in Luke 18, the Pharisee left the temple thinking he was right with God, but he was wrong (Luke 18:14). How important then that Protestants and Catholics not so much agree with each other on this matter but that they agree on what the Bible teaches concerning this matter. How sad that Protestants and Catholics should agree to disagree, or find a moderating position over an issue that is the difference between heaven and hell.

Before proceeding to outline the biblical meaning and means of justification, let us define the theological and historical term so that we might establish a benchmark for the purposes of contrast and comparison. Simply defined: Justification is the gracious act of God in declaring righteous the sinner who believes on Jesus. Philip H. Everson defines it more fully in his book, *The Great Exchange*, when he writes:

Justification is a legal pronouncement made by God in the present, prior to the day of judgment, declaring sinners to be not guilty and therefore acquitted, by pardoning all their sins and reckoning them to be righteous in his sight, on the basis of Christ, their representative and substitute, whose righteousness in life and death is put to their account when in self-despairing trust they look to him alone for salvation.[7]

Having established this datum line let us set it alongside the straight edge of God's revealed Word to see how true it really is.

The Meaning of Justification

The use of the word *justify* in the Bible indicates that justification is a legal declaration by God. It means to be declared righteous, to be accounted righteous. This term emerges from the law courts and describes the act of a judge in acquitting an accused person. It is a judicial word indicating the action of declaring righteous, and of special note are the two legalistic words: "acquitting" and "declaring." Special because the single most serious flaw in trying to understand justification is to suppose that it means "to make righteous" in the sense of actually producing righteousness in the one justified, which is the understanding given to justification by Roman Catholicism. This is problematic because justification only indicates that the person involved has a right standing before the bar of God's justice. It does not indicate how he or she got to be that way, which is why the other salvation-related terms—redemption and propitiation—are so necessary.

From another angle, justification can be viewed as the opposite of condemnation. When a defendant is found standing on the wrong side of the law, he or she is condemned or pronounced guilty by the judge. Condemnation of that defendant does not make the person guilty. The fact is that he or she is only declared to be so and thus recognized to be so. Similarly, with justification the person is declared to be just or in a right relationship to the law, not to be made righteous. Of course a person *could* be declared righteous on the grounds of his or her own righteousness; in that case such a one would be pronounced innocent in the eyes of the court. But in salvation, since we lack any righteousness to claim as our own and are not innocent, we are through grace declared righteous on the basis of Christ's atonement.[8]

In its theological sense, justification is a forensic, or a purely legal term. It is not a work done within the sinner, but a work done on behalf of the sinner. It describes what God declares about the believer, not what he does to change the believer. As John MacArthur in his book, *Faith Works*, points out:

> In fact, justification effects no actual change whatsoever in the sinner's nature or character. Justification is a divine judicial edict. It changes our status only, but it carries ramifications that guarantee other changes will follow. Forensic decrees like this are fairly common in everyday life.

> When I was married, for example, Patricia and I stood before the minister (my father) and recited our vows. Near the end of the ceremony, my father declared, "By the authority vested in me by the state of California, I now pronounce you man and wife." Instantly we were legally husband and wife. Whereas seconds before we had been an engaged couple, now we were married. Nothing inside us

changed when those words were spoken. But our status changed before God, the law, and our family and friends. The implications of that simple declaration have been lifelong and life-changing (for which I am grateful). But when my father spoke those words, it was a legal declaration only.

Similarly, when the jury foreman reads the verdict, the defendant is no longer "the accused." Legally and officially he is instantly becomes either guilty or innocent—depending on the verdict. Nothing in his actual nature changes, but if he is found not guilty he will walk out of the court a free man in the eyes of the law, fully justified.

In biblical terms, justification is a divine verdict of "not guilty- fully righteous." It is the reversal of God's attitude toward the sinner. Whereas He formerly condemned, He now vindicates.[9]

At this point, the question must be asked and answered: How do we know that in Scripture, justification means constituting a person righteous by declaration? In answer to that fundamental question, I would suggest several pieces of evidence that prove the case.

- The Bible presents justification as the opposite of condemnation. In Deuteronomy 25:1, it is written that judges are to acquit (justify) the innocent and condemn the guilty. Here it is obvious that the question is not one of moral improvement. The judges are not to make the righteous man better, rather their job is to vindicate his position as satisfactory to the law. Clearly to condemn in this context does not mean "to make them guilty," but rather "to declare them to be guilty" and so to constitute them "guilty" by the verdict. By virtue of the parallelism between the two expressions acquit cannot mean "to make innocent' but must mean to declare a person to be innocent, to constitute them 'innocent' by declaration (Gen. 44:16; Ex. 23:7; 1 Kings 8:31-32; Prov. 17:15; Isa. 50:7-9; Rom. 8:33-34).

+ The terms with which "righteous" is associated have a judicial flavor as emphasized in Genesis 18:25 with God as Judge. Similar evidence is found in Psalm 143:2.

+ The expressions used as synonyms or substitutes for justify do not carry the sense of "making righteous" but bear this declarative and constitutive sense (Gen. 15:6; Psalm 32:1-2; and Paul's use of both texts in Rom. 4:3, 6:8).

+ It may also be noted that Jesus is said to be justified (1 Tim. 3:16). Who among us would dare to advance the notion that this statement implies an infusion of grace with a view to overcoming the power of indwelling sin? In this context justification once again carries the idea of vindication. Paul is referring to the vindication of Christ by God through the triumph and victory of the resurrection. By the resurrection, Christ was declared to be in a right relationship with God (Rom. 1:4).[10]

However, while the Hebrew judge may justify the innocent, and the perfect Son of God has been vindicated through His resurrection; it is a legitimate question to ask, How can God justify the sinner without actually making him righteous? Paul gives the answer in Romans 4:1-25 by demonstrating that the act of justification is accomplished by the legal imputation of Christ's righteousness. Using a bookkeeping term repeatedly (Greek logizomai—to reckon or impute), Paul shows how God through a double transaction both negative and positive graciously justifies the believing sinner. Employing Abraham as an example, Paul outlines how God did not reckon Abraham's sin against him but reckoned the righteousness of Christ to him. In an act both glorious and gracious, God removed Abraham's sins from his ledger, but that was only because he had first transferred them to the ledger book of Jesus Christ. The negative transaction inferred in Paul's writing is when Jesus Christ took the liability of those transgressions in Himself and paid for them in full by means of his ruby red blood given in death. Abraham's sin was not laid to his charge because it was transferred to Jesus' account.

Parallel to that, Paul proceeds to tell us that based upon his understanding of Genesis 15:6, God then took the righteousness of Christ and wrote it in Abraham's ledger (Rom. 4:22-25). The positive transaction occurs when God imputes His righteousness to us. So when God justified Abraham, He imputed divine righteousness to him. Christ's own infinite merit thus became the very ground upon which Abraham stood before God. Thus, what was true of Abraham is true of every believing sinner (Rom 5:19; 1 Cor. 1:30; Phil. 3:9). Therefore, because of justification, believers not only are perfectly free from any charge of guilt (Rom. 8:33) but also have the full merit of Christ reckoned to their personal account (Rom. 5:17). In April 1516, Martin Luther wrote to George Spenlein about this wonderful exchange:

> Learn to despair of yourself and say to Him, Thou Lord Jesus art my righteousness, and I am thy sin. Thou hast taken what was mine, and Thou has given me what was Thine. What Thou was not, Thou didst become, so that I might become what I was not.[11]

Returning to the marriage metaphor used by John MacArthur, when one marries they assume mutual ownership of both the debts and the wealth of their spouse. Even though nothing was done to gain either, they become one's own. Similarly, when you are married to, that is united with, Christ by faith, you share in the accrual of His work. In His love, He assumes the debt of all your sin against God and pays what is due. But He also allows you to share in His wealth—acceptance by God and eternal life. The value and accomplishments of what Jesus did two thousand years ago become yours now and forever when the Spirit of God weds you to Christ.

To summarize the meaning of justification based on the information thus far, justification is considered an act of God whereby the position of a guilty sinner before Him changes from condemnation to perfect acceptance because God counts the sinner to be righteous. Justification is more than pardon. Pardon is negative, the putting away of sin. Justification is positive in that the perfect righteousness of Christ is imputed to the sinner. In the law court, a man proved to be guilty might be granted a pardon. If however, he is proved to be innocent of the charge leveled against him, he is not pardoned but justified, so he leaves the court with no stain upon his character. In contrast to this, the Apostle Paul declares that though we are guilty, God not only offers pardon through Christ, He justifies us. This is the wonder of the Christian Gospel. Christ is so united to the Christian, that God reckons our sins to Him; and the Christian is so united to Christ, that God reckons His righteousness to us. God sees us in Him and reckons us as righteous as He is.

Near, so very near to God,
Nearer I cannot be,
For in the Person of His Son,
I am as near as He.
Dear, so very dear to God,
Dearer I cannot be,
For in the Person of His Son,
I am as dear as He.

Before closing this extended look at the meaning of justification, two other matters need to be touched upon as we anticipate our look at the Roman Catholic understanding of this doctrine. These two points are derived from the very nature of forensic justification itself. First, there are no degrees of justification. Justification rests upon the finished work of Christ and not the unfinished work of the Christian. As one writer put it, "Backslidden Lot was still fully justified (2 Pet. 2:7), as were also the carnal Corinthians (1 Cor. 6:11)." Thomas Watson well sums up this aspect: "The weakest believer is as perfectly justified as the strongest; Mary Magdalene is as much justified as the Virgin Mary."[12]

Second, justification is a once and final transaction. While referring to the hand of God in salvation that reaches back to eternity past and forward to eternity future, Paul writes: "Whom he justified them he also glorified." (Rom. 8:30). While it would be logical to speak of justification in the past tense, because it is a past transaction from the moment the sinner believes, Paul also embraces glorification in the past tense. The apostle could not and would not write in this manner if there were any chance of the believer becoming unjustified.

Truly the saint of God can say with the psalmist. "Let such as love your salvation say continually 'The Lord be magnified'" (Psalm 40:16).

The Means of Justification

How marvelous then, that the justified believer has had his day in court and nothing is laid to his charge. But how does this come about? The best answer to that question comes from the pen of Paul as he writes to the living saints at Rome detailing their justification by means of grace alone (Romans 3:24), through faith alone (5:1) in the blood atoning death of Christ alone (5:9). According to the apostle, salvation is unmistakably by grace—by blood—by faith. Paul is not writing that there are three methods of justification, but all three are necessary to convey the whole truth. Let me explain by way of illustration. Los Angeles' water supply comes largely from the Colorado River. Ask the citizens of Los Angeles how they get their water and you will get a variety of answers. One might say, "From the Colorado River." A second might suggest "Through the pipes that crisscross the city." A third might comment, "I get it by turning on the tap." All three are correct, but to express the whole truth all three must be stated. So it is with the great subject of justification. Its source and origin are in the grace of God. It is mediated and conveyed to us through the sacrifice of the Cross. It is obtained and realized by our act of faith.

Let's unpack the nature of this right relationship with God:

It Knows No Reason—Only Grace (Rom. 3:24)

Although difficult for the suspicious mind to accept and the religious heart to embrace, the Word of God is clear that justification is a gift from God and free of charge to those who believe. Following his explanation in Romans 1:18-3:20 that no one will ever be able to make himself righteous before God (Rom. 3:20), Paul then explains the wonder of the gospel that although men have fallen short of God's glory, God has in love reached down in Christ to save by grace. The apostle tells us that we are justified freely by God's grace (Rom 3:24). The term "freely" is translated "without a cause" in John 15:25. It is therefore to be understood that God makes men right with Him by grace not by merit. Justification is a free gift from God that finds no reason or cause in mankind (Acts 20:28; Eph. 1:7, 2:8; Titus 3:5-7). The word grace itself means favor that is not deserved and cannot be earned.

The thought that rises to the surface in all of this is the sole agency and efficacy of God in salvation (Jonah 2:9). Because we are completely unable to earn favor with God, the only way we could be declared righteous is if God freely provides salvation for us by grace, totally apart from our work. This He did through the appearing of His Son Jesus Christ who came in an act of grace to put away sin by the sacrifice of Himself (Titus 2:11; Heb. 9:26). God is the only reason things can be made right with Him. Salvation is not then a meritorious work of man but a gracious act of God. Man can justify the innocent and pardon the guilty, but only God can justify the guilty. It is all of God, all of grace, and all for His glory. Works, rituals, and philanthropy are not the way to gain God's attention, because grace signals that we have already been noticed. John tells us that we love God because He first loved us (1 John 4:10, 19). The writers of Holy Scripture are uncomplicated in telling us that the action of justification finds its cause in the heart of God not the piety of men. Consequently and conclusively, salvation is a gift of grace to the ungodly and not a reward of grace to the godly (Rom. 5:6-11). Again Paul is unmistakable in proclaiming that a right relationship with God is not a pay back but a free and sovereign offer of God to the lost and perishing sinner (Rom. 4:5, 11:6).

In application, grace voids the need for human contribution or cooperation in the act of justification. Grace is undeserved and nothing is expected in return. Such a concept however cuts across the grain of human thinking and the intent of most religious endeavors. Religion at large teaches that every good work done puts God in debt to man and therefore obligates Him to return the favor. Religion often seeks a salvation experience that is something God owes man rather than a free gift God offers man. It results in God becoming the secondary cause of salvation, with man presented as winning God over and making God love him through his good endeavor. If this were so, salvation would then be a concession on the part of God to man's merit rather than a gift given to those who are undeserving as the Bible says.

In Romans 4:4-5, Paul is explicit in countering this religious thinking, stating that when God saves He does it out of grace and not out of debt. Grace cannot be purchased.

To make his point Paul takes an illustration from the life of a working man. Paul pictures a man working for a wage and at the end of the day or week he receives it and when he does he does not go and throw his arms around the boss. In fact if the truth be known he thinks he is worth twice as much as what he is getting. The wage is owed to him and if the employer was not forthcoming with his wages a lawcourt would come to his defense. His wages are owed to him as debt.

Paul's point is that God will not accept us on the basis of our works for that will put Him in the position of owing man salvation. Justification is not an obligation foisted on God by the work of man, but remains a free and gracious gift from God established by the work of Christ upon the Cross. Justification knows no reason or cause other than grace. It is truly amazing grace.

In the light of these facts we would do well to enlist the prayer of the old Scots saint as he stressed the preeminence of grace in the Christian life:

> Lord Jesus from whom all grace comes, give me grace to feel my need of grace, and give me grace to ask for grace, then give me grace to receive grace, and when grace is given give me grace to be grateful and to use grace. Amen.

It Knows No Other—Only Christ (Rom. 3:24-26)

Building on what we have thus far presented, justification is available not because men are good but God is good to men. God offers it to humankind in Christ; He is not obligated to give it. The very heart and distinction of the Christian message is that salvation is not to be found in the righteous actions of a man but in the gracious and righteous action of God Himself in sending His Son to die for the ungodly, unworthy and unlovely (1 John 4:9-10). To read Romans and Corinthians is to discover this very point—that the justification of the sinner is tied to and bound up in the sufferings of Christ upon Calvary's brow (Rom. 3:24, 5:9; 2 Cor. 5:21).

The connection between the two is both simple and staggering because in the death of Christ we have a payment for sin (1 Cor. 15:3-4). The Bible is candid in showing that there are wages attached to sin and a price to be paid for sinning (Rom. 6:23; Jas. 1:14-15). Somebody has to pay the bill for sin. Justification is not and cannot be a divine denial or fictional thing where God says, "I will shut my eyes and forget they ever sinned." Because He must deal with sin, God must remain just and yet show Himself to be the justifier of the ungodly; the voice of law and justice must be silenced and satisfied. Fortunately for mankind, that tension was wonderfully overcome in the atoning death of Christ upon the cross. To satisfy divine justice, the impeccable Christ offered himself as a sacrifice for the sin of all, and thus provided from Calvary's Hill the ground upon which God could be both just and justifier (Rom. 3:24-26). David told us that God has not rewarded us according to our iniquities (Psalm 103:10). And the prophet Isaiah offers further explanation that this is so, not because God turned a blind eye to sin, but because God dealt with our sin in the person and work of His dear Son (Isaiah 53:3-6, 11). The cross work of Christ therefore justifies justification (1 Peter 3:18). God has not gone soft on sin in justifying the sinner.

In possibly the single most important paragraph to be written on this subject in Scripture, the Apostle Paul attributed the satisfying of God's righteousness and his ability to justify to the propitiatory nature of Christ's death (Rom. 3:25). Of this concept of propitiation John MacArthur writes in his commentary on Romans 1-8:

> Hilasterion (propitiation) carries the basic idea of appeasement, or satisfaction. In ancient pagan religions, as in many religions today, the idea of man's appeasing a deity by various gifts or sacrifices was common. But in the New Testament propitiation refers to the work of God, not of man. Man is utterly incapable of satisfying God's justice except by spending eternity in hell.[13]

Therefore, the only satisfaction that could ever be acceptable to God and that could reconcile Him to man had to be made by God. For this reason, God is to be seen in Christ reconciling the world to Himself, not imputing their trespasses to them (2 Cor. 5:19). In Christ alone, refuge is afforded from the wrath of God because He has singularly appeased the wrath of God by means of the infinite value of His death and precious blood given on behalf of sinners (Gal. 3:13; Col. 2:11-14; 1 Peter 1:18-19, 2:24).

It is significant that the Hebrew equivalent of *hilasterion* (propitiation) is used in the Old Testament in reference to the mercy seat. As a Jew, Paul knew that the priest had to sprinkle blood seven times on the mercy seat to make atonement for God's people and to turn away God's wrath at their sins (Lev. 16:14). The Ark contained the Law of the Ten Commandments, and the ceremony portrayed the fact that a broken Law stood between a holy God and mankind. But through the shedding of blood, this place of judgment becomes the place of reconciliation. In Christ's death the demands of God for justice against a sinful race are fully met, leaving him free to be merciful to those who formerly merited only judgment. Therefore, from the mercy seat of Christ's finished work, God could be both just and the justifier of those who believe. What Christ did on the cross towards God protected God's integrity and paved the way for God's mercy in justification. God can forgive us and justify us without shaking the base of His throne because in sparing the sinner, He did not spare His own Son (Rom. 8:32-34).

Men are not saved by the philosophy Christ taught, nor by the example Christ set, nor by the works Christ prescribed, but by the death of Christ on their behalf. The message of the New Testament is that total dependence upon the death of Christ triggers for us that wonderful exchange whereby all that we are and have done becomes His, and all that He is and has accomplished becomes ours (2 Cor. 5:21). The only basis for justification, which the New Testament recognizes, is the work of Christ.

A wise and just ruler established a series of laws for his people to follow. One day his mother broke one of the laws and was brought to the ruler after being caught. The penalty was twenty lashes. How could the ruler remain just and still fulfill the demands of his love for his mother? He took the lashes on his back. Justice was satisfied, while love was revealed in full measure.

In a similar fashion but in greater measure, God through the substitutionary death of His Son on behalf of sinners, met the demands of His righteousness while revealing His love for a lost world (John 3:16; Rom 5:1-11; Eph. 2:1-10; 1 John 4:9-10). Christ willingly placed Himself under the curse of God, in order to set us at liberty from it. This is the solid and singular ground of our justification. In this section we have touched upon the very heart of the Gospel, and in so doing the very heart of God. With a firm grip we have laid hold of the truth that justification is based solely and completely upon the merits of another—Jesus Christ.

In his beautiful hymn, Horatius Bonar wrote:

Not what my hands have done
Can save my guilty soul:
Not what my toiling flesh has borne
Can make my spirit whole.
Not what I feel or do
Can give me peace with God;
Not all my prayers and sighs and tears
Can bear my awful load.
Thy grace alone, O God,
To me can pardon speak;
Thy power alone, O Son of God,
Can this sore bondage break.

No other work save thine,
No other blood will do;
No strength save that which is divine
Can bear me safely through.

It Knows No Works—Only Faith (Romans 3:22, 25-26; 3:28; 5:1)

As we have defined, justification is an act undertaken by God, wholly separate from anything done by us as believers. It is an act of sovereign grace, because it finds its cause in the heart of God. Biblical and evangelical justification is the result of the work of Christ not the work of Christians. Christ's death on Calvary has made it a free gift to men but not free to God for it cost Him His Son and it cost the Son His life. As a gift, justification cannot therefore be earned by works but must be received by faith alone (Acts 13:39; 16:30,31; Rom. 3:28; Gal. 2:16; Phil. 3:8-9). This is righteousness apart from the law of human achievement (Rom. 3:21-22). Consequently, the fingerprint of man is not to be found upon the jewel of justification. It is His treasure alone to give. The New Testament repeatedly presents eternal life as a gift from God through the gift of His Son and as such it must be received by faith alone apart from works (Rom. 6:23; 2 Cor. 9:15; Eph. 2:8-9). In John 1:12-13, the Apostle John uses the word, receive synonymously for believe. Faith alone is the link that relates the repentant sinner to God's salvation.

But what is faith? Faith is a total dependence and trust directed towards the Lord Jesus Christ as its object. The eye of faith sees only one Savior and only one satisfactory sacrifice for sin (John 14:6; Acts 4:12; 1 Tim. 2:5; Heb. 10:10-12). Faith is not the cognition of man's intellect, but is the heart and totality of a man throwing himself upon Jesus Christ (Rom. 10:9-10). As presented by Jesus and Paul, it is a total transfer of trust from confidence in the flesh and the merit of human work to the eternal and finished work of Christ upon the Cross for sinners (Luke18:9ff; Phil. 3:2, 8-9). Our faith should be targeted to Christ alone.

Bishop Munsey tells a parable of a man whom, while walking along, suddenly falls off the edge of a cliff. As he was hurled down he was able to reach out and grab a limb jutting out of the rock. He grasped it and hung there between life and death. Below, he saw the jagged rocks awaiting his fall. Suddenly an angel appeared to him, and the man pleaded for the angel to save him. The angel responded, "Do you believe I can save you?" The man saw the strong arms of the angel and said, "Yes, I believe you are able to save me." the angel asked, "Do you believe I will save you?" He saw a smile on the angel's face and replied, "Yes, I believe you will save me." "Then," said the angel, "if you believe I can save you and will save you, let go!"[14]

The "letting go" is faith. Christ wants us to rest our full intellectual, emotional, and spiritual weight on Him alone. That is saving faith in Christ, who alone is qualified to reconcile us to God. Those who make such a transfer of dependence no longer owe God any righteousness. This was the ground upon which the Reformation was fought. Philip H. Eveson pinpoints this when he writes:

> The Reformers also stressed that it is through faith in Jesus Christ that sinners are justified. For them, saving faith is not merely the faith of assent to the facts of the gospel or a willingness to accept what the church believes, but a personal reliance on the Lord Jesus Christ. Justification, however, is not based on faith. It is based on Christ and received through faith. Luther was also quick to emphasize

that it is through faith alone that sinners are declared righteous. He was, and still is, criticized for adding 'alone' to his German New Testament translation of Romans 3:28. His reply was to the effect that the sense of the passage demanded it. Both he and Calvin point out that, in the very same part of Romans, Paul goes on to stress that works do not justify. If it is not faith plus works that justifies then it must be by faith alone.[15]

This concentration upon faith must not, however, be misunderstood as viewing faith as the basis of our justification. Faith simply unites us to Christ and Christ alone saves. We are not saved because of faith but by means of the object of faith. Faith is never more than the instrument, the channel by which we receive God's grace and justification. This point finds support in the New Testament, with the use of prepositions in conjunction with faith. In the letters to the Romans and Galatians we find the prepositions *ek* and *dia* being used alongside faith (Rom. 3:28, 5:1; Gal. 2:16). In each case, the preposition carries the idea of *through* or *by*, emphasizing that faith is the instrument that appropriates justification. Faith is never represented as the meritorious ground for our justification. We are justified not merely by faith, but by faith in Christ; not because of what faith is but because of what faith lays hold of and receives. In the application of justification, faith is not a builder but beholder; it has nothing to give or achieve, but has all to receive (Eph. 2:8-10, Titus 3:5-8). Faith is neither the ground nor the substance of our justification, but the hand that receives the divine gift extended to us in the gospel. As little as a beggar, who puts forth his hand to receive a piece of bread, can say that he earned the gift granted him, so little can believers claim that they have merited justification. Faith contributes nothing, brings nothing, pays nothing and performs nothing. It only receives, takes, accepts, grasps, and embraces the glorious gift of justification which Christ bestows.

Furthermore, it is not the amount of faith that matters, but the trustworthiness of Him in whom we place our faith. Faith takes the doctor's medicine because it trusts his qualifications. Faith entrusts money to the banker because it believes in his integrity. Faith hands over a broken watch to be repaired because it believes in the skill of the watchmaker. So faith in Christ means taking from Him the medicine we need to cure the disease of sin, committing to His safe keeping the treasure of our souls, and surrendering our broken lives to Him who is the perfect life-mender.

What is strikingly transparent in the revelation of Scripture is the absence and rejection of works on the part of man for the obtainment of justification. In his New Testament letters, Paul rings this bell repeatedly, announcing the inability of mankind to obtain a right relationship with God through works (Rom. 3:28; 4:4-5; Gal. 2:16; Eph. 2:8-9; Phil. 3:8-9; Titus 3:5-8). If it is salvation by grace, which it is, then it can no longer be of works (Rom. 11:6). The only work acceptable to God the Father for the atonement of sin is the work of His Son (John 17:1-4; 19:30; Phil. 2:5-11). As J. Vernon McGee commented, "Salvation by work? That is like jumping out of a airplane clutching a sack of cement instead of a parachute!" Or as George Whitefield said, "Heaven by works? I had just as soon climb to the moon on a rope of sand." Salvation is not earned; it is embraced by faith. Justification is not a prize to be sought but a gift to be welcomed gratefully. Righteousness is not for sale to the highest bidder with the most works, but has been purchased at a price by the Savior who in turn donates it to down and out sinners who by faith receive it (Rom. 3:21-26, 10:1-4).

The story is told of a man who came eagerly but very late to a revival meeting and found the workmen tearing down the tent in which the meetings had been held. Frantic at missing the evangelist, he decided to ask one of the workers what he could do to be saved. The workman, who was a Christian, replied, "You can't do anything, It's too late." Horrified the man said, "What do you mean? How can it be too late?" "The work has already been accomplished," he was told. "There is nothing you need to do but to believe it."

Such is the message of the New Testament and the Reformation. There is nothing we need do or can do to be justified but to believe that in union with Christ our sins are removed and His righteousness is received. An alien righteousness not due in any measure to a work or deed on our part. Faith alone embraces this understanding wholeheartedly.

What about the Book of James, when the apostle wrote extensively about works? Does James not tie works to justification? Was not Martin Luther himself suspicious of this when Luther labeled this letter a "rather strawy epistle" meaning that he felt it lacked solid, biblical doctrine? For some, there appears to be a contradiction between Paul who writes that justification is "apart from works" (Rom. 3:28; 4:6), and James who writes " that a man is justified by works, and not by faith only" (James 2:24). It should be kept in mind that the two authors are speaking about different aspects of the same doctrine. Charles Swindoll helps us to see this distinction as he writes:

> First, it's crucial to understand that the emphasis of Paul's and James' writings are different. Paul stresses the root of salvation, which is faith in Christ plus

nothing. James calls attention to the fruit after salvation. Every believer rooted in Christ by faith will bear fruit, like branches on a vine (see John 15:4-5). Paul talks of the root, James talks of the fruit.

A second contrast between Paul and James is perspective. Paul looks at life from God's perspective, while James looks at life from a human perspective. Paul sees the fire in the fireplace, while James eyes the smoke coming out the chimney. To James, the world should be able to tell that a faith burns in our hearts by the works they see coming out of our lives.

The third contrast, and the perhaps the most important one, is the difference in terms. Both Paul and James use the same word, justified, but with two different meanings. When Paul mentions justification, he means the act of God at salvation whereby He declares the believing sinner righteous while still in a sinning state. James, on the other hand, uses it to mean to 'validate or evidence.' We justify or prove our faith, James says, by our works.[16]

The reality of Charles Swindoll's statement is further reinforced when Paul writes of Abraham being justified apart from works (Rom. 4:1-5). He takes his quotation from Genesis 15; and when James refers to the patriarch being justified by works through the offering up of Isaac (James 2:21), he has in mind the events recorded in Genesis 22 which took place some twenty years after the events in Genesis 15. James, however, is not ignorant of the earlier incident and explains that in the testing of Abraham's faith through the offering of Isaac, that "The scripture was fulfilled which says Abraham believed God and it was accounted to him for righteousness" (James 2:23). The later experience demonstrates the reality of the faith which twenty years earlier had laid hold of the God who justifies.

The Apostles Paul and James are not soldiers of different armies fighting against each other, but soldiers of the same army fighting back to back against enemies coming from opposite directions. Paul shows us that we are saved by faith alone and James complements this doctrine by showing that saving faith is never alone. Works are not the ground of salvation but they are the result of salvation (Eph. 2:8-10; Titus 3:5-8). Our standing effects our state. The book of Ephesians was written for the purpose of showing how our union with the risen and exalted Christ effects and regulates our walk and behavior on earth. The first three Chapters show us our wealth in Christ, and the last three chapters show us our walk in Christ.

Before pressing on to consider the Roman Catholic view of justification, let us take a last look by way of summary at the biblical basis of justification. This will help us to compare beliefs and facilitate a foundation upon which to build our argument.

- Justification is a declarative and judicial act of God and not a process.

- Justification is a gift from God not a reward to men.

- Justification is received by faith alone.

- Justification is rooted in union with Christ.

- Justification is based upon the substitutionary work of Christ

- Justification involves the imputation of Christ's righteousness to us.

- Justification once granted cannot be lost or undone.

- Justification and sanctification are distinct.

The Betrayal of Declared Righteousness

Having traced the contours of biblical justification we now turn to consider the shape of Roman Catholic teaching on this matter. While the beginning of this chapter has been given to the Evangelical and Protestant position, this has not been without design. Similarly, in the fight against forgery and counterfeit money, it is said that federal agents train their eye to be discerning not by studying the counterfeit but by fostering a familiarity with the genuine dollar bill. This familiarity makes the job of detecting the fraudulent much easier. What is true with regard to counterfeit money is also true of false theology—That to know what is true is also to know what is false.

With the truth of biblical justification clearly set before our eyes, it is therefore time to engage the Roman Catholic Church on this issue of being made right with God. To the theologically trained eye it will soon become apparent that the gospel according to Rome is a poor imitation of the real thing. It is a counterfeit gospel that robs Christ, cheapens grace, and if embraced will cost men the forfeiture of heaven. What we shall discover as we continue the journey, is that Roman Catholicism is a movement away from the gospel of free grace and full forgiveness. Although unpalatable to the appetite of the ecumenists, I believe it is true in stating that Rome is the product and purveyor of a false gospel. Despite rumors to the contrary, the gospel of justification by grace alone, through faith alone, in Christ alone is a gospel foreign to Roman Catholicism.

To those who consider this perspective to be an overstatement of the facts, consider the words of Roman Catholic priest Richard Neuhaus, a signatory to ECT himself. In contributing to the book, *Evangelicals and Catholics Together*, which he co-edited with Charles Colson, Neuhaus writes:

The advocates of justification by grace alone through faith alone because of Christ alone may well believe that it most adequately reflects the teaching of the Bible, but the formula itself is in fact a six-teenth-century theological construct that is not found in the Bible.[17]

Is it unfair to say that what you have in these words is an overt rejection of the New Testament gospel and a rebuttal of the Reformation? Is it not strange that the Pauline formula of faith alone (Rom. 5:1), by grace alone (Rom. 3:24), in Christ alone (Rom. 5:9) should be considered by Mr. Neuhaus to be unbiblical? Students of church history will recognize that this aversion towards the Evangelical gospel is by no means new on the part of Rome. In referring to *sola fide* as a sixteenth-century theological construct, Richard Neuhaus is showing his colors and siding with the Council of Trent in its rejection of the Protestant view of justification as a gift and declarative act of God received by faith alone. History is a witness to the fact that the Council of Trent which convened to counter the threat of the Reformation, cursed and anathematized the blessed gospel of free grace and imputed righteousness as it is detailed, for example in Romans 4:5-8.

The most relevant canons that reject the Protestant theology of justification include the following:

+ If anyone says that by *faith alone* the sinner is justified, so as to mean that nothing else is required to cooperate in order to obtain the grace of justification . . . let him be anathema (Trent, sess. 6, canon 9).

+ If anyone says that men are justified either by imputation of the righteousness of *Christ alone*, or by remission of sins alone, to the exclusion of the grace and love that is poured forth in their hearts by the Holy Spirit and is inherent in them; or even that grace by which we are justified is *only the favor of God*—let him be anathema (Trent, sess. 6, canon 11).

+ If anyone says that the righteousness received is not preserved and also not increased before God *by good works*, but that those works are merely the fruits and signs of justification obtained, but not a cause of its increase, let him be anathema (Trent, sess. 6, canon 24).

These canons proclaimed by the Council of Trent are a frontal attack on the gospel of justification by grace alone, through faith alone, in Christ alone. Should not these statements require a reality check on the part of many misty eyed Evangelicals who advocate the acceptability of Roman Catholicism as a biblical religion? In these Trentine articulations, it is plain that Romanism past and present has never afforded a pulpit to the true preaching of the gospel and if anyone is guilty of overstating the facts it is anyone who would deny these facts.

In building on the ground already covered, let us proceed to weigh the Roman Catholic view of justification in the balance of the biblical data gathered. As a format for clarity and contrast we will consider this viewpoint under the same categories used to explain the Protestant perspective.

The Meaning of Justification

In Roman Catholicism, justification is a comprehensive term that includes, among other things, what Protestants understand by regeneration and sanctification. For Rome, justification is not an objective *pronouncement* of righteousness but a lifelong process of making righteous. As stated earlier, Rome teaches that justification is a work done in man by God in cooperation with man whereby the soul is progressively and actually made righteous and acceptable to God. From this perspective, justification embraces and entails the whole process of sanctification.

Writing in the *Pocket Catholic Dictionary*, John Hardon defines justification as:

> The process of a sinner becoming justified or made right with God. As defined by the Council of Trent, "Justification is the change from the condition in which a person is born as a child of the first Adam into a state of grace and adoption among the children of God through the Second Adam, Jesus Christ our Savior" (Denzinger 1524). On the negative side, justification is a true removal of sin, and not merely having one's sins ignored or no longer held against the sinner by God. On the positive side it is the supernatural sanctification and renewal of a person who thus becomes holy and pleasing to God and an heir of heaven.[18]

It is of profound importance that Hardon states that justification according to this statement of Catholic belief comes to the godly and not to the ungodly. On the basis of Mr. Hardon's words justification is a goal towards which every good Catholic moves. It is the end of the Christian life rather than the beginning. Catholic dogma teaches that the establishment of a right relationship with God is brought about by process, not a declarative act, during which the soul is actually made perfect and righteous before God. This *process* assumes and encompasses the proper use of the sacraments, including baptism, confession of one's sins verbally to a priest, and death without having committed a mortal sin. In fact, the *process* does not end there but is said to continue beyond the grave, in purgatory, where the remaining corruption's and transgressions are purged.[19] Roman Catholic justification is, therefore, not a change of status but a change of nature.

Consequently, justification is not a once-for-all-declaration of righteousness grounded in the imputed righteousness of Christ as the Bible teaches, but a process given to variation in that it is dependent upon the righteousness of man produced through infused grace. It may be fairly noted that according to the gospel of Rome, persons are justified not on the basis of what Christ has done *for* them but what God is doing *in* them. Roman Catholics trust God's infusion of a new nature and plead the worth of their God-enabled works.

As biblicists we must reject this perspective on justification. It is essential to the heart of the gospel to insist that God declare us to be just or righteous, not on the basis of our actual condition of righteousness or holiness, but rather on the basis of Christ's perfect righteousness, which God declares as belonging to us. This was the battleground on which the Reformation was fought, and it remains a position that must not be surrendered. To surrender here would force Protestants to sacrifice the plain truth of the biblically revealed gospel. The Roman Catholic equation of justification and sanctification clearly rejects Paul's declaration in Romans 4:1-5, that justification comes only to those who are wicked and stop working for it. Remember that when the Bible speaks of believers' justification it always speaks of a past tense event that took place at the moment of faith (John 5:24). According to Jesus, the repentant publican who cried out to God for mercy without personal merit "went down to his house justified" (Luke 18:14). His justification was immediate, complete, and devoid of human endeavor, based solely on his repentant faith. When writing to the Romans the apostle Paul places the justification of the believer in the past rather than the future (Rom. 5:1, 9; 8:1). Paul did not view justification as a border yet to be crossed, but ground already possessed. In his letter to the Church in Rome, Paul declared that the believers' rightness with God is an accomplished fact, not an unfinished project.

To surrender the ground of *sola fide* is not only to sacrifice the biblically revealed gospel with its doctrine of instantaneous justification, but to also sacrifice the sure hope that this gospel brings. If justification changed us internally and then declared us to be righteous based on the merit of our works, then we could never be declared perfectly righteous in this life. Sin would remain in our lives. Equating justification with the entire renewal of the inner man is to relinquish any certainty of a right relationship with God.[20] If justification is a process, then salvific assurance becomes a dream. Yet it was this dream that was a reality to the believers of the New Testament, knowing that things were right with heaven. They knew without doubt the certainty of their salvation. Salvation was money in the bank because the righteousness of Christ had been put to their account (Rom. 4:21-5:1). They knew their sins had been forgiven; and they knew that they had a home in heaven. They also knew that they had received eternal life.

In the New Testament it is written, "We know that we have passed from death unto life" (1 John 3:14). "We know that we are of God" (1 John 5:19). We know "in whom we have . . . forgiveness of sin" (Ephesians 1:7). "We know that, when he shall appear, we shall be like him" (1 John 3:2). We know that "to be absent from the body" is "to be present with the Lord" (2 Cor. 5:8). We know that nothing can "separate us from the love of God, which is in Christ Jesus our Lord" (Romans 8:39). We know that we know! Affirmation piled on top of affirmation. They not only knew, but they knew that they knew!

The testimony of first century Christianity is that salvation is by no means an uncertain process. Forgiveness and acceptance before God is not received in installments or through a graduated process. Salvation for every true child of God is an instantaneous spiritual event by the grace of God when we put our faith in Jesus Christ (Luke 23:42). To be sure, spiritual birth (John 3:3) must be followed by spiritual growth (2 Peter 3:18), but the growth is the evidence of the birth, not the cause of it. One of the old hymns says it perfectly:

> *Tis done, the great transaction's done!*
> *I am my Lord's and He is mine.*
> *(Philip Doddridge)*

Comparing the Roman Catholic meaning of justification against the Evangelical Protestant position is to set night against day and light against darkness. They are not, as some would have us believe, the same gospel (Gal. 1:5-9). Roman doctrine declares that God inspires men to work for righteousness, but Protestants aver that God gives men righteousness as the fruit of the finished work of Jesus Christ. In Catholicism men depart from Calvary towards the goal of justification, but in Protestantism men arrive at Calvary for the gift of justification.

The Means of Justification

Evangelicals and Catholics not only part company over the meaning of justification, they also sit at opposite ends of the room when it comes to the means of justification. From a Protestant viewpoint, as already detailed, justification has its complete source and origin in the grace of God. It is mediated and channeled to us directly through the person and atoning work of Christ. It is obtained and realized by simple dependence upon Christ by faith. Catholicism, however, sees things differently. According to the faith of the Vatican; Justification is brought about by the grace of God mediated through the sacraments of the Catholic Church to the obedient soul. It is not a simple act of faith on the part of the repentant sinner who rests upon the finished work of Christ, but a complex process of rituals, works and submission to the Church of Rome. As we shall see, this results in the simplicity of the gospel being complicated and the sufficiency of Christ being compromised. In the end we are left with a hybrid gospel of God and man, grace and merit, faith and works, Christ and the Church.

Not Solus Christus

Returning to a point already touched upon, it is important to realize that for Roman Catholics, acceptance before God is secured not by the alien righteousness of Christ alone credited to the sinner, but a personal righteousness created by Christ within the sinner. The Roman Catholic Church interpretation of the phrase *the righteousness of God*, does not mean Christ's own personal righteousness reckoned in grace to the believer, but the righteousness which Christ infuses into the life of the believer in his own living and behavior. Consequently, justification is founded not upon Christ's personal and perfect righteousness, but in the believer's personal righteousness, which he performs, by the grace of God. It is Christ's righteousness versus the believer's own righteousness. Vatican dogma proclaims that a right relationship with God is the product of man cooperating with the grace of God infused into the life, which produces inherent justice. The justified are in themselves beautiful and holy in God's sight.[21]

Read again the proclamation from the Council of Trent so that there is no misunderstanding on this matter of Rome's rejection of *Solus Christus*:

> If anyone says that men are justified either by the sole imputation of the justice of Christ or by the sole remission of sins, to the exclusion of the grace and the charity which is poured forth in their hearts by the Holy Ghost and remains in them (i.e.' the Catholic view of infused justification), or also that the grace by which we are justified is only the good will of God, let him be anathema. (Trent, sess. 6, canon 11).

The support structure behind this repudiation of imputed righteousness and endorsement of infused righteousness is the sacramental system. Rome not only undermines the cause of *Solus Christus* by replacing Christ's worth by personal and meritorious righteousness in the believer, but also in making Christ the indirect cause of justification. Consider the following for clarification. In Roman Catholic teaching there is no salvation apart from participation in the sacraments mediated through its priesthood.[22] The Roman Church presents herself as the mediator between Christ and the individual.

Within the Roman system, there are three main sacraments necessary for justification and ultimate salvation. In order for justification to begin, one must first be baptized and then (as an adult) continue in faith. Through baptism an individual is brought into a state of regeneration and sanctifying grace. It is said to remove original sin, the sin inherited from Adam, and pours sanctifying grace into the soul.[23] This doctrine is stated in The New Catechism, as the following extract demonstrates:

Justification is conferred in Baptism, the sacrament of faith.

Baptism not only purifies from all sins, but also makes the neophyte a new creature, an adopted son of God, who has become a partaker of the divine nature, member of Christ and co-heir with him, and a temple of the Holy Spirit.[24]

Once this initial justification through baptism is embraced, the Roman Catholic must then rigorously seek to increase and preserve grace in his soul. This progression and protection of sanctifying/justifying grace is furthered according to the New Catechism by sacraments and good works.[25] Through the sacraments, actual grace is obtained, enabling the devotee to avoid sin and thereby preserve the grace received in baptism. Of special note in this matter is the role played by the sacraments of the mass and penance. While original sin and all sin committed up to the point of baptism is forgiven in the sacrament of baptism, iniquity committed after baptism must be dealt with through these two sacraments. This is especially true for mortal sin, which is said to kill spiritual life in the soul and cause an undoing of justification. In order to regain the state of grace and the hope of justification, the sinner must repent and confess all his mortal sins to a priest in the sacrament of penance.[26] He must also seek refuge and comfort in the propitiatory value of the mass.[27]

Thus, we see that the work of a priest and the work of the penitent are supplementary to the work of Christ in the obtainment of justification.

In probing Rome's understanding of justification, the point not to be missed is that this doctrine robs Christ of his central place. The foundation of *Sola Christus* is being eroded. I say this because personal righteousness produced by infused grace takes the spotlight off Christ and onto man. Righteousness is no longer the fruit of God's work in Christ (2 Cor. 5:19), but man's work in God. The Catholic Church has snatched from the hand of Christ the gift of righteousness, which was purchased by His blood, intended for poor sinners, and turned it into a reward given to man by God for a life well lived. Such robbery is a crime when judged by the Bible, as John MacArthur points out in his excellent book *Reckless Faith*:

> The Bible teaches that justification means righteousness imputed not infused. Righteousness is "reckoned," or credited to the account of those who believe (Rom. 3:3-25). They stand justified before God not because of their own righteousness but because of a perfect righteousness outside of themselves that is reckoned to them by faith (Phil. 3:9). Where does that perfect righteousness come from? It is God's own righteousness (Rom. 10:3), and it is ours in the person of Jesus Christ (1 Cor. 1:30; cf. Jer. 23:6; 33:16). We are united to Christ by faith— we are "in Christ"—and therefore accepted by God in His beloved Son (Eph. 1:6-7). Christ's own righteousness is credited to our personal account (Rom. 5:17, 19), just as the full guilt of our sin was imputed to Him (2 Cor. 5:21). So once again we see that the ground on which we stand before God is the perfect righteousness of Christ imputed to us by faith and not (as the Catholic Church teaches) the imperfect righteousness that is wrought by God's grace into us. The point is that the only merit God accepts for salvation is that of Jesus Christ; nothing we can ever

do could earn God's favor or add anything to the merit of Christ.[28]

The Bible is unequivocal in its teaching that our righteousness does not result from His righteousness; it is His righteousness.

This theft of Christ's centrality continues in His displacement by the Romanist's sacramental system. Rather than dealing directly with the Savior, sinners have been rerouted through the Catholic Church in order to find peace with God. Rather than dealing directly with the one mediator who offered the one sacrifice for sin, sinners are being lost amidst a crowd of mediators offering a multiplicity of sacrifices. In all of this Christ is minimized and Calvary neutralized, which is biblically and patently unacceptable (Col. 1:18; Gal. 6:14-15).

In his dealings with Rome's false doctrine of justification, John Calvin perceived these consequences when he wrote:

> Wherever the knowledge of it (justification) is taken away, the glory of Christ is extinguished, religion abolished, the church destroyed, and the hope of salvation utterly overthrown.[29]

Not Sola Gratia

Even though grace is part and parcel of the Roman Catholic understanding of justification, it is presented as the enabling of a right relationship with God rather than establishing it. While the Bible is adamant in knocking down any attempt to secure justification before God on the basis of works as previously indicated, Rome refuses to surrender this thought. She espouses a theology of salvation by grace, but her doctrine of merit reveals her true heart in that salvation is not by grace alone. The Vatican teaches that meritorious works are necessary and acceptable in the process of justification, at least for those that live beyond infancy.[30] Justified persons are said to merit eternal life through good works prompted by grace. Having been given a start by the infusion of grace through baptism, the individual cooperates with God's grace that results in the performance of good works. These works include compliance to the commandments of God and the Church, acts of charity, self-denial, and the practice of virtues. As a result, these good works produced in cooperation with the grace of God earn a reward from the hand of God called *merit*. This merit then becomes the ground for an increase in sanctifying/justifying grace. The picture that emerges is one in which grace given in baptism produces works, and these works merit reward, and that reward is an increase in one's justification before God.

The Council of Trent confirms this understanding of merit, in negative fashion when it states:

> "If anyone says that the good works of a justified man are gifts from God to such a extent that they are not the good merits of the justified man himself; or that, by the good works he performs through the grace of God and the merits of Jesus Christ (of whom he is a living member), the justified man does not truly merit an increase of grace, life everlasting, and, providing he dies in the state of grace, the attainment of that life everlasting, and even an increase in glory: let him be anathema." (Trent, sess. 6, canon 32).

The very idea, however, that one can "merit an increase in grace" is to stand the Bible on its head. For if something is of grace, how can it be merited? If something is a gift, how can it be earned? Can good works be smuggled into the message of the gospel under the guise of grace?

I believe the Lord Jesus stops such a theology in its tracks. In Luke's gospel, Jesus told a parable about two men who went up to the temple to pray (Luke 18:9-14). The Pharisee was a religious leader and respectable citizen; the publican was regarded as the scum of the earth. The Pharisee "gave thanks to God" that he was not like other men, and then cataloged his good works—fasting, tithing, prayer. He did not take credit for his accomplishments, realizing that these were the produce of grace.

The publican on the other hand knew full well that he was a sinner. He made no attempt to blow the trumpet of morality. And to say it was because he had not performed any good works is to miss the point. The fact is that standing in the presence of God he knew that anything he would mention would be as dung (Paul's description in Philippians 3) in the presence of a holy God. Thus, seeing his utter poverty of character, he cast himself entirely upon the mercy of God. Jesus concluded that he went home justified; the religious man did not.

The deeds the Pharisee had done in response to God's grace did not justify him. The publican was made right with God because he knew that no good work could save him.

As Erwin Lutzer says:

> This parable confirms the words of Isaiah, 'All our righteous deeds are like a dirty garment' (Isaiah 64:6). No human merit is ever accepted by God for justification. Just as it is possible to add a billion bananas and never get an orange, so all human goodness added together can never be transformed in God's righteousness. Only Christ's merit is accepted.[31]

Not *Sola Fide*

Finally, while Roman Catholicism emphasizes faith in the justification of the believer it redefines the Protestant and biblical concept of a simple trust and singular dependence upon Christ. To the Roman Catholic, justifying faith is *dogmatic faith*. It is a belief in God and the firm acceptance of all that the Church proposes for belief.[32] Essentially it means intellectual assent and practical consent to everything the Roman Catholic Church holds as true. Consequently, in order to be saved an individual must be in creedal and dogmatic communion/agreement with Rome. To reject any official teaching of the Roman Church is, according to Vatican I, to reject saving faith, and places one at risk with a loss of justification and eternal life:

> Further, all those things are to be believed with divine and Catholic faith which are contained in the Word of God, written or handed down, and which the Church, either by a solemn judgment, or by here ordinary and universal magisterium, proposes for belief, as having been divinely revealed. And since, without faith, it is impossible to please God, and to attain to the fellowship of his children, therefore without faith no one has ever attained justification, nor will any one obtain eternal life unless he shall have persevered in faith unto the end.[33]

What this constitutes is a redefinition of the biblical informed understanding of faith as a simple dependence upon the finished work of the risen Christ. Protestants, however, believe that faith is founded upon a certain knowledge, which is the essence of the biblical gospel (1 Cor. 15:1-8). Faith in Christ who died for sinners and rose the third day is the means of justification.

The Bible declares unequivocally that justification is possessed by faith alone centered upon God and His provision of righteousness through the work of Jesus Christ. The apostle Paul was a man who once defined his faith and acceptance before God in terms of conformity to the theological guidelines and by-laws of a religious system. However, one day under grace he traded it all in for the righteousness which is from God by faith in the person of Jesus Christ (Phil. 3:1-9). Theology is not to be the object of saving faith but is a support in pointing the way to Jesus Christ; and in that sense it is not what we believe that saves, but in Whom we believe (2 Tim. 1:12). Christianity is neither a philosophy nor an ethic, but a person. Christianity is belief in Christ.

Clearly, the facts identify that it is not we who have conspired to criticize Rome, but Rome by her own mouth has invited condemnation upon herself. For in anathematizing the gospel of justification by grace alone, through faith alone in Christ alone, Roman Catholicism has anathematized itself. As quoted earlier, "Take away the Gospel from a Church and that Church is not worth preserving."

Yet the truth of all this seems to be falling on deaf ears and blind eyes within the camp of Evangelicalism. In light of the material covered in this chapter, are we not dumbfounded to find Evangelicals and Catholics publicizing a supposed agreement on the Reformation principle of justification by faith alone. In an article entitled "The Gift of Salvation," published in the December 8, 1997 edition of *Christianity Today*, many of the original signers of ECT tout that what is contained in this remarkable statement is "agreement with what the Reformation traditions have meant by justification by faith alone (*sola fide*)."[34] In reading the document it sounds rather orthodox at first glance; however, it is totally mystifying to see how so many Roman Catholic leaders can add their endorsement to a statement that is said to embrace the principle of *sola fide*. Should this be true it means that they are agreeing that the Reformation was needed to correct the errors of the Roman Catholic Church, and that they are now repudiating what the Roman Catholic Church still believes in error. If this agreement embraces what the Reformers meant by *sola fide*, then the signers will also deny that which contradicts it. Based on the quotations of this chapter, that would involve a denial of the Council of Trent, Vatican I, and the New 1994 Catholic Catechism. Since this is highly unlikely on the part of men such as Avery Dulles, Richard John Neuhaus, and Peter Kreeft, one is left to wonder about the measure and weight of this agreement.

The third paragraph, before the end of the document, raises further suspicion in that we find important questions that touch upon the heart of the Reformation battle over justification left unanswered. Consider the issues detailed in the following ECT statement:

> The meaning of baptismal regeneration, the Eucharist, and sacramental grace; the historic uses of the language of justification as it relates to imputed and transformative righteousness; the normative status of justification in relation to all Christian doctrine; the assertion that while justification is by faith alone, the faith that receives salvation is never alone; diverse understanding of merit, reward, purgatory, and indulgences; Marian devotion and the assistance of the saints in the life of salvation; and the possibility of salvation to those who have not been evangelized.[35]

How can these questions remain unanswered and agreement be declared? The Reformers' articulation of *sola fide* did not leave these areas open for further discussion. *Sola fide* did not leave room for diversity on such issues as merit, reward, purgatory, and indulgences. In fact, the matter of indulgences was the very spark that lit the fuse of the Reformation and its fight for the doctrine of faith alone . One could be forgiven in concluding that either the Roman Catholics who signed this document are no longer Roman Catholics, which is hard to believe, or that the Evangelicals who signed it cannot tell the difference, rendering dissident Catholics or deceived Protestants.

In closing this chapter, I must be honest and say that my fear over these matters runs in the direction of Protestants being deceived by the craft of Roman Catholic double talk. Some individual Roman Catholics may feel at liberty to say one thing, but the creeds and councils of Rome say another. To that end my heart lies with Bishop Ryle's caution and warning when he writes:

> Unity in the abstract is no doubt an excellent thing:
> but unity without truth is useless. Peace and unifor-
> mity are beautiful and valuable: but peace without
> the Gospel—peace based on a common Episcopacy,
> and not a common faith—is a worthless peace is not
> deserving of the name. When Rome has repealed the
> decrees of Trent, and her additions to the Creed—
> when Rome has formally renounced image-worship,
> Mary-worship, and transubstantiation—then, and
> not till then will it be time to talk of reunion with
> her. Till then there is a gulf between us which cannot
> be honestly bridged. Till then I call on Christians to
> resist to the death this idea of reunion with Rome.[36]

1. William Webster, *The Gospel of the Reformation*, (Washington: Christian Resources Inc., 1997) 90.

2. Ibid., 80.

3. B.B.Warfield, *Studies in Theology*, (London, 1932) 465.

4. J.C.Ryle, *Five English Reformers*, (London: Banner of Truth, 1960) 36.

5. John Calvin, *Institutes of the Christian Religion*, (Battles edition, Westminister Press, Vol 1) 726.

6. Thomas Watson, *A Body of Divinity*, (London: Banner of Truth Trust, 1970) 226.

7. Philip H. Eveson, *The Great Exchange*, (England: Day One Publications, 1996) 193.

8. Taken and adapted for the most part from, James Boice, *Romans*, Volume 1, (Grand Rapids: Baker, 1991) 383.

9. John MacArthur, *Faith Works*, (Dallas: Word Publishing, 1993) 89.

10. Taken and adapted for the most part from, Sinclair Ferguson, *The Christian Life*, (Scotland: Banner of Truth Trust, 1989) 82.

11. Ian Barclay, *What Jesus Thinks About The Church*, (England: Kingsway Publications, 1986) 89.

12. Thomas Watson, *A Body of Divinity*, (London: Banner of Truth Trust, 1958) 159.

13. John MacArthur, *Roman 1-8 New Testament Commentary*, (Chicago: Moody Press, 1991) 209.

14. Erwin Lutzer, *All One Body - Why Don't We Agree?* (Illinois: Tyndale House, 1989) 99.

15. Philip H. Eveson, 64.

16. Charles Swindoll, *Bible Study Guide - James*, (Dallas: Word Publishing, 1991) 83-84.

17. Charles Colson & Richard John Neuhaus, *Evangelicals and Catholics Together*, (Dallas: Word Publishing, 1995) 200.

18. John A. Hardon, *Pocket Catholic Dictionary*, (New York: Image Books, 1985) 214.

19. *Catechism of the Catholic Church*, (Missouri: Ligouri Publications, 1994) para. 2019-20, 1129, 980, 1030-31.

20. Ibid., para. 1036, 2005.

21. Ibid., para. 1992, 1999-2000, 2024.

22. Ibid., para. 1127-1129, 1212.

23. Ibid., para. 1262-1274.

24. Ibid., para. 1992, 1265.

25. Ibid., para. 1212, 1392, 2010.

26. Ibid., para. 980, 1446.

27. Ibid., para. 1366, 1407, 1416, 1566.

28. John MacArthur, *Reckless Faith*, (Illinois: Crossway Books, 1994) 144.

29. John Calvin, *The Necessity of Reforming the Church, in Tracts and Treatises* (Grand Rapids: Eerdmans, 1958) 1:42.

30. *Catholic Catechism*, para. 2010, 2027.

31. Lutzer, 98.

32. *Catholic Catechism*, 181-182, 1814.

33. Philip Schaff, *The Creeds of Christendom*, (New York: Harper, 1877) Volume II, 244-245.

34. *Christianity Today*: December 8, 1997, p. 36.

35. Ibid., 38.

36. J.C.Ryle, *Knots Untied*, (London, 1959) 319.

CHAPTER 11

AMBASSADOR TO THE VATICAN

2 Cor. 5:12-21

Some will remember the name Claire Booth Luce. She was an outstanding playwright and the wife of Henry Luce, the founder of Time magazine. Mrs. Luce was converted to the Roman Catholic faith. President F. D. Roosevelt appointed her as ambassador to Italy. During the course of her ambassadorial engagements Mrs. Luce had an official appointment with the pope. The story goes that after an hour, the pope had a brief chance to speak and exclaimed: "But, Madame Ambassador, I am a Catholic!"[1]

How would you like to be a *ambassador* to the Vatican? During Bible times, the word ambassador had little to do with politics. Rather, it carried the meaning of "personal messenger," one sent on a special mission (2 Chr. 35:21; Isa. 18:1-2; Luke 14:32). The ambassador was under the authority of a ruler or a government official. He was sent to declare a message but not to negotiate the response.

In Paul's day, the Roman Empire cast its imperial shadow over two different types of provinces, both of which were related to the Roman government but in a divergent manner. *Senatorial provinces* were comprised of people who bowed before the imperial insignia and peacefully obeyed the law. *Imperial provinces*, however, were often stiff-necked and would often disturb the empire's *Pax Romana*. Rome sent ambassadors to the imperial provinces but not to the senatorial provinces.

Christians are God's ambassadors to this world because it is a world in rebellion to God (Rom. 5:10, 8:5-8). Through the sacrifice of Jesus Christ upon Calvary's brow, the obstacle of sin has been removed, and God has been reconciled to the world (2 Cor. 5:18-19). Yet the world fights on and God must therefore deal with this warring world as Rome dealt with their imperial provinces. He must dispatch His ambassadors with His declaration of peace. This is a mission of mercy, for God would be well within His rights to mobilize the armies of heaven and crush earth's anarchy.[2]

This reality is what makes every child of the King of Kings, an ambassador to the Vatican. With an evangelistic zeal akin to that of Mrs. Luce, it is imperative that we bring to Roman Catholics the glad message of the "gospel of peace" (Eph. 6:15). Let us announce joyfully and firmly that God has made peace through the blood of Christ's atoning death (Rom. 15:33; Col. 1:20). While men were shaking their fist at God, God was stretching His hands out upon a cross as the "chastisement for our peace" (Isa. 53:4-6). It is not the responsibility of men to try to make peace with God but to accept the peace that God has already made through His Son. The perfect work of the perfect Son of God establishes the basis for a perfect peace with a perfect God (Eph. 2:14). This is the victorious and glorious message that must be delivered to the doorstep and over the threshold of every Roman Catholic home and heart.

This is a must because although some Roman Catholics' genuinely know Christ despite their Church, there are hundred's of thousands who remain blind to the light of the gospel.

Hundreds of years of Roman Catholic traditions have veiled the true Gospel of Christ. As a consequence, many Catholics put their trust in a complex sacramental system and are lost to Christ in a maze of religious rituals and requirements. There is an absence of the "gospel of peace" in the Catholic Church. Instead, Catholics are loaded down with more requirements for salvation than the Jews were before Christ's atonement. Peace with God alludes the Catholic; for as previously noted, Roman salvation is a never-ending journey, from baptism to purgatory in which the Catholic can never be sure that enough grace has been merited to make him acceptable before God. A gospel that does not bring peace is not a gospel at all. Addressing this very point, James White wrote:

> A message of works-righteousness, for example, that calls someone to strive to obtain peace with God through various ceremonies or duties, could not logically be called a gospel, for such would not qualify as good news. Such a message would bring about not peace but turmoil to the hearts of those who struggle to meet the impossible standards built into such systems.[3]

In light of this obligation is it not both a tragedy and travesty to find present day Evangelicals announcing peace with Rome rather than preaching the "gospel of peace" to the adherents of Rome? Is it not bizarre and sad to discover that many Protestants support a recall of Christ's ambassadors to the Vatican? I say this because ECT, in blurring the historical and theological lines between Protestantism and Roman Catholicism, has had the effect of redrawing the boundaries of legitimate evangelism. After all, what is the point of sending ambassadors to those who are already at peace within God's kingdom? This landmark document in effect redirects Protestants away from evangelizing devout Catholics. In fact, it goes so far as to stigmatize such efforts as "sheep stealing." The relevant sections from the ECT are as follows:

We are called and we are therefore resolved to explore patterns of working and witnessing together in order to advance the one mission of Christ (4).[4]

All who accept Christ as Lord and Savior are brothers and sisters in Christ. Evangelicals and Catholics are brothers and sisters in Christ (5).

Today, in this country and elsewhere, Evangelicals and Catholics attempt to win "converts" from one another's fold . . . In many instances, however, such efforts at recruitment undermine the Christian mission . . .

It is understandable that Christians who bear witness to the gospel try to persuade others that their communities and traditions are more fully in accord with the gospel. There is a necessary distinction between evangelizing and what is today commonly called proselytizing or "sheep stealing." We condemn the practice of recruiting people from another community for purposes of denominational or institutional aggrandizement. At the same time, our commitment to full religious freedom compels us to defend the legal freedom to proselytize even as we call upon Christians to refrain from such activity (20,22)

We as Evangelicals and Catholics affirm that opportunity and means for growth in Christian discipleship are available in our several communities (22).

In view of the large number of non-Christians in the world and the enormous challenge of our common evangelistic task, it is neither theologically legitimate nor a prudent use of resources for one Christian community to proselytize among active adherents of another Christian community (22-23).

There are, then, differences between us that cannot be resolved here. But on this we are resolved: All authentic witness must be aimed at conversion to God in Christ by the power of the Spirit. Those converted - whether understood as having received new birth for the first time or as having experienced the reawakening of the new birth originally bestowed in the sacrament of baptism - must be given full freedom and respect as they discern and decide the community in which they will live their new life in Christ (24).

Please take a deep breath and submerge yourself in the implications of these words. First, the Catholic Church is a legitimate Christian community and therefore to seek to win Catholics to Christ is, in essence, seeking to save the saved. Catholics are brothers and sisters in Christ and therefore it would be a more prudent use of our time and energy to seek the lost in the world not those who belong to another Christian fold. Second, to involve oneself in such evangelistic efforts among Roman Catholics is to be branded an Evangelical rustler guilty of "sheep stealing." Third, the gospel of this common mission is inclusive of a false view of baptism that imparts the regenerating life of God to the one being baptized. Yet, while the document is clear about that, it nowhere attempts to outline in a clear manner the content of the gospel itself.

In short, this document gives legitimacy to Catholicism that it has never had before among Evangelical Protestants. As a result, it stigmatizes the centuries old practice of viewing the Catholic system as a false Christianity whose devotees need to be reached with the message of Christ's finished work and God's full forgiveness. The life-giving gospel itself is diluted and reduced to what's common among the two sides rather than what the Bible teaches. By inference, the martyrs were mistaken, converts from Rome deceived, and Martin Luther wrong in his estimation that Rome was without the biblical gospel.

The purpose of this chapter is to show the fallacy and tragedy of such thinking. It is to be feared that the greatest causality in this declared truce between both sides is the never dying souls of Roman Catholics. To reclassify Roman Catholics as brothers and sisters in Christ runs the risk of making them Christians on paper but not in reality. To re-label a bottle of poison as medicine doesn't change the content of the bottle; in fact, it heightens the danger because the poison is now mistaken as medicine. That is what ECT has done in effect by having declared what has always been labeled a false gospel to be true and in turn made what is false more dangerous to both Catholics and Protestants. In the face of such danger, it is incumbent upon us to take the medicine of the true gospel to Roman Catholics who are drinking poison from a re-labeled bottle.

The Need of Evangelism Among Catholics

In this climate of compromise and convergence the reader should clearly understand that theological convergence between Roman Catholicism and Evangelicals can only take place with compromise by Evangelicals or by conversion on the part of Roman Catholics. There is no neutral ground for resolving the critical issues that divide both sides. We do not share a common evangelistic task with Roman Catholics. We have an evangelistic task to the entire lost world, which includes the vast majority of Roman Catholics. This is not the time to recall Christ's ambassadors to the Vatican. Consider the following as I buttress this statement.

The Theology of Catholocism

Does not a common evangelistic task assume a common evangel? Does not a shared mission presuppose a shared message? The reality, however, is that while Protestants and Catholics share some common theological ground (e.g., the doctrine of the Trinity, the incarnation of Christ through means of the virgin birth, the sinlessness of Jesus, the death of Christ for sin, the bodily resurrection of the Savior), there remains a great unbridgeable gulf over key doctrines, especially the content and character of the gospel itself. The fundamental mistake of the Catholic Church is to deny that there is a great and free salvation available, and a God, who is able to make it effective.

The fallacy of ECT is that one can consistently believe in two opposing propositions at the same time. It is implied, that at worst, the choice between the theology of Catholicism and Protestantism is a choice between what's good and what's best. But that is not true. One cannot possibly believe, as Protestantism does, that salvation is by faith, apart from works, and at the same token believe that good works contribute to the obtaining of eternal life. Surely this is theological oil and water.

To give Roman Catholicism an Evangelical make over is most diabolical. Rome's creeds, catechisms, decrees, and dogmas have anathematized the one true biblical gospel, for which she has never repented. Therefore, to be saved a Catholic would have to believe the true gospel and reject Catholicism's false gospel. Roman Catholicism is no safe house for troubled sinners but a prison where men are bound to tradition, shackled to ritualistic works, and tied to a false hope of heaven.

Let us be reinforced to the reality of this by recounting some of the differences detailed in this book between biblical Christianity and Roman Catholicism.

- Protestants believe that only "Christ is the head of the Church which is His Body"; Roman Catholics believe that the pope is the head of the visible Church on earth as the Vicar of Christ.

- Protestants believe that Peter was one of Christ's chief apostles; Roman Catholics believe that he was the "the Rock" upon which the Church is founded.

- Protestants believe in justification by faith alone—that salvation comes only by the grace of God; Roman Catholics believe that salvation is secured by faith plus good works—only as channeled through the Roman Catholic Church.

- Protestants believe that there are indications of diversity in worship in the New Testament, nevertheless the preaching of the Word and the administration of Baptism and the Lord's Supper was universal and underlines the Church's unity. Therefore, Protestants have only two sacraments or ordinances, namely, Baptism and the Lord's Supper. Roman Catholics have seven sacraments: Baptism, Confirmation, Holy Eucharist, Penance, Extreme Unction, Holy Orders, and Matrimony.

- Protestants believe that water baptism is not essential to salvation; Roman Catholics believe that baptism is essential to salvation.

- Protestants believe that the Lord's Supper is commemorative and the elements remain as they are; Roman Catholics believe that the bread and wine are actually changed by the miracle of transubstantiation into the real flesh and blood of Christ.

+ Protestants see the Lord's Table as a commemoration of the finished work of Christ through his once-and-for-all-death; Roman Catholics see the Lord's Supper as an unbloody propitiatory sacrifice of Christ in the ongoing work of Calvary.

+ Protestants believe that no one has the right or power to forgive sins save God alone; the Roman Catholic Church teaches that the priest can and does forgive sins.

+ Protestants believe that all people after death enter either Heaven or Hell; Roman Catholics also believe in Heaven and Hell, but have added an intermediary stage to heaven know as purgatory. There the Catholic atones by means of punishment for certain unforgiven sins.

+ Protestants believe that the Scriptures are all sufficient for the Christian life and practice; the Roman Catholic Church teaches that *Tradition* must be accepted with the Scriptures as equally authoritative.

+ Protestants believe that they have the right to interpret the Scripture under the Holy Spirit; the Roman Catholic Church insists upon being the interpreter for the individual.

+ Protestants honor Mary as the mother of Jesus; Roman Catholics venerate her as the Mother of God and inter-cessor for sinners in the provision of redemption through her Son.

+ Protestants believe that full forgiveness of sins can be known and received from God and that it is not necessary for those who are forgiven to pay for sins after death. Roman Catholics believe that some sins cannot be entirely atoned for upon earth and that the granting of indulgences helps to alleviate the unpaid debts of temporal punishments in purgatory.

• Protestants believe that good works should result from the faith of the Christian in union with Christ, but that they are not an essential part of justification before God; the Roman Church teaches that one can earn the eternal reward of heaven by performing the corporal works of mercy.[5]

In the wake of these differences, the common ground becomes rather uncommon. It is evident that Roman Catholicism works from a different authority base; a different understanding of grace and faith; a different understanding of atonement and the means to forgiveness; and a different understanding of works, Church ordinances, and the concept of priesthood. At the heart of Roman Catholicism, justification becomes an unfinished business and atonement for sins an unfinished work. Is this the gospel Christ bequests and Paul preached? The arguments of this book would answer with an emphatic negative.

A few years ago two ministers got into a fight about what they considered to be an important doctrinal matter. They settled the fight when the first minister told the second, "Look, what are we fighting over? We're both striving to do the Lord's work. You do it your way and I'll do it His way!"

Surely the difference between Catholicism and biblical Christianity is the difference between our way and His way. It is the difference between human effort and divine accomplishment. It is the difference between human tradition and divine revelation. It is the difference between man helping God in the act of salvation and God alone saving helpless men.

People without the gospel are people in need of the gospel. The Catholic, like the Jew, may have a zeal for God, a reverence for Scripture, and a desire to live a holy life, but still remain ignorant of the gospel, seeking to establish their own righteousness (Rom. 10:1-4).

Our hearts' desire and prayer to God must therefore be for their salvation. It is erroneous to say that Protestants and Catholics are brothers and sisters in Christ, for to make such a statement is to say that they believe the same Gospel. The tragedy of such thinking is to prevent the gospel from being presented to lost millions who have now been wrongly re-labeled by Evangelical leaders as Christians. Is it not the case that the falsehood of Roman Catholicism is the truest answer to those who would discourage evangelism among Catholics? A new label doesn't change the content of the bottle.

The History of Protestantism

Another encouragement as to the propriety of evangelizing Roman Catholics is the history of Protestantism itself. Protestants have been driven historically by a desire to positively present the gospel to those who lack its assurance and freedom. Protestants glory in the fact that the Protestant Reformation was the rediscovery of a sufficient Bible and a simple gospel. When Martin Luther felt himself reborn through the life giving gospel of justification by faith alone, a burden was lifted from him. The burden of his sin and guilt was lifted from tired shoulders by the nail pierced hand of Christ. Yet while one burden was lifted, another burden was put in its place. This second burden was a sense of obligation towards those who remained in bondage to Rome's enslaving doctrines. Luther and the Reformers, therefore, saw to it that the gospel of free and sovereign grace was preached from every available pulpit and printed from every available press. Therefore, to be a Protestant was to be a witness to the gospel of justification by faith alone. The Protestant Reformation was Christianity reasserting its simplicity and purity, divesting the gospel of the burdens and corruption imposed upon it by man, renouncing mere human authority, and asserting the supremacy of the Lord Jesus Christ.

While the word Protestant is commonly understood to mean 'somebody who protests against the errors of the Roman Catholic Church,' it only represents half of the truth. It is often used in that fashion, but the Latin root of the word means first of all 'to declare something formally in public, to testify, to make a solemn declaration'. Thus, the connotation of 'protesting against error' is only a secondary meaning. That means that the Protestant is first and foremost an evangelist and then an apologist. The Protestant Reformation was at its heart an Evangelical movement bent on presenting the authentic gospel of Jesus Christ to those ignorant of it and that included Roman Catholics.

The original 'Protestants' were people in the German town of Spires. In 1529, they made a solemn *Protestation* on behalf of the Evangelical cause in Europe. The pope and the Holy Roman Emperor were attempting to stamp out the new Evangelical teaching by use of secular power; and it appeared that it would be a fight to the death. So the supporters of the Evangelical cause, the 'Protestants', declared:

> There is, we affirm, no sure preaching or doctrine but that which abides by the Word of God. According to God's command no other doctrine should be preached. Each text of the holy and divine Scriptures should be elucidated and explained by other texts. This Holy Book is in all things necessary for

the Christian; it shines clearly in its own light, and is found to enlighten the darkness. We are determined by God's grace and aid to abide by God's Word alone, the holy gospel contained in the biblical books of the Old and New Testaments. This Word alone should be preached, and nothing that is contrary to it. It is the only truth. It is the sure rule of all Christian doctrine and conduct, it can never fail us or deceive us. Whoso builds and abides on this foundation shall stand against all the gates of hell, while all merely human additions and vanities set up against it must fall before the presence of God.[6]

What we see in the *Protestation* is a powerful declaration of commitment to the gospel of our Lord Jesus Christ, as it is recorded in the Bible. A gospel that was opposed by the power of the papacy and later condemned by the canons of the Council of Trent. To be a 'Protestant' was to owe ones allegiance to the protection and free proclamation of the Gospel of Jesus Christ. The Church of Rome was by no means an ally in that mission. Therefore, the word 'Protestant' is not a word to be forgotten, but a term to be understood with fresh appreciation and coated with renewed honor.

It is plain that the ECT document is a betrayal of historic Protestantism in its message and mission. Rome has neither repealed the canons of Trent nor embraced the doctrine of justification by faith alone and thus remains a threat to biblical Christianity. Evangelicals faced with such facts must once again pick up the mantle of the *Protestation* and testify to dear Roman Catholics that our hope is built on nothing less than Jesus blood and righteousness.

Despite the hazard of being considered a 'sheep stealer' and an 'Evangelical mugger' there is truly a great need for evangelism among the Roman Catholic community. This is based upon the realization that: (1) they lack a true understanding of the Gospel; and (2) it is our history and responsibility to take the message of the true gospel to them.

The Nature of Evangelism Among Catholics

Having talked about the need to witness, the question now is how might that best be achieved? How does one play his or her part in the great enterprise of the *Protestation?* This is an important question because we cannot assume that those who believe the right way will necessarily present that belief in the right manner.

Let us consider, therefore, a plan of action that can help Catholics find their way out of the labyrinth of sacramental salvation to Christ.

Be Real

There is nothing more contagious and infectious than the Christian life well lived. The best witness for Christ is an authentic walk. This was true of the Thessalonians and ought to be true of us (1 Thess. 1:6-10). The best gospel tract a Roman Catholic is ever likely to read is the living letter of a Christian who is manifesting the peace and joy of life in Jesus Christ. Paul, in his second letter to the Corinthians, wrote that every Christian is a letter of reference or recommendation to Christ (2 Cor. 3:1-3). People will judge Christ and His gospel by what they read in the lives and conduct of those who profess Him. If the world judges a shopkeeper by what he sells and a craftsman by the work he produces, will they not also judge Christ by His followers? This is God's preferred method of evangelism for in the incarnation of Jesus Christ "the word was made flesh". The gospel was not only spelled out in the words of Jesus but in the actions of Jesus.

In this regard, to manifest the peace and joy that faith alone in Christ brings can have such an impact on the Roman Catholic. For the most part this kind of joy and assurance is lacking in the experience of the Catholic. Roman Catholics can never be sure of their salvation and labor continually under the fear of their eternal fate. It is a sin of presumption to even imagine that one possesses eternal life, in spite of the clear teaching of the Scriptures on the subject. Beyond the pale of death looms the ugly shadow of purgatory. What a contrast and challenge to be faced with a real Christian who rejoices in the assurance of sins forgiven and a home in heaven (Ps. 40:1-3). Such a radiant testimony can light up the path to Christ.

In the light of what was mentioned, consider the true and challenging words of D.L. Moody when he said: "For many we are the only Bible they will ever read and some of us need revising."

Be Longsuffering

Patience and sympathetic understanding are indispensable in dealing with Roman Catholics for the purpose of evangelism. Much effort has been wasted for lack of proper understanding of the Roman Catholic mind and reaction. Roman Catholics have been brought up and trained in the belief that theirs is the only true church of Christ; that the pope, as the Vicar of Christ on earth, is infallible, and that the Protestant churches are man-made. Their minds have been filled with the poison of error and superstition, and they will react violently against any attempt on our part to inject into their souls the saving truth of the Gospel of Jesus Christ. Just as the skillful physician will proceed cautiously but firmly in removing a cancerous growth from one of his patients, so the witness to Roman Catholics will exercise caution and forbearance. And at the same time show determination to eradicate from them the malignant growth of error that robs them of many of the joys and blessings of true Christianity (2 Tim. 2:24).

Be Informed

The better you understand Roman Catholicism, the better you will be able to effectively communicate the gospel to Catholics. Lack of knowledge or misinformation of the subject will spoil the best efforts. It takes the average Roman Catholic priest many years of intensive study to really grasp the intricacies, distinctions and contra-distinctions of Roman Catholic teaching and practice. Too often the Christian witness thinks that he knows it all by merely having read a few articles or having browsed through a couple of books. To this end a working knowledge of the New 1994 Catechism is a good place to start. The purchase and reading of the Pocket Catholic Dictionary is also helpful.

The purpose of this is to meet the Catholic on his own ground and stimulate thought. It is rather disconcerting and convicting for the Catholic to be confronted with things he didn't know about the doctrines of his Church when set against the Bible. The fact is that most Roman Catholics don't ask much of the Church, and the Church doesn't ask much of them. It makes an impact therefore when the witnessing Protestant knows more about the Roman Catholic Church than the average Catholic.

In one of his speeches on the requisites for military success General Douglas MacArthur placed more emphasis on having a knowledge of the enemy than on anything else. He said, "The greater the knowledge of the enemy, the greater potential of victory."

In the battle for the soul of the Roman Catholic a knowledge of Roman dogma, particularly as it stands in opposition to the gospel, can spell greater success. To be well armed with the facts of the matter is to lay the groundwork for effective evangelism.

Be Focused

One of the great dangers in witnessing to Roman Catholics is to be sidetracked by "red- herrings" and nonessentials. While there are many issues raised by the controversy between Protestantism and Catholicism, the gospel is the heart of the matter. The Roman Catholic's greatest problem is not the Roman Catholic Church, but rather his own sin. Therefore, it is unwise to make the injustices and history of the Roman Church and its Popes the focus of attention.

When the arguments in a debate get sidetracked, the cause of truth is not served. Every moment spent talking about topics that are not relative comes at the cost of time available to discuss important issues (2 Tim. 2:23). The key to effective evangelism is keeping the plain things the main things. The end should be the winning of a lost sinner not the defeat and embarrassment of a proud Catholic by fine argument.

Be Tactful

Remember you cannot argue someone into salvation. There are, of course, times when it is necessary to defend ones position, but care must be taken lest in winning the argument we lose the one we are seeking to win. God has called the Christian to be a faithful witness, not a judge or prosecuting attorney. Words spoken should be seasoned with grace and zeal to see that the lost is won with speech that is tempered by gentleness (Col. 4:5-6; Phil. 4:5). Many Roman Catholics have been turned off from the gospel because aggressive Evangelicals handled them with undue care. Christ must be presented in a considerate and compassionate manner. Evangelicals ought to be light to Roman Catholics not lightening. Remember that tact is the knack for making a point without making an enemy.

> A young man was applying for a job as a clerk in a shoe store. The store owner asked him, "Suppose that a lady customer asked you if you thought that one of her feet was bigger than the other. What would you say?" The young man responded promptly, "I would say. Oh no lady! If anything one is a little smaller than the other."

Be Sociable

Since Catholicism tends to run along family and ethnic lines, many Catholics do not have a single non-Catholic Christian friend. As a result few have ever heard a clear presentation of the Gospel. Let God therefore open a window of opportunity to befriend a Roman Catholic workmate or neighbor. Don't be afraid to reach out to priests and nuns. Many are lonely and searching for answers.

Was not the Savior known as the friend of sinners? Friendship is therefore a necessary bridge to effective evangelism.

Be Prayerful

The reality is that God does nothing but by prayer and everything with it. Effective witnessing must be underpinned by effectual praying. In the New Testament, we see prayer advancing the cause of God's Word (2 Thess. 3:1-2). Prayer opens the door of opportunity for effective Christian witness (Col. 4:3). Prayer gives backbone and boldness to the gospel courier (Acts 4:29). Prayer effects the harvest of souls (Luke 10:2), and is the real work of the evangelist.

In evangelizing Roman Catholics, prayer must never become a prefix or a suffix to our work. God will work in the hardest of hearts as we pray and while we pray. Through prayer we work with God and not just for God.

> A kneeling marble-cutter with chisel and hammer in hand was changing a stone into a statue. A preacher looking on said, "I wish I could deal such powerful blows on stony hearts." The sculptor answered, "Maybe you could if you worked more on your knees like I do?"

> To truly love Roman Catholics is to pray for them fervently.

Be Biblical

According to the Bible the instrument of change in bringing dead sinners to life in Christ is the Bible (Acts 2:40-41; Rom. 10:17; Jas. 1:21). Therefore, we can help the Roman Catholic most by encouraging him to read the Bible, and when in conversation with him we ought to make the Bible the sure ground of our argument. Consequently, the Protestant must know his Bible and make it known.

We must counter the Roman Church that keeps Bible truth from the people, because she knows that those who know the Bible will not remain in Romanism. People will not pray to saints, when they know they have the right to pray to the enthroned Lord himself, who has all power in heaven and on earth (Heb. 4:14-16). They will no longer go to an earthly priest to confess their sin, when they know that only Christ has the right to hear confession and grant absolution (1 John 2:1-2). They will not trust in their own good works, when they know that salvation is free through the finished work of Christ (Titus 3:5-8). They will not adore the wafer, when they know that the glorified body of Christ is in heaven, and that the wafer is not the flesh and blood of Christ (Col. 3:1-3).

If we hope to reap a harvest of souls from the Catholic community we must be diligent in sowing the imperishable seed of God's Word (Isa. 55:11; Luke 8:11; 1 Pet. 1:23). Echoing this theme, Martin Luther made a telling comment on the Protestant Reformation when he stated:

> "I did nothing. The Word did it all. I simply taught, preached, wrote God's Word, otherwise I did nothing. And while I slept and drank Wittenburg beer with Philip and Amsdorf, the Word weakened all who opposed me."[7]

Be Complete

The great commission calls upon every Christian witness to make disciples of all nations, not just decisions (Matt. 28:19-20). The work of evangelism is not completed until the Roman Catholic is saved, baptized, and incorporated into a sound, Bible-teaching assembly.

The task of evangelizing Roman Catholics must include the counsel to burn any bridges back to the Roman system. It must be taught that the light of the Gospel disallows any fellowship with spiritual darkness (2 Cor. 6:14-18; Rev. 18: 4-5). The prospective and new convert must be encouraged to flee the idolatrous practices of the Church of Rome (1 Thess. 1:9-10; 1 John 5:21).

Patient instruction and regular encouragement must accompany the evangelization of the Roman Catholic. Do not underestimate the magnitude of how ingrained Roman Catholicism can be even in those who have left the Church. If this separation is not encouraged, the new born babe in Christ can be placed in great danger.

> Samuel Chadwick, one time principal of Cliff College in Wales, blamed himself on one occasion for disrupting the spiritual growth of a new convert by sending him to a church which was cold and dead. He said, "It was like putting a baby in the arms of a corpse."[8]

While not a complete and comprehensive methodology on how to evangelize Roman Catholics, I nevertheless trust that what has been shared here will encourage what ECT discourages. We must take these principles and evangelize Roman Catholics. The need for Evangelicals to witness is imperative because Roman Catholic doctrine is void of the gospel. In the era of ECT, this increasingly seems to be an unpopular line, but we must endeavor to remain faithful to the Word of God for the work of Christ demands it.

As the writing of this book tapers to an end and goes to print, the movie *Titanic* is breaking all box office records. Perhaps a sad fact about the sinking of that great vessel will help reemphasize in closing the concern and purpose of this book from the start.

> Survivor Eva Hart remembers the night, April 15, 1912, on which the Titanic plunged 12,000 feet to the Atlantic floor, some two hours and forty minutes after an iceberg tore a 300-foot gash in the starboard

side: "I saw all the horror of its sinking, and I heard, even more dreadful, the cries of drowning people."

Although twenty lifeboats and rafts were launched - too few and only partly filled - most of the passengers ended up struggling in the icy waters while those in the boats waited a safe distance away. Some were already overloaded, but in virtually every other boat, those already saved rowed their half-filled boats aimlessly in the night, listening to the cries of the lost. Each feared a crush of unknown swimmers would cling to their craft, eventually swamping it.[9]

In drawing an analogy to the Titanic, this book bears witness to a generation of Evangelical Protestants scrambling in panic for safety in the lifeboat of ecumenical alliances. This panic has been brought about by the horrifying sight of a morally shipwrecked society, sinking in a sea of relativism due to the iceberg of pluralism. What becomes plain, however, is that the seeming safety of this ecumenical lifeboat comes at the cost of throwing truth overboard and leaving dear Roman Catholics to drown without the hope of the gospel. Without fear the purpose of this book has been to rock that boat.

---

1. G. Avery Lee, Elijah: *Yahweh is My God,* (Nashville: Broadman Press, 1987) 16.

2. Adapted from Warren Wiersbe, *Be What You Are,* (England: Scripture Press, 1988) 130-131.

3. James R. White, *The Roman Catholic Controversy,* (Minnesota: Bethany House, 1996) 39-40.

4. *"Evangelicals and Catholics Together: The Christian Mission in the Third Millennium,"* (29 March 1994), All page numbers refer to the 25-page version of the document as originally distributed by Prison Fellowship.

5. Taken for the most part from Stanley Stuber, *Primer on Roman Catholicism for Protestants*, (New York: Associate Press, 1960) 262-269.

6. Peter Toon, *What's the Difference?* (England: Marshalls Books, 1983) 13.

7. David Roper, *Seeing Through*, (Oregon: Multnomah Books, 1995) 55.

8. Selwyn Hughes, *The Introvert's Guide to Spontaneous Witnessing*, (Minnesota: Bethany House, 1983) 173.

9. Graig Brian Larson, *Illustrations for Preaching & Teaching*, (Grand Rapids: Baker, 1993) 67.

FOR FURTHER READING

A View of Rome,
By John H. Armstrong. Published by Moody Press.

Protestants & Catholics: Do They Now Agree?
By John Ankenberg & John Weldon. Published by Harvest House.

The Faith of the Vatican
By Herbert Carson. Published by Evangelical Press.

The Woman that Rides the Beast
By Dave Hunt. Published by Harvest House.

The Gospel According to Rome
By James McCarthy. Published by Harvest House.

Reckless Faith
By John MacArthur. Published by Crossway Books.

The Roman Catholic Controversy
By James White. Published by Bethany House Publishers

The Church of Rome at the Bar of History
By William Webster. Published by Banner of Truth.

About the Author

Philip De Courcy

Born September 27, 1961—Born again January 28, 1978.

Home Church: Rathcoole Baptist, N. Ireland.

Prior to entering the ministry he worked for seven years as an aircraft fitter in Short Brothers and also served for six years as a Reserve Constable in The RUC, in Belfast.

Trained and graduated for the pastorate from the Irish Baptist College in Belfast.

After graduating, he served for six years as the Pastor of Carr Baptist Church in N. Ireland.

Since 1994 he has been Senior Pastor of Placerita Baptist Church in Newhall, California. This church is part of the GARBC movement.

He is also studying at the Master's Seminary in Los Angeles for the purpose of obtaining a Master of Divinity degree. Graduation D.V. May 1999.

He is married to June, a native of Scotland and graduate of the Whitfield College of Bible. They have three lovely daughters, Angela, Laura, and Beth.

Placerita Baptist Church
22004 W. Placerita Canyon Road
Newhall, California 91321